GREAT LIVES

ALBERT
EINSTEIN

First edition for the United States, Canada, and the Philippines
published in 2019 by B.E.S. Publishing

All inquiries should be addressed to:
B.E.S. Publishing
250 Wireless Boulevard
Hauppauge, NY 11788
www.bes-publishing.com

ISBN: 978-1-4380-1202-5

Library of Congress Control No.: 2018963803

Conceived, designed, and produced by The Bright Press,
an imprint of The Quarto Group.
The Old Brewery, 6 Blundell Street,
London, N7 9BH, United Kingdom
T (0) 20 7700 6700 F (0) 20 7700 8066
www.QuartoKnows.com

Publisher: Mark Searle
Creative Director: James Evans
Managing Editor: Jacqui Sayers
Editor: Judith Chamberlain
Project Editors: Anna Southgate, Lucy York
Art Director: Katherine Radcliffe
Design: Lyndsey Harwood and Geoff Borin

Date of Manufacture: March 2019
Manufactured by: Hung Hing Printing, Shenzhen, China

Printed in China

9 8 7 6 5 4 3 2 1

GREAT LIVES

ALBERT
EINSTEIN

By Ned Hartley
with illustrations by Tom Humberstone

PUBLISHING

CONTENTS

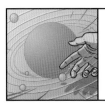

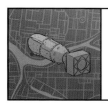

INTRODUCTION

Albert Einstein was a quiet child. At first, his parents were worried that he might have learning difficulties and took him to see a specialist. In fact, he was quiet because he was always deep in thought—something that would stay with him for the rest of his life. Einstein's father ran an electrical equipment business, and this enabled him to support young Albert throughout his academic career. Both of Einstein's parents were Jewish. Although the family was not religious, being Jewish was always very important to Albert.

Einstein was amazingly clever, but he was not a great student at school. His report cards said that he was a disruptive pupil who always thought he knew more than his teachers did. Albert saw no point in learning facts without having a reason to do so, but when he was interested in something there was no stopping him— he taught himself geometry and algebra over the course of a summer.

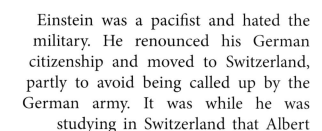

Einstein was a pacifist and hated the military. He renounced his German citizenship and moved to Switzerland, partly to avoid being called up by the German army. It was while he was studying in Switzerland that Albert met his first wife, Mileva Marić. They had two sons together, but their marriage did not last.

The most important year of Einstein's life was 1905, when he published four groundbreaking scientific papers, all while working as a patent clerk in Switzerland. These papers challenged everything that was known about the Universe—in the last of them Einstein established a link between mass and energy, which he summed up in the most famous equation in the world: $E=mc^2$. Once the scientific community understood the importance of Einstein's work, everything changed for him and he became a celebrity.

Perhaps the darkest moment of Einstein's life was when he realized that his theory of relativity could be used to create incredibly destructive atom bombs. Being a pacifist, he despised the idea that his work could be used in such a deadly manner. Einstein was able to return to Germany after World War II, but he decided to spend the last years of his life at Princeton University, New Jersey, in the United States.

During his lifetime, Albert Einstein showed that he was a true genius. The theories he developed continue to form the basis of modern physics today. They have taught us that space and time can bend and warp in ways we would not have thought imaginable. Thanks to Einstein, by understanding how matter and energy are linked, we can learn more about the building blocks of the Universe!

CHAPTER 1

EINSTEIN'S CURIOSITY AWAKENS

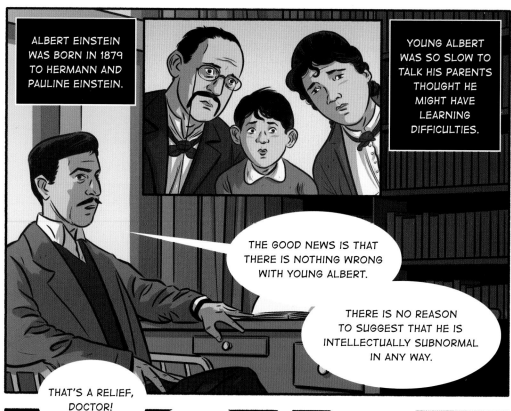

ALBERT EINSTEIN WAS BORN IN 1879 TO HERMANN AND PAULINE EINSTEIN.

YOUNG ALBERT WAS SO SLOW TO TALK HIS PARENTS THOUGHT HE MIGHT HAVE LEARNING DIFFICULTIES.

THE GOOD NEWS IS THAT THERE IS NOTHING WRONG WITH YOUNG ALBERT.

THERE IS NO REASON TO SUGGEST THAT HE IS INTELLECTUALLY SUBNORMAL IN ANY WAY.

THAT'S A RELIEF, DOCTOR!

BUT WHEN WILL HE TALK?

HE WILL TALK WHEN HE IS READY. PERHAPS HIS MIND IS ON OTHER THINGS.

EINSTEIN LATER SAID THIS GAVE HIM TIME TO STUDY THINGS OTHERS TOOK FOR GRANTED.

ALBERT SOON BEGAN TO TALK. IN 1884, WHEN HE WAS FIVE, HE HAD A BRIEF ILLNESS. HIS FATHER GAVE HIM A PRESENT THAT WOULD CHANGE HIS LIFE FOREVER.

I HAVE A SPECIAL GIFT FOR YOU...

...IT'S A COMPASS.

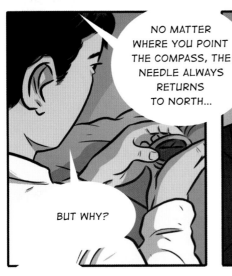

NO MATTER WHERE YOU POINT THE COMPASS, THE NEEDLE ALWAYS RETURNS TO NORTH...

BUT WHY?

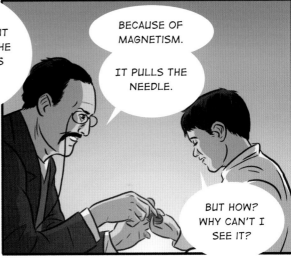

BECAUSE OF MAGNETISM.

IT PULLS THE NEEDLE.

BUT HOW? WHY CAN'T I SEE IT?

IT'S A FORCE...LIKE GRAVITY.

GRAVITY IS THE FORCE THAT HOLDS US TO THE GROUND.

THE UNIVERSE IS MADE UP OF INVISIBLE FORCES THAT AFFECT OUR LIVES IN HUNDREDS OF DIFFERENT WAYS.

AMAZING! I MUST DISCOVER THESE DEEPLY HIDDEN FORCES.

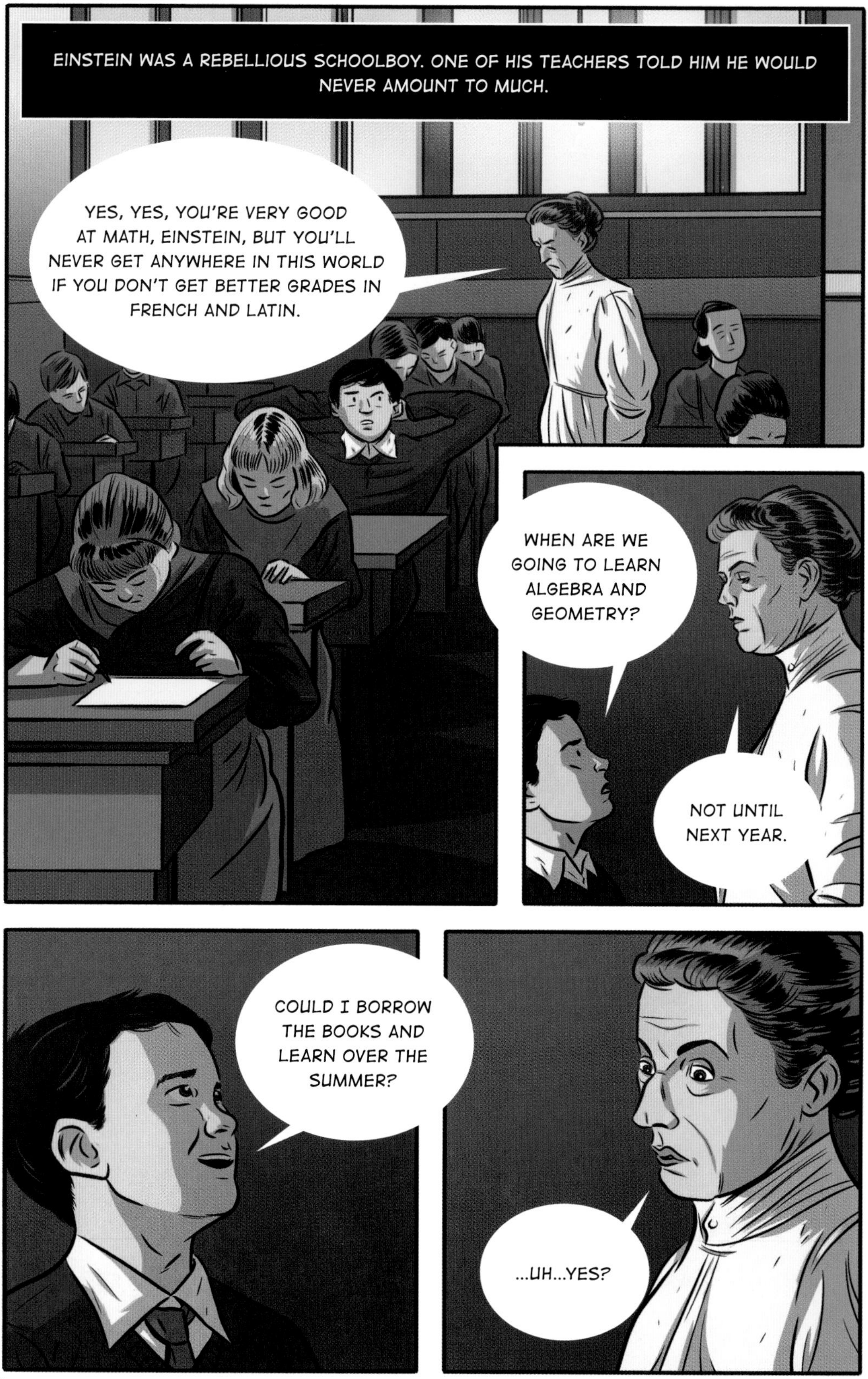
EINSTEIN WAS A REBELLIOUS SCHOOLBOY. ONE OF HIS TEACHERS TOLD HIM HE WOULD NEVER AMOUNT TO MUCH.
YES, YES, YOU'RE VERY GOOD AT MATH, EINSTEIN, BUT YOU'LL NEVER GET ANYWHERE IN THIS WORLD IF YOU DON'T GET BETTER GRADES IN FRENCH AND LATIN.
WHEN ARE WE GOING TO LEARN ALGEBRA AND GEOMETRY?
NOT UNTIL NEXT YEAR.
COULD I BORROW THE BOOKS AND LEARN OVER THE SUMMER?
...UH...YES?

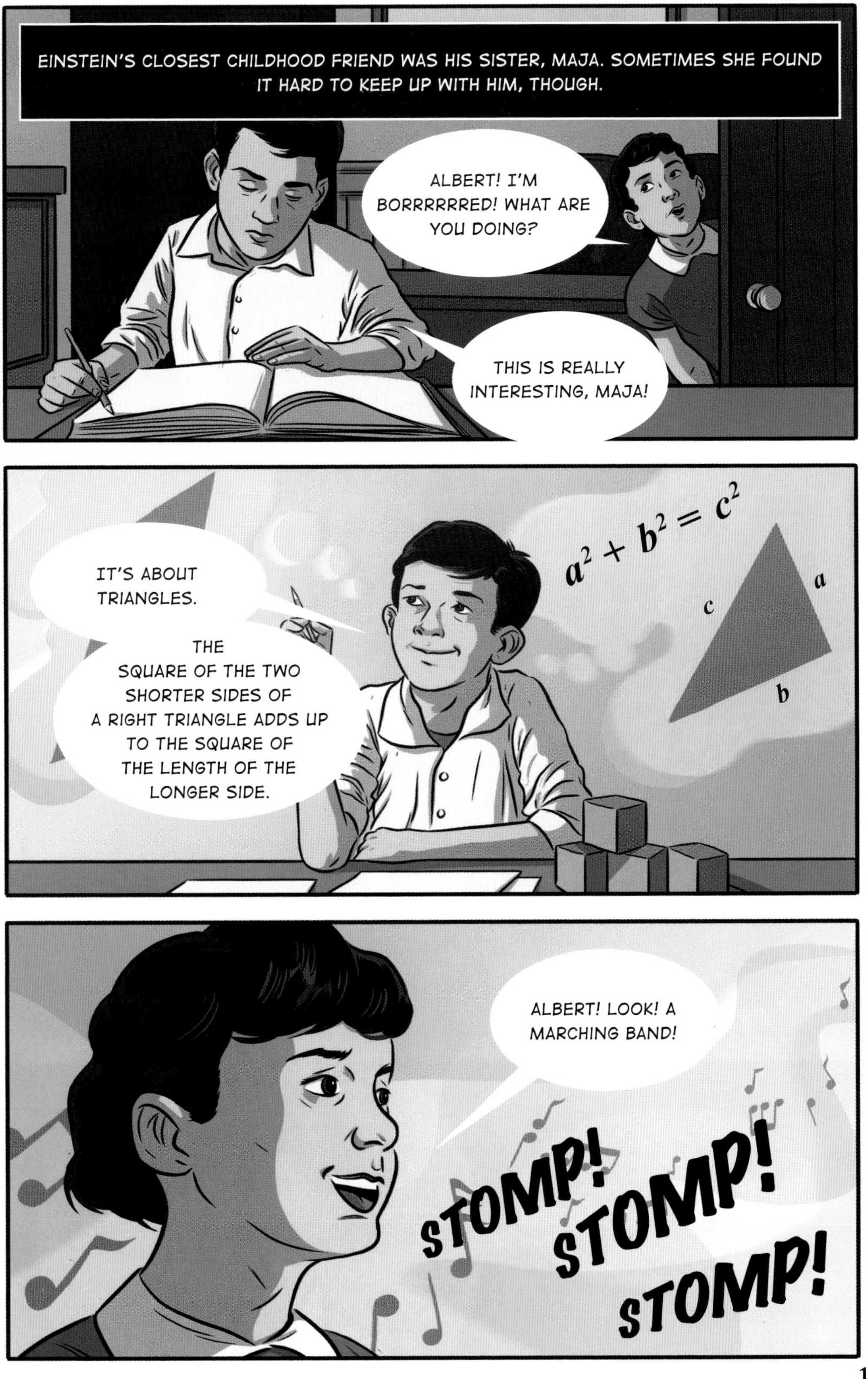
EINSTEIN'S CLOSEST CHILDHOOD FRIEND WAS HIS SISTER, MAJA. SOMETIMES SHE FOUND IT HARD TO KEEP UP WITH HIM, THOUGH.
ALBERT! I'M BORRRRRRED! WHAT ARE YOU DOING?
THIS IS REALLY INTERESTING, MAJA!
IT'S ABOUT TRIANGLES.
THE SQUARE OF THE TWO SHORTER SIDES OF A RIGHT TRIANGLE ADDS UP TO THE SQUARE OF THE LENGTH OF THE LONGER SIDE.
$a^2 + b^2 = c^2$
c
a
b
ALBERT! LOOK! A MARCHING BAND!
STOMP! STOMP! STOMP!

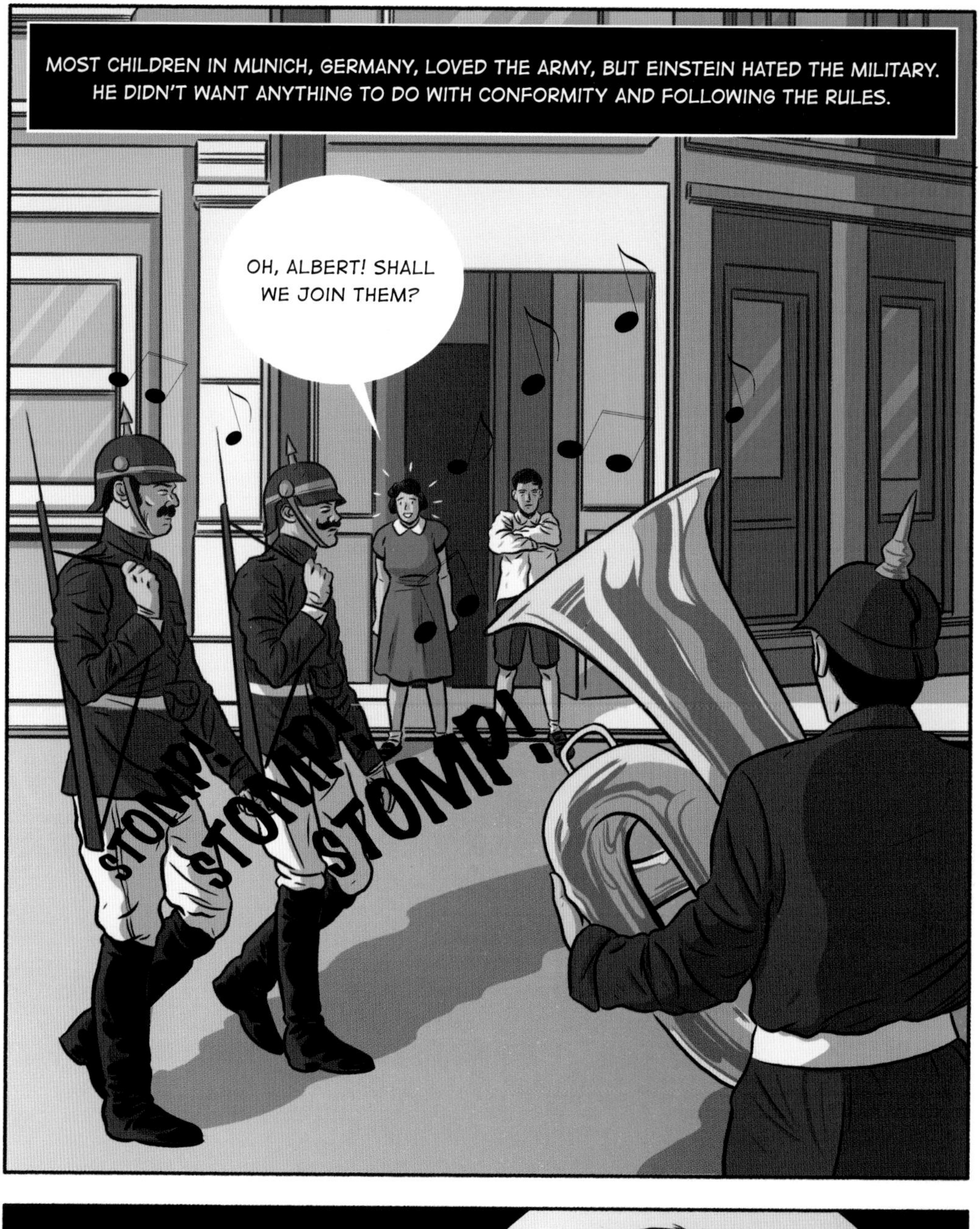
MOST CHILDREN IN MUNICH, GERMANY, LOVED THE ARMY, BUT EINSTEIN HATED THE MILITARY. HE DIDN'T WANT ANYTHING TO DO WITH CONFORMITY AND FOLLOWING THE RULES.
OH, ALBERT! SHALL WE JOIN THEM?
STOMP!-STOMP!-STOMP!

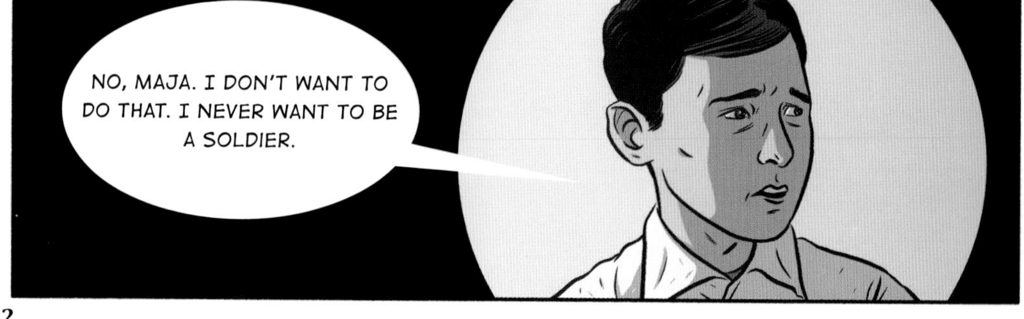
NO, MAJA. I DON'T WANT TO DO THAT. I NEVER WANT TO BE A SOLDIER.

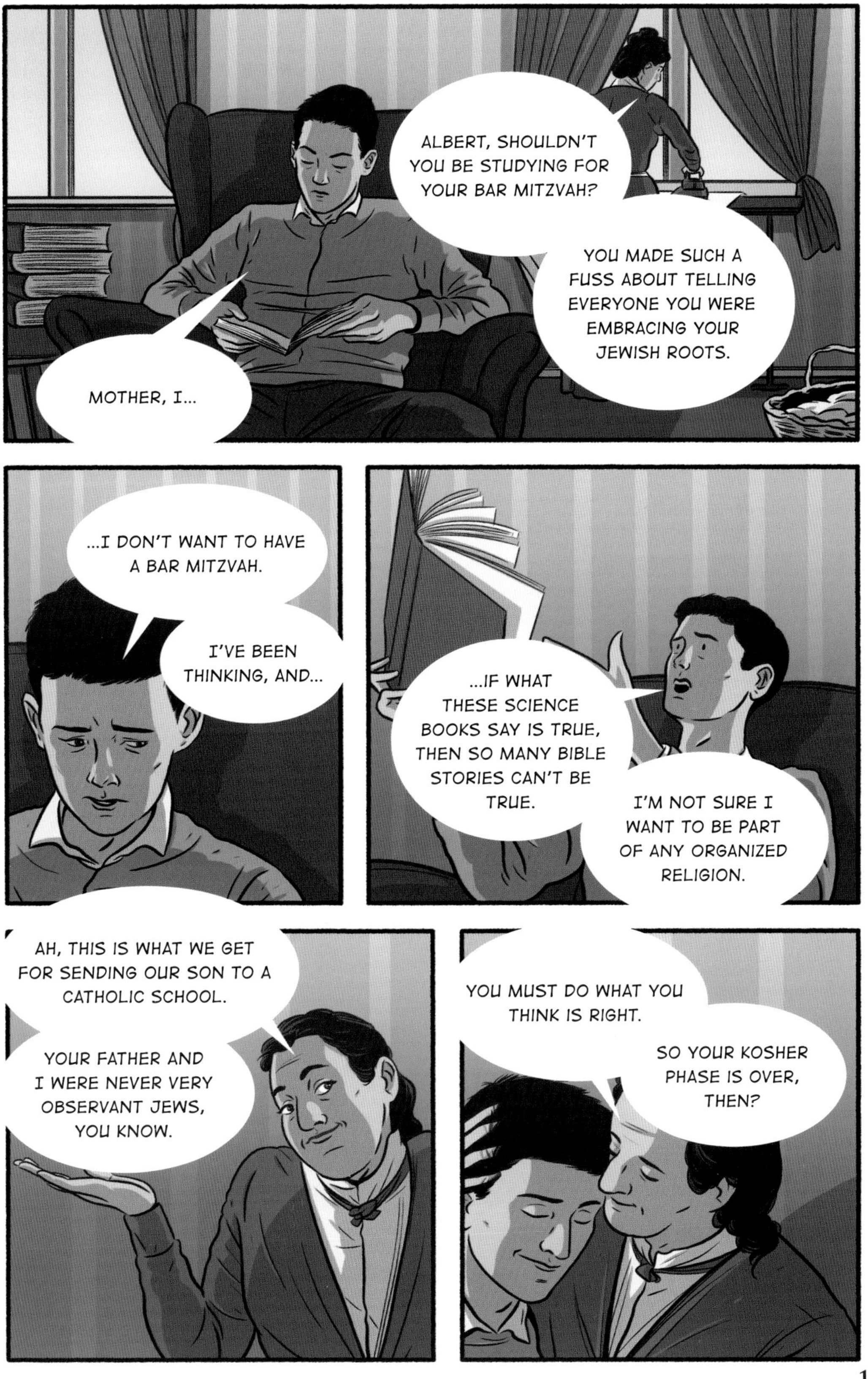
ALBERT, SHOULDN'T YOU BE STUDYING FOR YOUR BAR MITZVAH?
YOU MADE SUCH A FUSS ABOUT TELLING EVERYONE YOU WERE EMBRACING YOUR JEWISH ROOTS.
MOTHER, I...
...I DON'T WANT TO HAVE A BAR MITZVAH.
I'VE BEEN THINKING, AND...
...IF WHAT THESE SCIENCE BOOKS SAY IS TRUE, THEN SO MANY BIBLE STORIES CAN'T BE TRUE.
I'M NOT SURE I WANT TO BE PART OF ANY ORGANIZED RELIGION.
AH, THIS IS WHAT WE GET FOR SENDING OUR SON TO A CATHOLIC SCHOOL.
YOUR FATHER AND I WERE NEVER VERY OBSERVANT JEWS, YOU KNOW.
YOU MUST DO WHAT YOU THINK IS RIGHT.
SO YOUR KOSHER PHASE IS OVER, THEN?

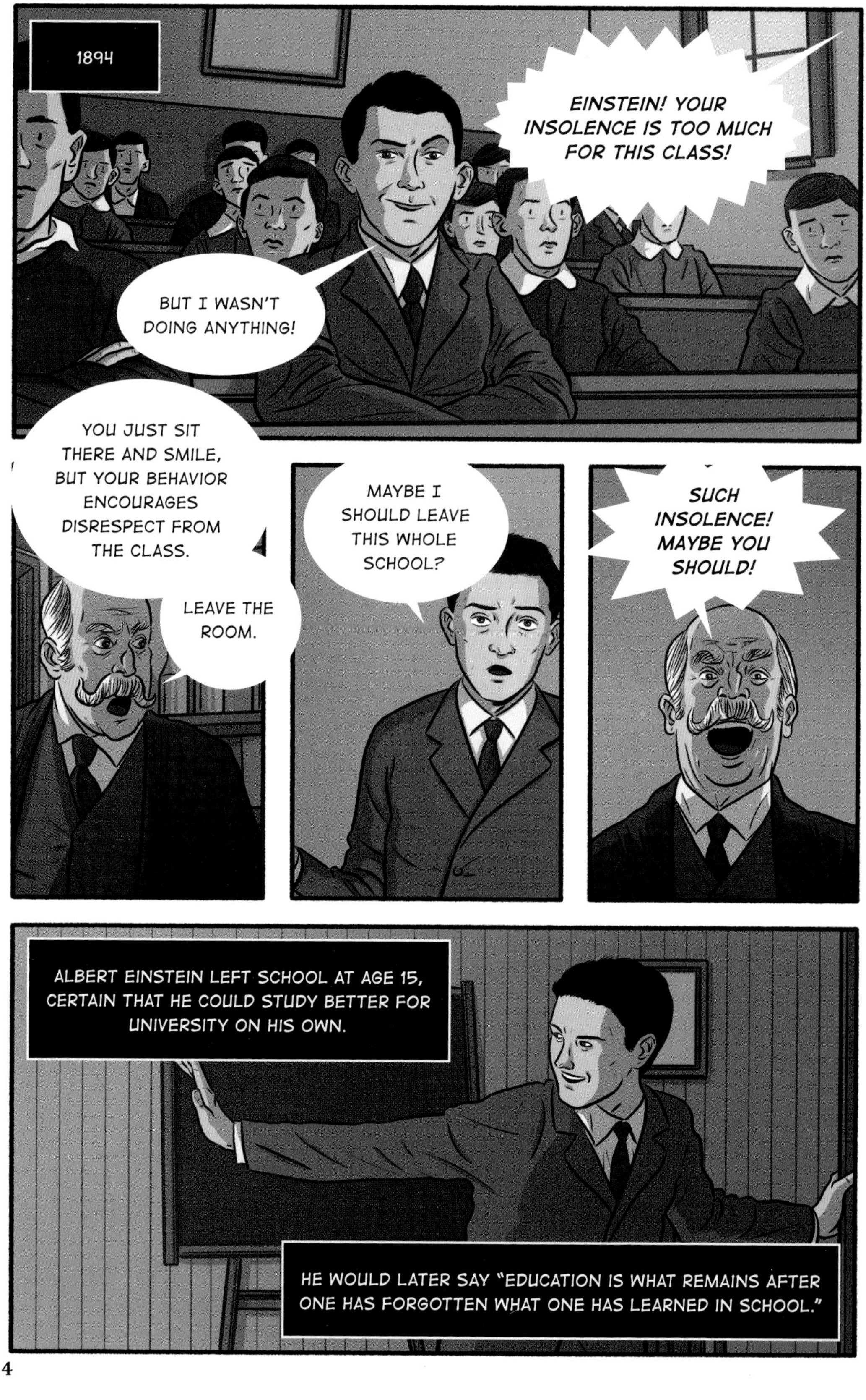
1894
EINSTEIN! YOUR INSOLENCE IS TOO MUCH FOR THIS CLASS!
BUT I WASN'T DOING ANYTHING!
YOU JUST SIT THERE AND SMILE, BUT YOUR BEHAVIOR ENCOURAGES DISRESPECT FROM THE CLASS.
LEAVE THE ROOM.
MAYBE I SHOULD LEAVE THIS WHOLE SCHOOL?
SUCH INSOLENCE! MAYBE YOU SHOULD!
ALBERT EINSTEIN LEFT SCHOOL AT AGE 15, CERTAIN THAT HE COULD STUDY BETTER FOR UNIVERSITY ON HIS OWN.
HE WOULD LATER SAY "EDUCATION IS WHAT REMAINS AFTER ONE HAS FORGOTTEN WHAT ONE HAS LEARNED IN SCHOOL."

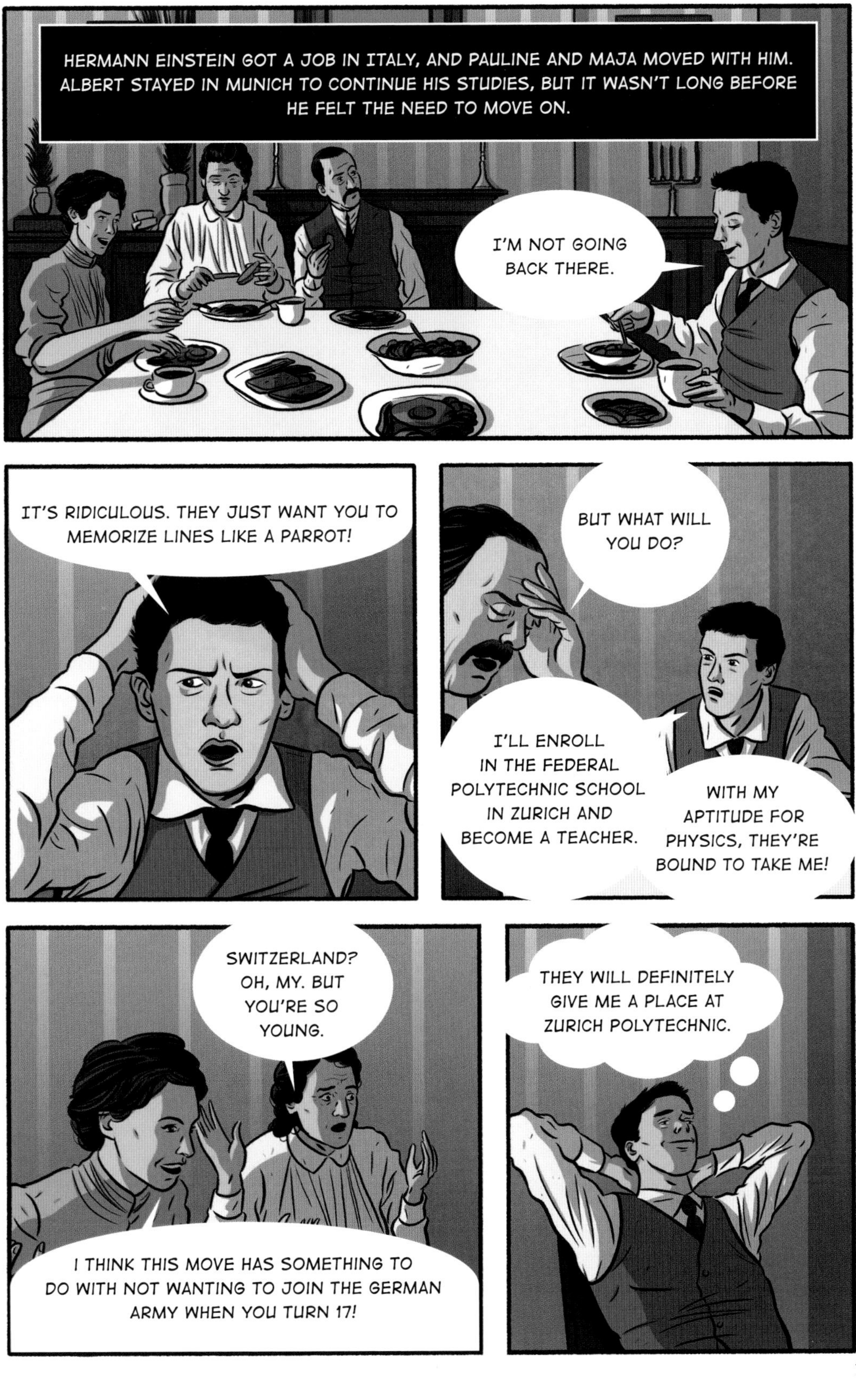
HERMANN EINSTEIN GOT A JOB IN ITALY, AND PAULINE AND MAJA MOVED WITH HIM. ALBERT STAYED IN MUNICH TO CONTINUE HIS STUDIES, BUT IT WASN'T LONG BEFORE HE FELT THE NEED TO MOVE ON.
I'M NOT GOING BACK THERE.
IT'S RIDICULOUS. THEY JUST WANT YOU TO MEMORIZE LINES LIKE A PARROT!
BUT WHAT WILL YOU DO?
I'LL ENROLL IN THE FEDERAL POLYTECHNIC SCHOOL IN ZURICH AND BECOME A TEACHER.
WITH MY APTITUDE FOR PHYSICS, THEY'RE BOUND TO TAKE ME!
SWITZERLAND? OH, MY. BUT YOU'RE SO YOUNG.
I THINK THIS MOVE HAS SOMETHING TO DO WITH NOT WANTING TO JOIN THE GERMAN ARMY WHEN YOU TURN 17!
THEY WILL DEFINITELY GIVE ME A PLACE AT ZURICH POLYTECHNIC.

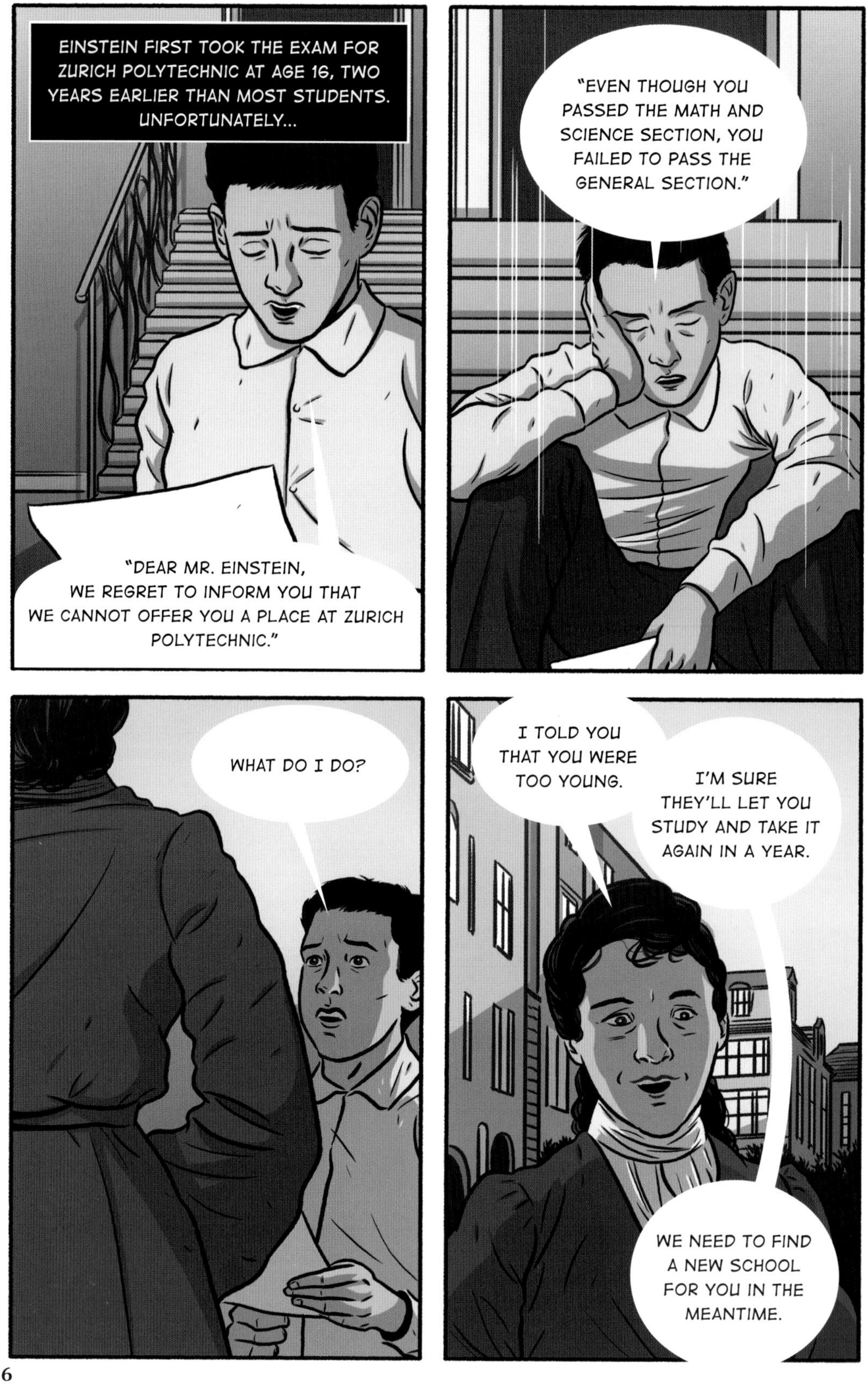
EINSTEIN FIRST TOOK THE EXAM FOR ZURICH POLYTECHNIC AT AGE 16, TWO YEARS EARLIER THAN MOST STUDENTS. UNFORTUNATELY...
"DEAR MR. EINSTEIN, WE REGRET TO INFORM YOU THAT WE CANNOT OFFER YOU A PLACE AT ZURICH POLYTECHNIC."
"EVEN THOUGH YOU PASSED THE MATH AND SCIENCE SECTION, YOU FAILED TO PASS THE GENERAL SECTION."
WHAT DO I DO?
I TOLD YOU THAT YOU WERE TOO YOUNG.
I'M SURE THEY'LL LET YOU STUDY AND TAKE IT AGAIN IN A YEAR.
WE NEED TO FIND A NEW SCHOOL FOR YOU IN THE MEANTIME.

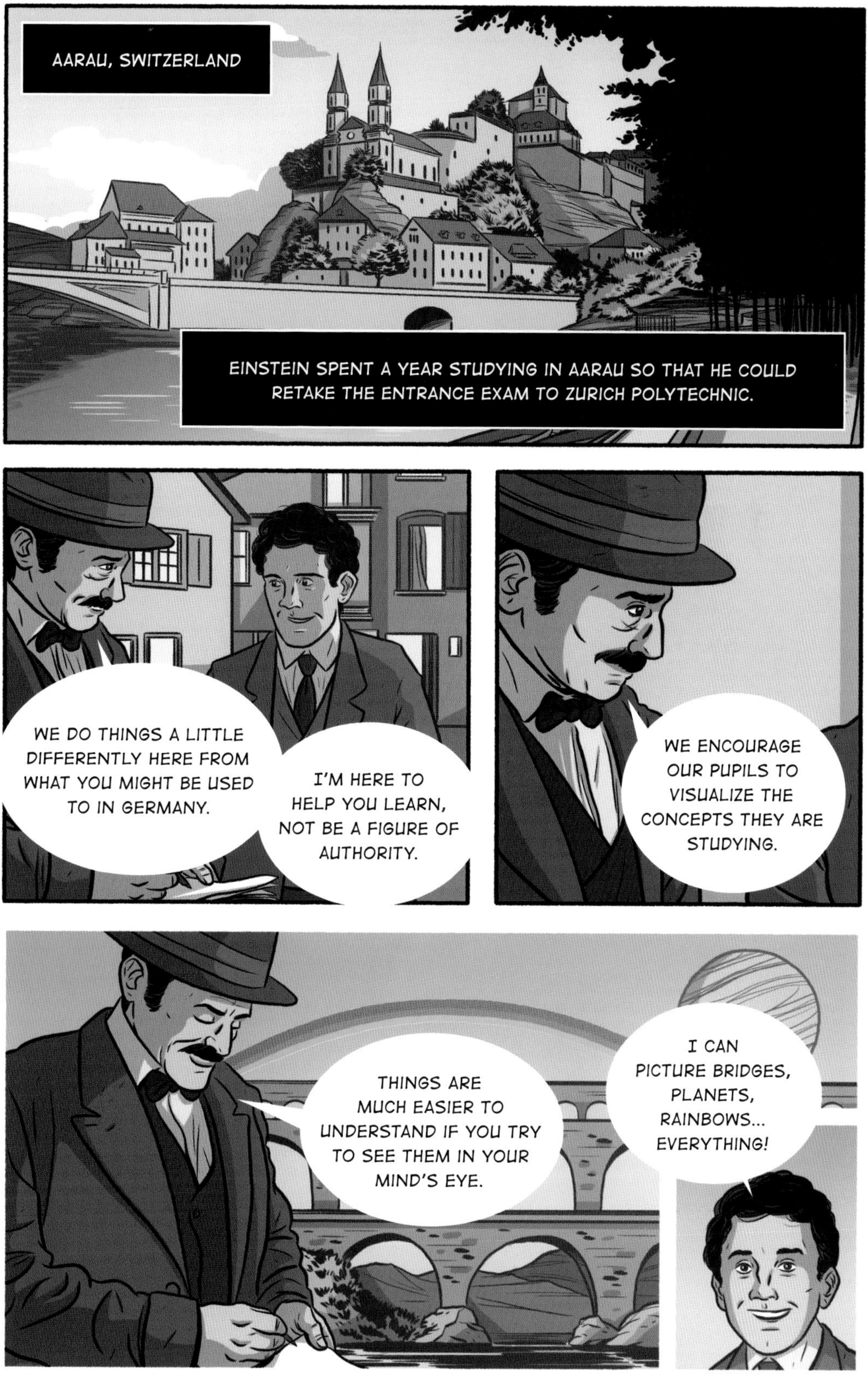
AARAU, SWITZERLAND
EINSTEIN SPENT A YEAR STUDYING IN AARAU SO THAT HE COULD RETAKE THE ENTRANCE EXAM TO ZURICH POLYTECHNIC.
WE DO THINGS A LITTLE DIFFERENTLY HERE FROM WHAT YOU MIGHT BE USED TO IN GERMANY.
I'M HERE TO HELP YOU LEARN, NOT BE A FIGURE OF AUTHORITY.
WE ENCOURAGE OUR PUPILS TO VISUALIZE THE CONCEPTS THEY ARE STUDYING.
THINGS ARE MUCH EASIER TO UNDERSTAND IF YOU TRY TO SEE THEM IN YOUR MIND'S EYE.
I CAN PICTURE BRIDGES, PLANETS, RAINBOWS... EVERYTHING!

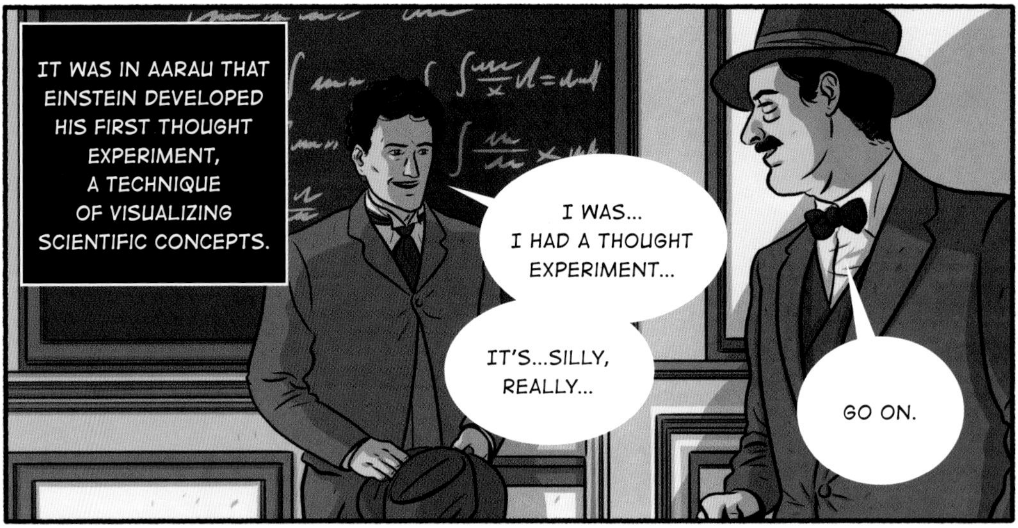
IT WAS IN AARAU THAT EINSTEIN DEVELOPED HIS FIRST THOUGHT EXPERIMENT, A TECHNIQUE OF VISUALIZING SCIENTIFIC CONCEPTS.
I WAS... I HAD A THOUGHT EXPERIMENT...
IT'S...SILLY, REALLY...
GO ON.

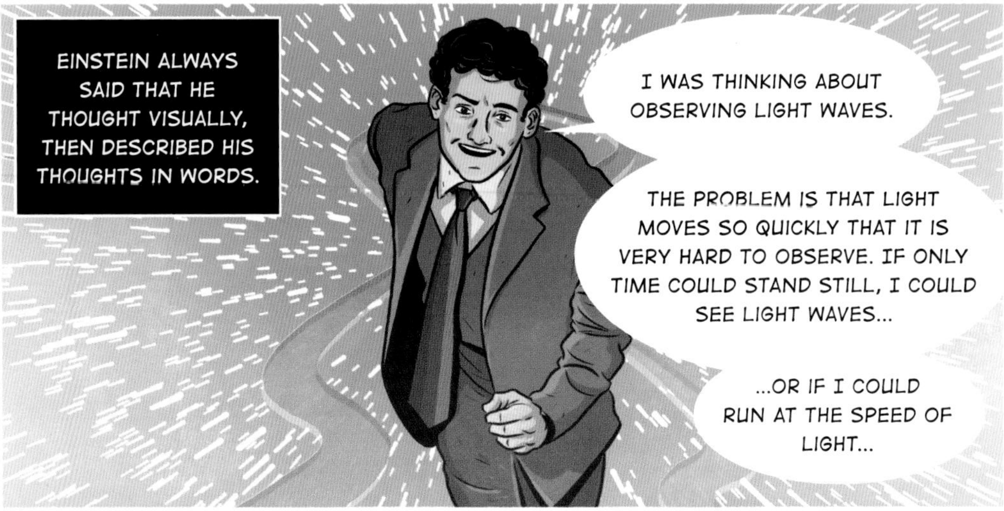
EINSTEIN ALWAYS SAID THAT HE THOUGHT VISUALLY, THEN DESCRIBED HIS THOUGHTS IN WORDS.
I WAS THINKING ABOUT OBSERVING LIGHT WAVES.
THE PROBLEM IS THAT LIGHT MOVES SO QUICKLY THAT IT IS VERY HARD TO OBSERVE. IF ONLY TIME COULD STAND STILL, I COULD SEE LIGHT WAVES...
...OR IF I COULD RUN AT THE SPEED OF LIGHT...

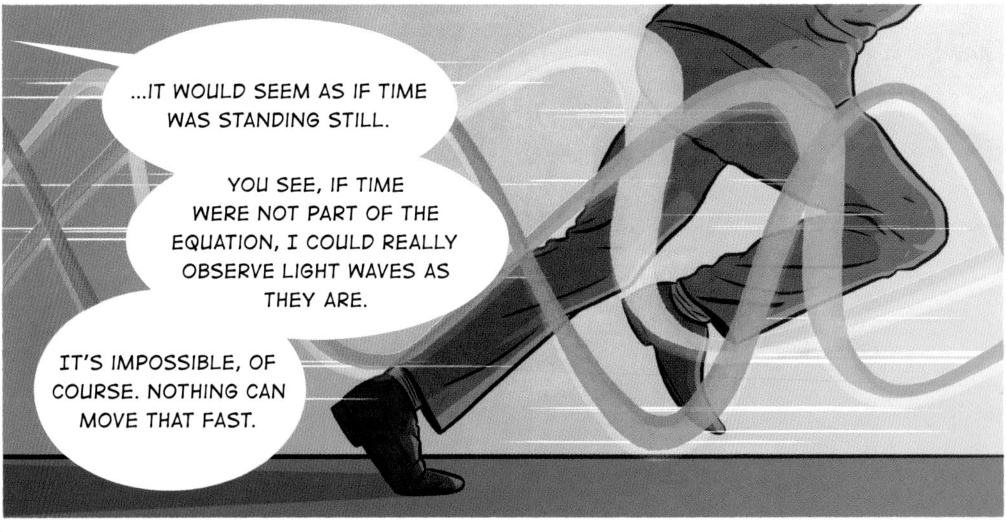
...IT WOULD SEEM AS IF TIME WAS STANDING STILL.
YOU SEE, IF TIME WERE NOT PART OF THE EQUATION, I COULD REALLY OBSERVE LIGHT WAVES AS THEY ARE.
IT'S IMPOSSIBLE, OF COURSE. NOTHING CAN MOVE THAT FAST.

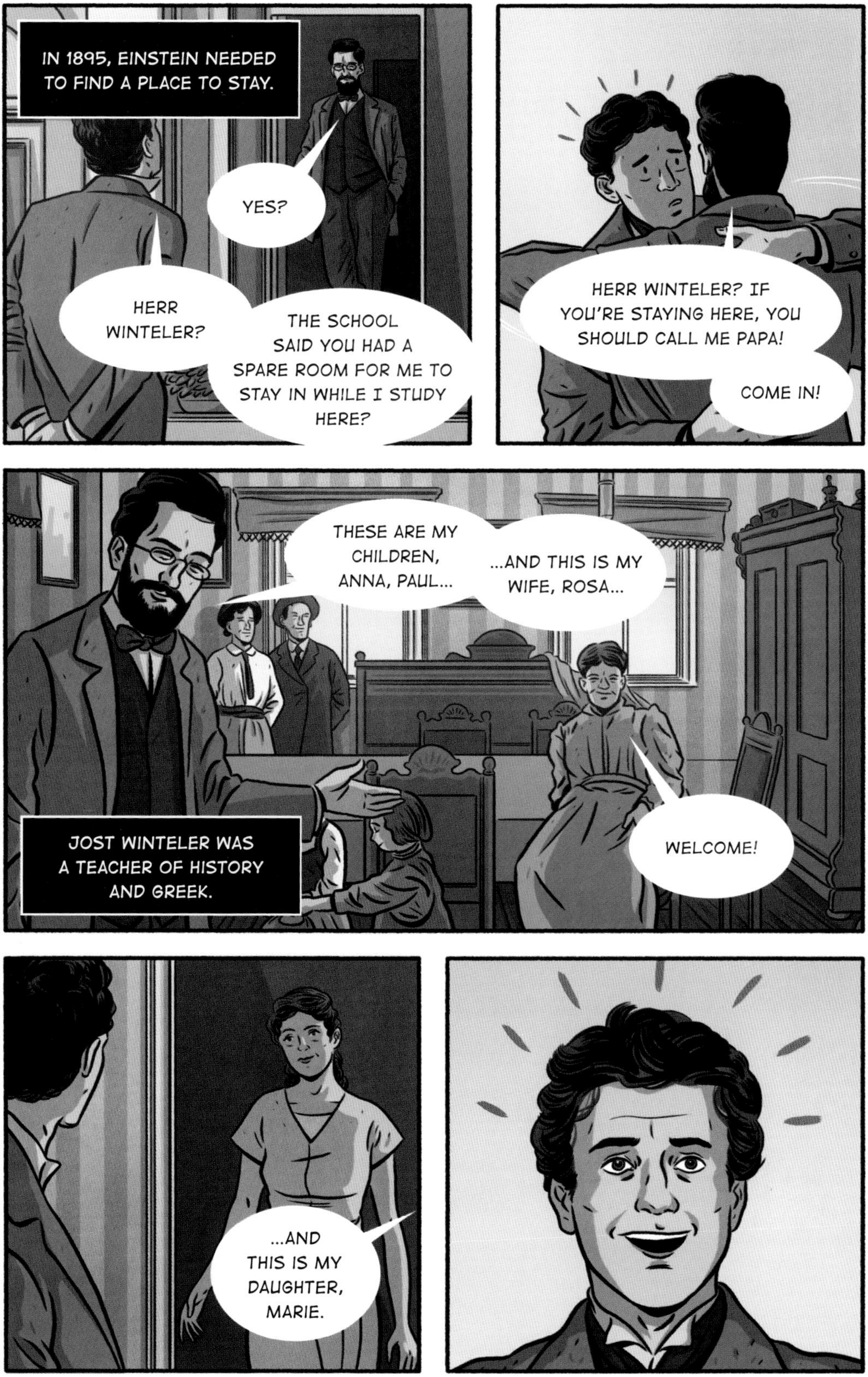
IN 1895, EINSTEIN NEEDED TO FIND A PLACE TO STAY.
YES?
HERR WINTELER?
THE SCHOOL SAID YOU HAD A SPARE ROOM FOR ME TO STAY IN WHILE I STUDY HERE?
HERR WINTELER? IF YOU'RE STAYING HERE, YOU SHOULD CALL ME PAPA!
COME IN!
THESE ARE MY CHILDREN, ANNA, PAUL...
...AND THIS IS MY WIFE, ROSA...
WELCOME!
JOST WINTELER WAS A TEACHER OF HISTORY AND GREEK.
...AND THIS IS MY DAUGHTER, MARIE.

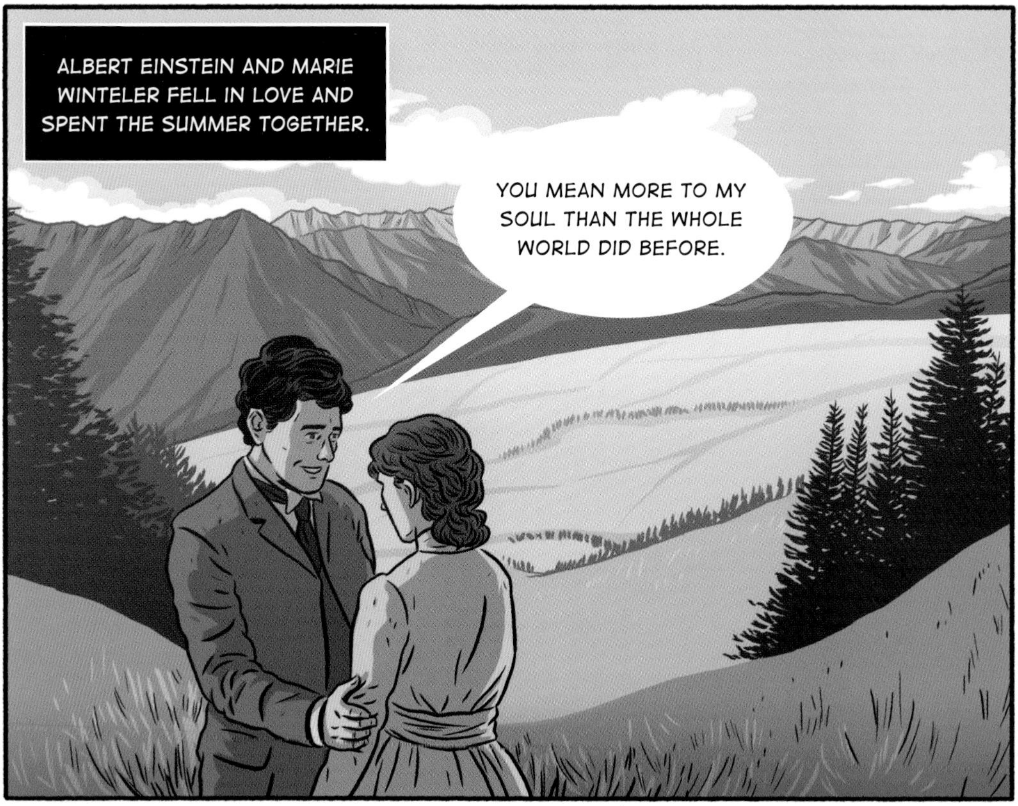
ALBERT EINSTEIN AND MARIE WINTELER FELL IN LOVE AND SPENT THE SUMMER TOGETHER.
YOU MEAN MORE TO MY SOUL THAN THE WHOLE WORLD DID BEFORE.

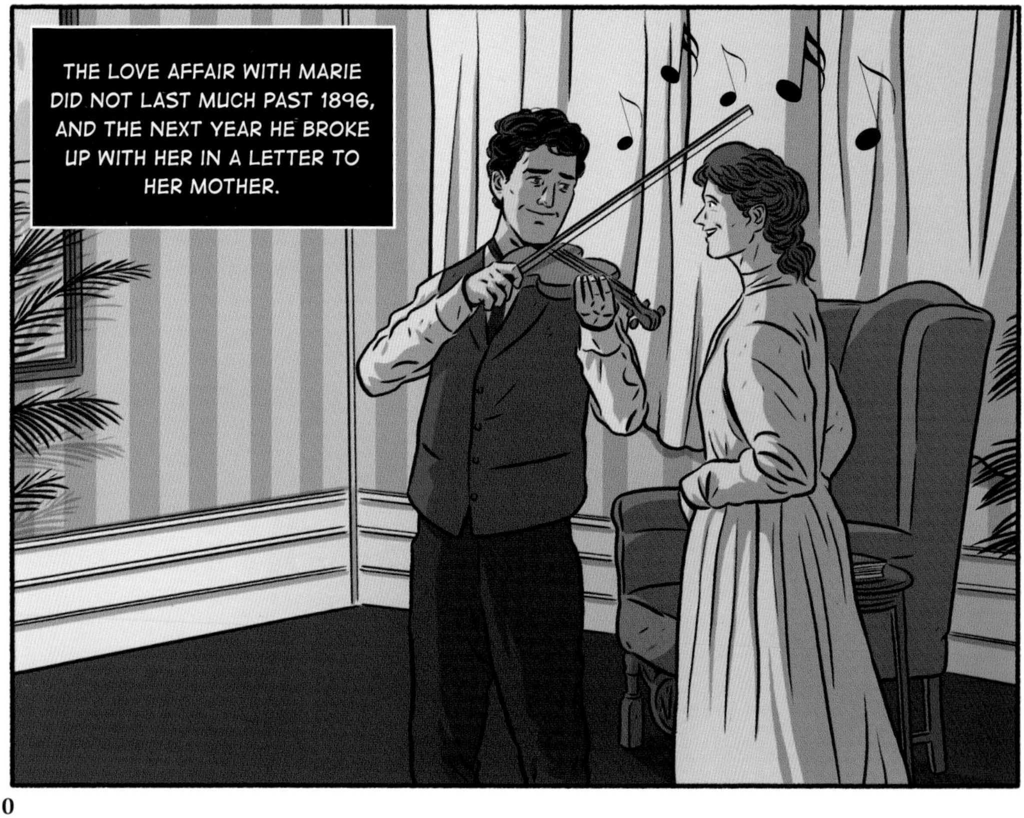
THE LOVE AFFAIR WITH MARIE DID NOT LAST MUCH PAST 1896, AND THE NEXT YEAR HE BROKE UP WITH HER IN A LETTER TO HER MOTHER.

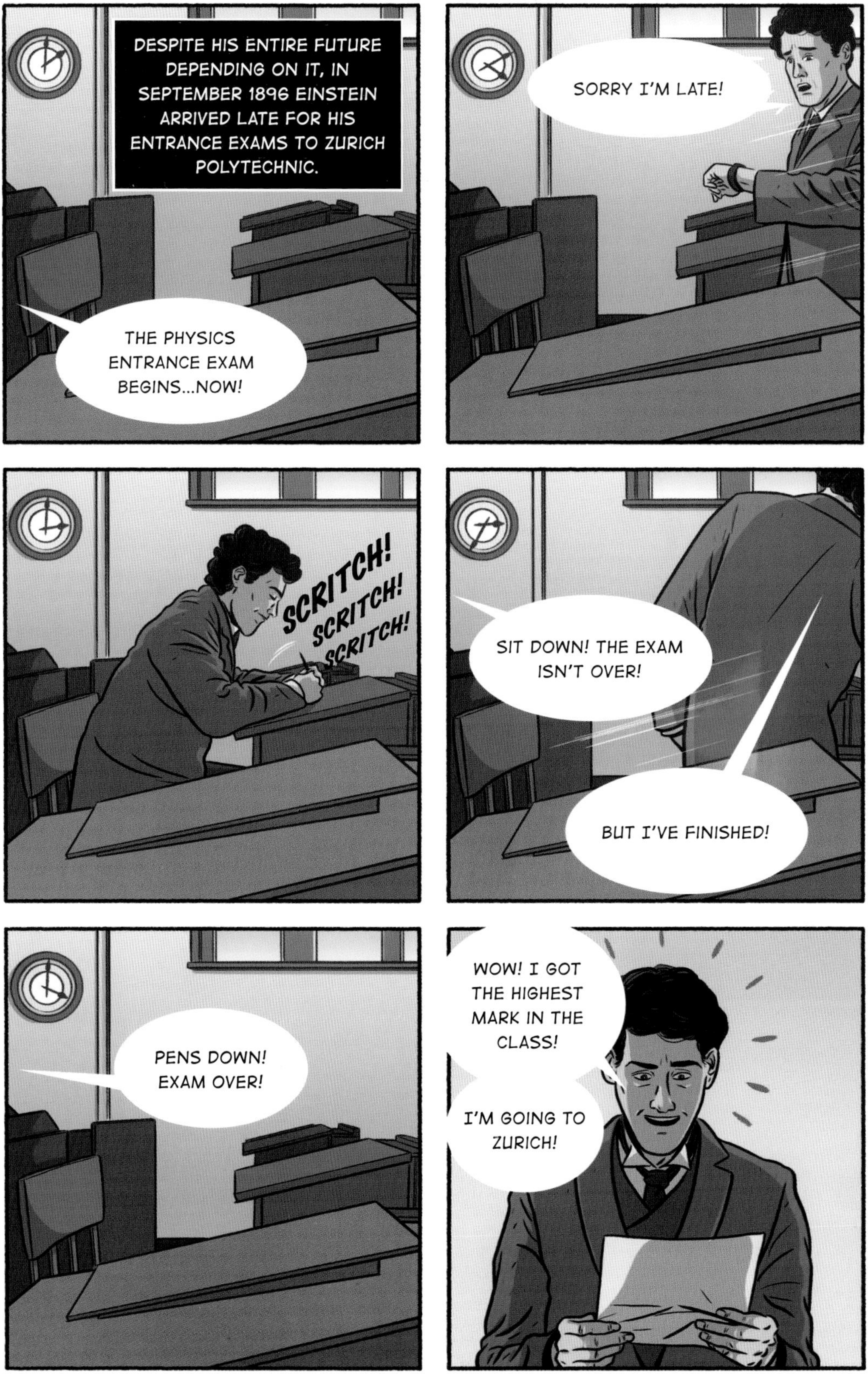
DESPITE HIS ENTIRE FUTURE DEPENDING ON IT, IN SEPTEMBER 1896 EINSTEIN ARRIVED LATE FOR HIS ENTRANCE EXAMS TO ZURICH POLYTECHNIC.
THE PHYSICS ENTRANCE EXAM BEGINS...NOW!
SORRY I'M LATE!
SCRITCH! SCRITCH! SCRITCH!
SIT DOWN! THE EXAM ISN'T OVER!
BUT I'VE FINISHED!
PENS DOWN! EXAM OVER!
WOW! I GOT THE HIGHEST MARK IN THE CLASS!
I'M GOING TO ZURICH!

CHAPTER 2

LIFE AT ZURICH POLYTECHNIC

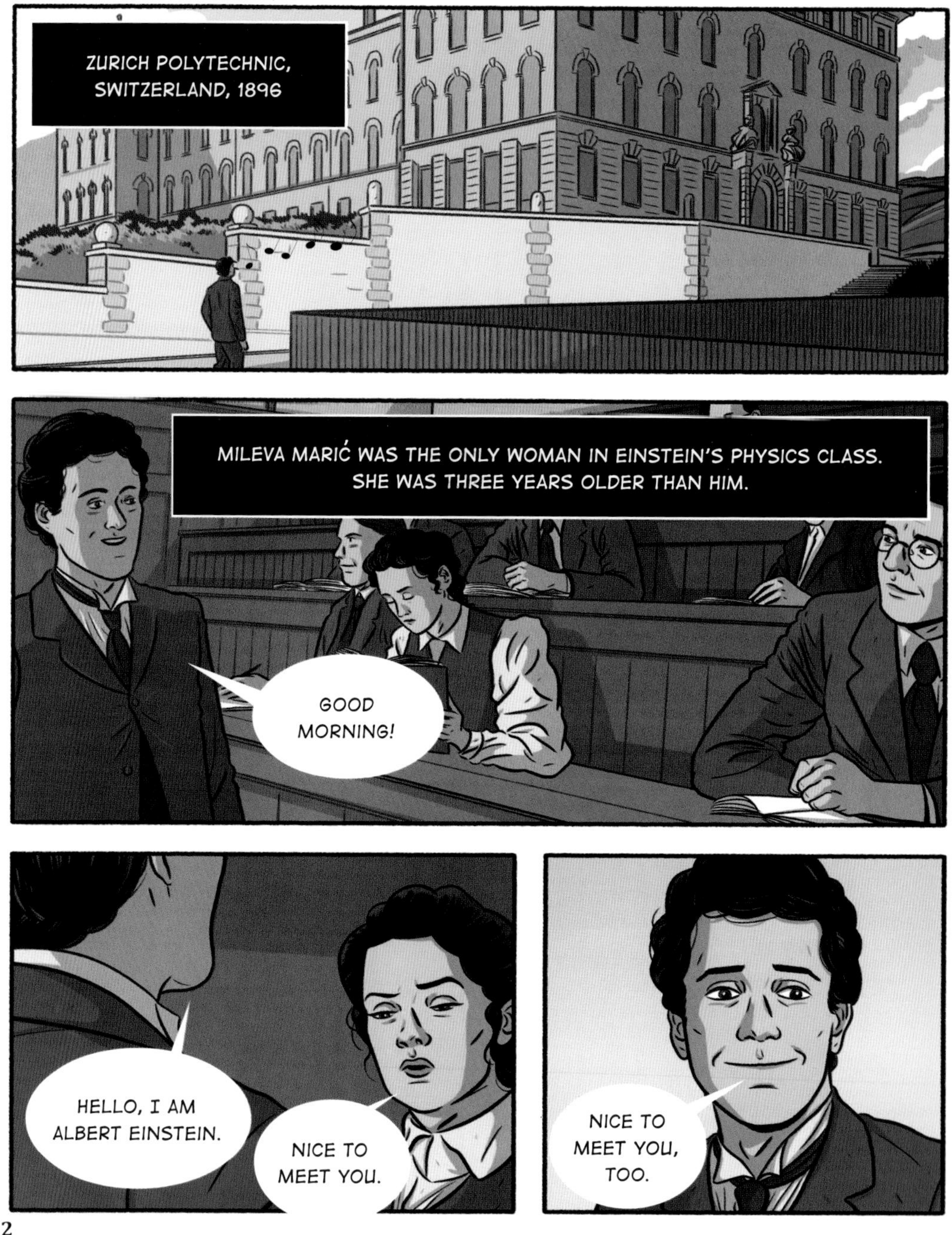
ZURICH POLYTECHNIC, SWITZERLAND, 1896
MILEVA MARIĆ WAS THE ONLY WOMAN IN EINSTEIN'S PHYSICS CLASS. SHE WAS THREE YEARS OLDER THAN HIM.
GOOD MORNING!
HELLO, I AM ALBERT EINSTEIN.
NICE TO MEET YOU.
NICE TO MEET YOU, TOO.

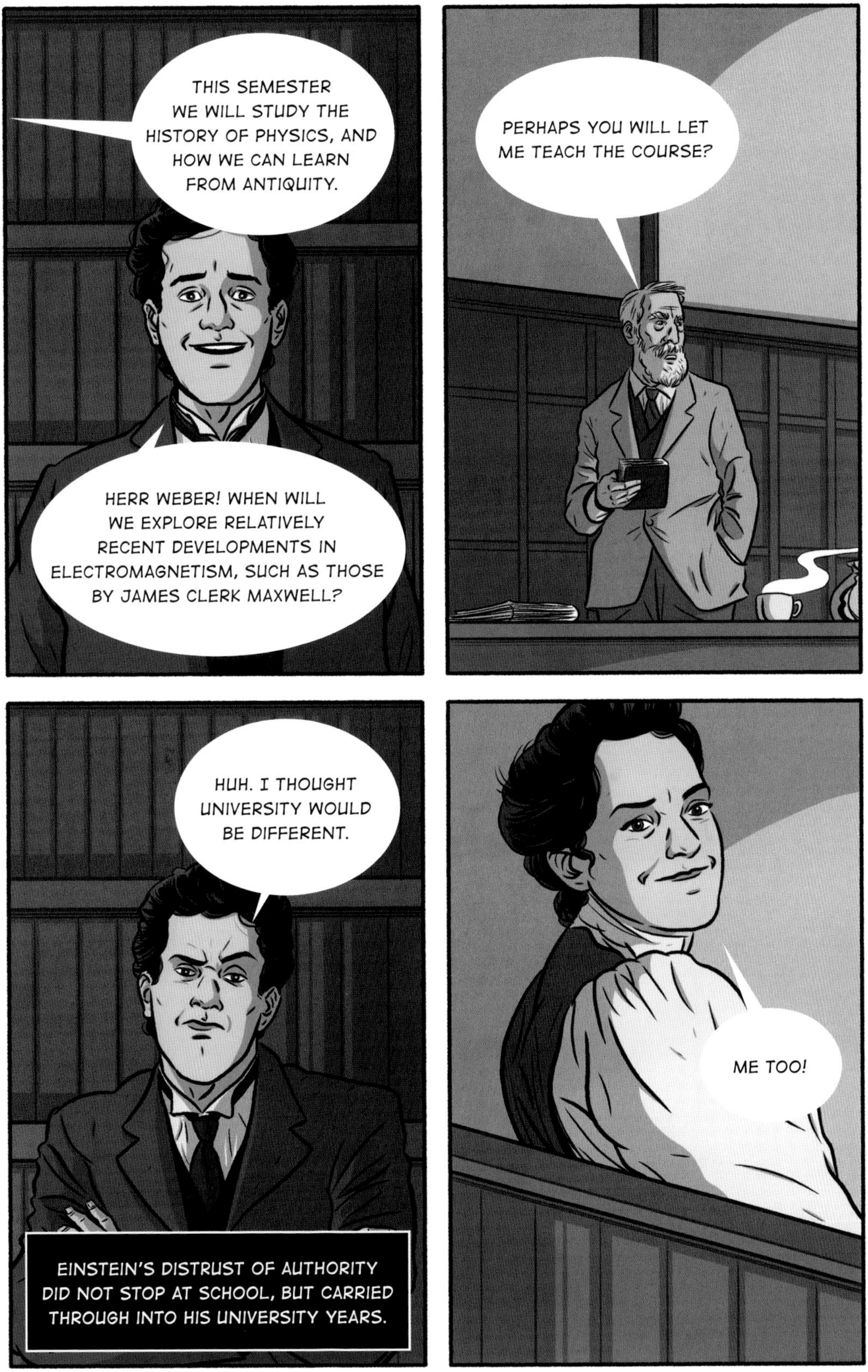
THIS SEMESTER WE WILL STUDY THE HISTORY OF PHYSICS, AND HOW WE CAN LEARN FROM ANTIQUITY.
HERR WEBER! WHEN WILL WE EXPLORE RELATIVELY RECENT DEVELOPMENTS IN ELECTROMAGNETISM, SUCH AS THOSE BY JAMES CLERK MAXWELL?
PERHAPS YOU WILL LET ME TEACH THE COURSE?
HUH. I THOUGHT UNIVERSITY WOULD BE DIFFERENT.
EINSTEIN'S DISTRUST OF AUTHORITY DID NOT STOP AT SCHOOL, BUT CARRIED THROUGH INTO HIS UNIVERSITY YEARS.
ME TOO!

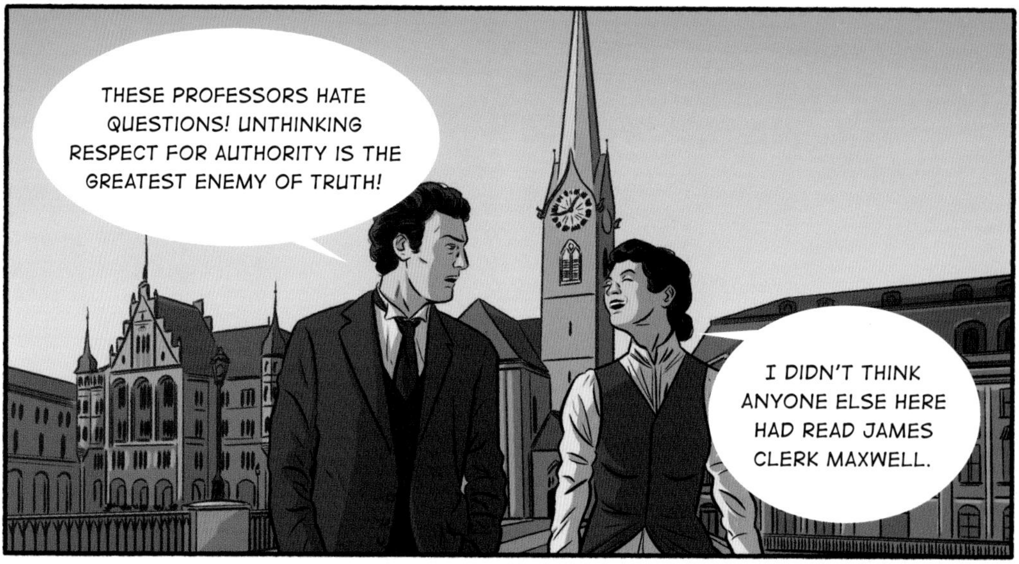
THESE PROFESSORS HATE QUESTIONS! UNTHINKING RESPECT FOR AUTHORITY IS THE GREATEST ENEMY OF TRUTH!
I DIDN'T THINK ANYONE ELSE HERE HAD READ JAMES CLERK MAXWELL.

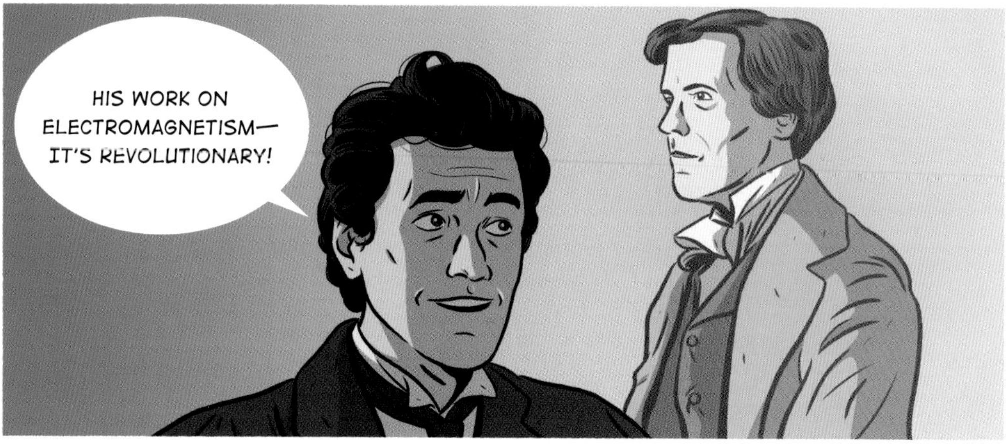
HIS WORK ON ELECTROMAGNETISM— IT'S REVOLUTIONARY!

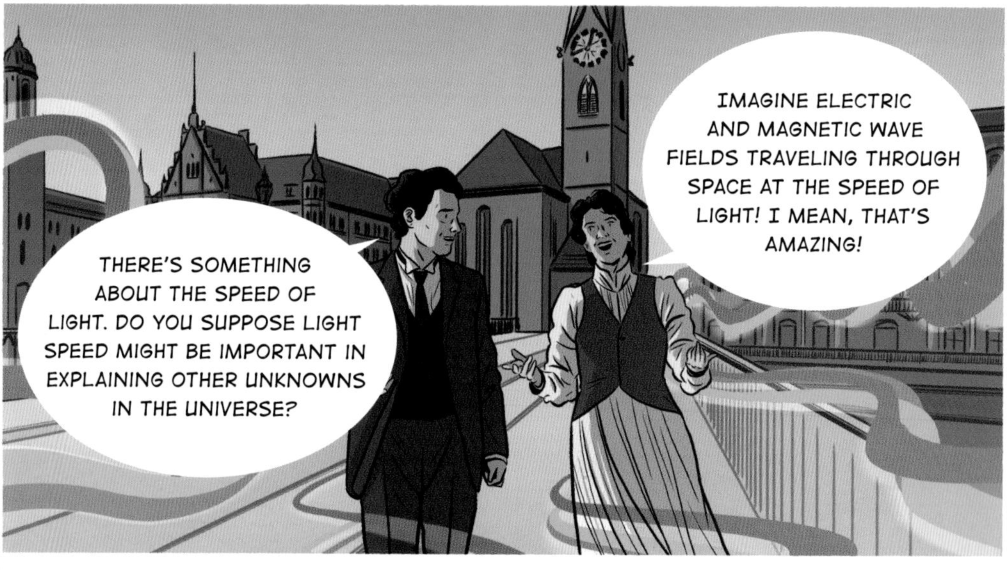
IMAGINE ELECTRIC AND MAGNETIC WAVE FIELDS TRAVELING THROUGH SPACE AT THE SPEED OF LIGHT! I MEAN, THAT'S AMAZING!
THERE'S SOMETHING ABOUT THE SPEED OF LIGHT. DO YOU SUPPOSE LIGHT SPEED MIGHT BE IMPORTANT IN EXPLAINING OTHER UNKNOWNS IN THE UNIVERSE?

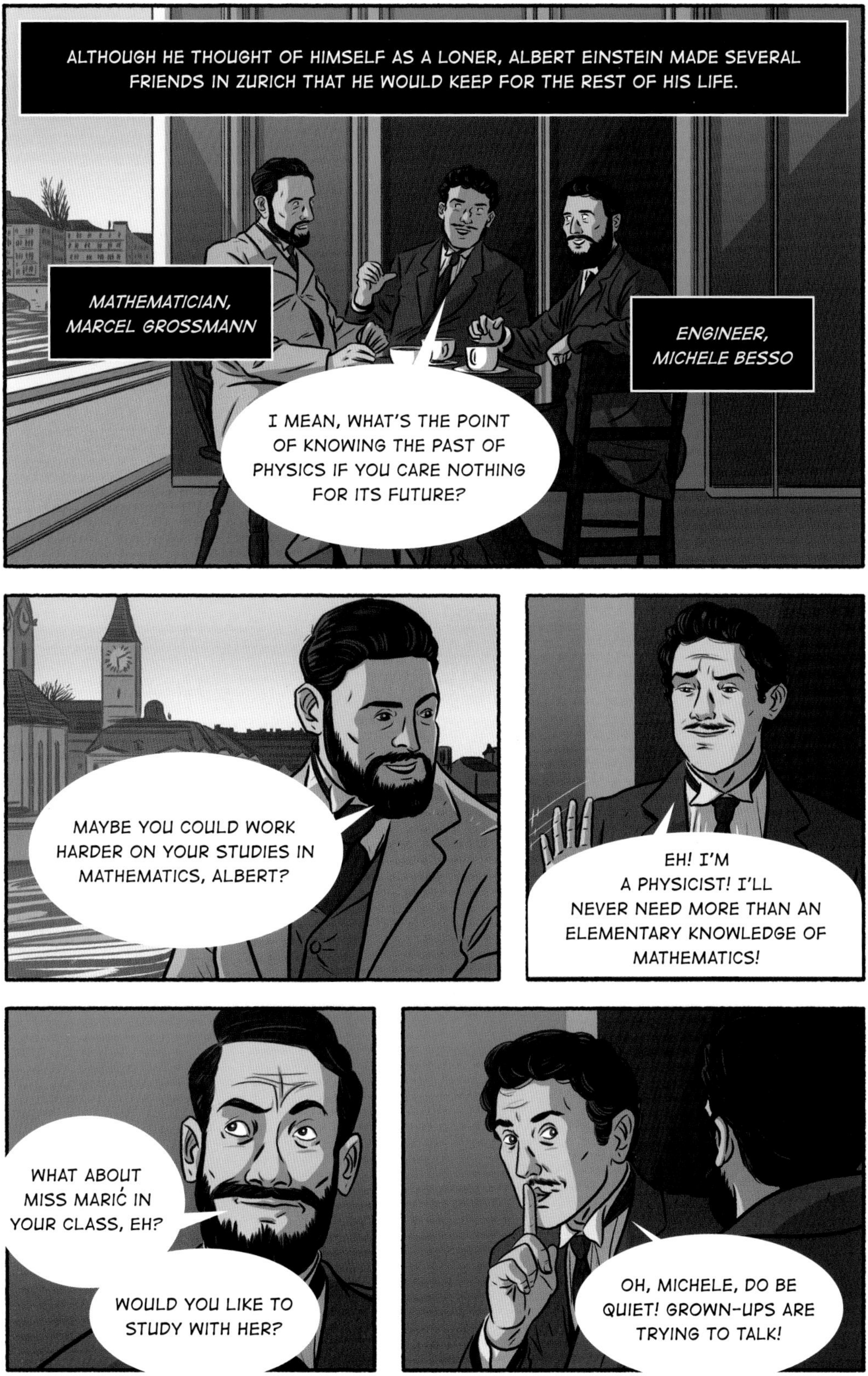
ALTHOUGH HE THOUGHT OF HIMSELF AS A LONER, ALBERT EINSTEIN MADE SEVERAL FRIENDS IN ZURICH THAT HE WOULD KEEP FOR THE REST OF HIS LIFE.
MATHEMATICIAN, MARCEL GROSSMANN
ENGINEER, MICHELE BESSO
I MEAN, WHAT'S THE POINT OF KNOWING THE PAST OF PHYSICS IF YOU CARE NOTHING FOR ITS FUTURE?
MAYBE YOU COULD WORK HARDER ON YOUR STUDIES IN MATHEMATICS, ALBERT?
EH! I'M A PHYSICIST! I'LL NEVER NEED MORE THAN AN ELEMENTARY KNOWLEDGE OF MATHEMATICS!
WHAT ABOUT MISS MARIĆ IN YOUR CLASS, EH?
WOULD YOU LIKE TO STUDY WITH HER?
OH, MICHELE, DO BE QUIET! GROWN-UPS ARE TRYING TO TALK!

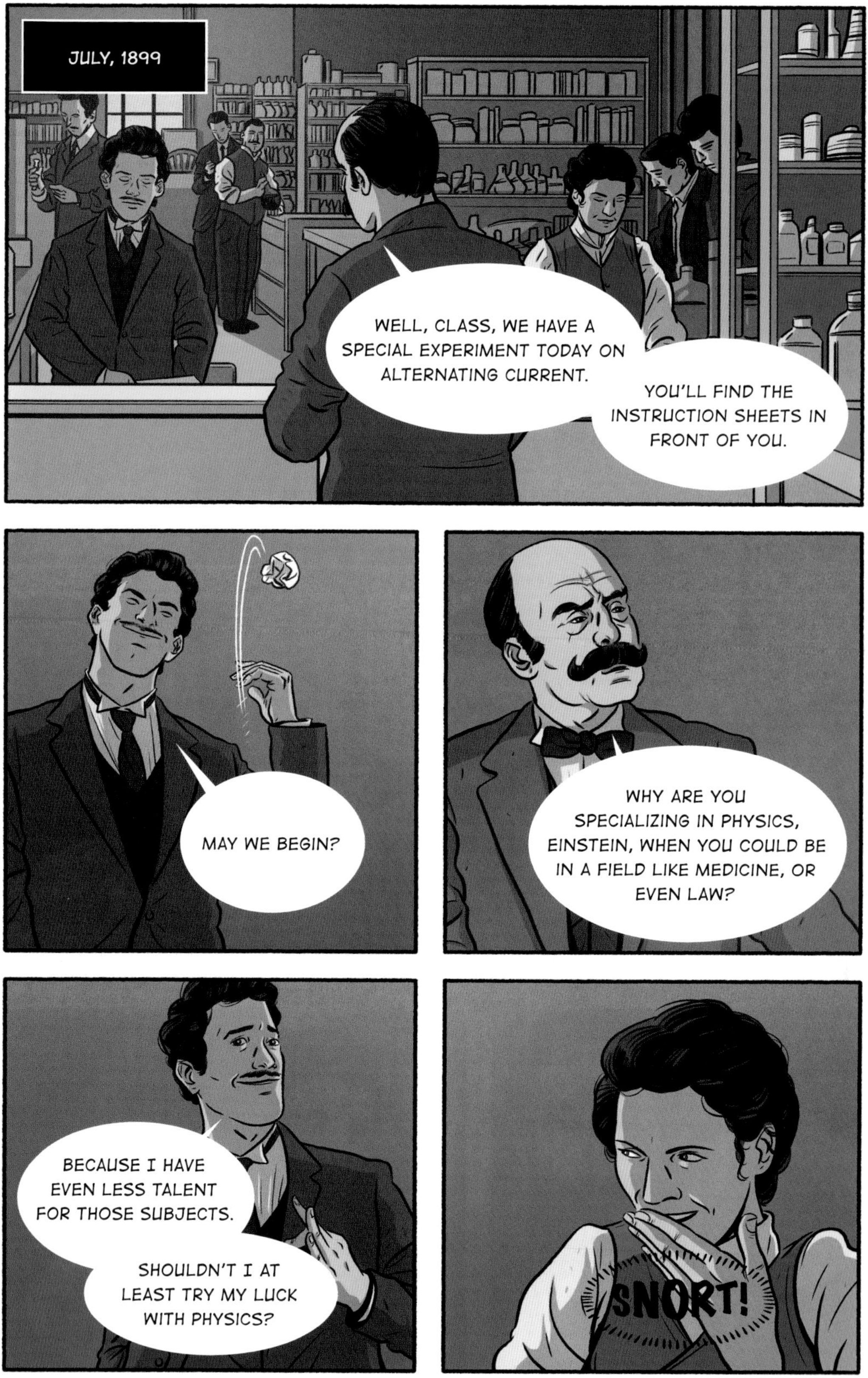
JULY, 1899
WELL, CLASS, WE HAVE A SPECIAL EXPERIMENT TODAY ON ALTERNATING CURRENT.
YOU'LL FIND THE INSTRUCTION SHEETS IN FRONT OF YOU.
MAY WE BEGIN?
WHY ARE YOU SPECIALIZING IN PHYSICS, EINSTEIN, WHEN YOU COULD BE IN A FIELD LIKE MEDICINE, OR EVEN LAW?
BECAUSE I HAVE EVEN LESS TALENT FOR THOSE SUBJECTS.
SHOULDN'T I AT LEAST TRY MY LUCK WITH PHYSICS?
SNORT!

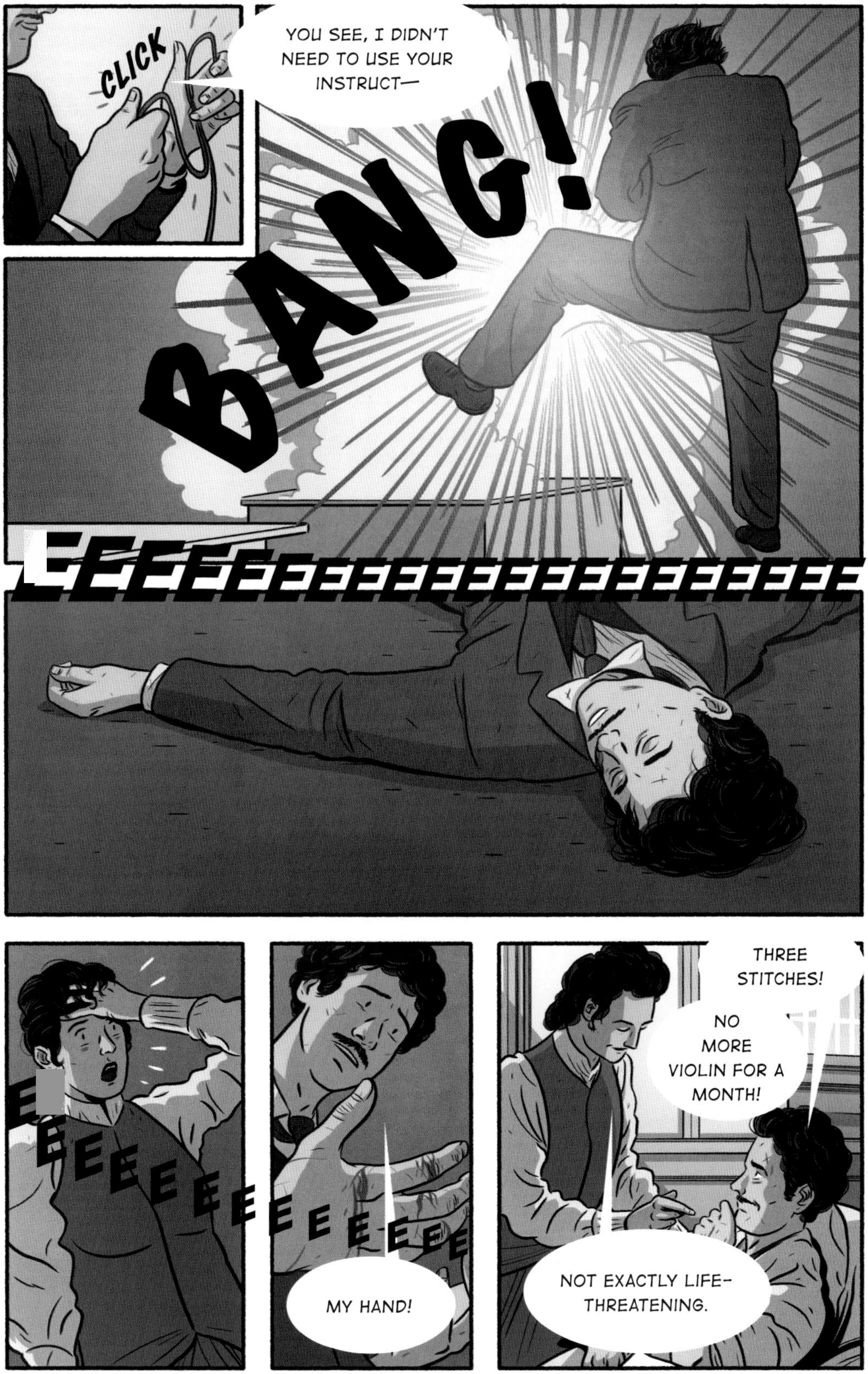
CLICK
YOU SEE, I DIDN'T NEED TO USE YOUR INSTRUCT—
BANG!
EEEEEEEEEEEEEEEEEEEEEEE
EEEEEEEEEEEEE
MY HAND!
THREE STITCHES!
NO MORE VIOLIN FOR A MONTH!
NOT EXACTLY LIFE-THREATENING.

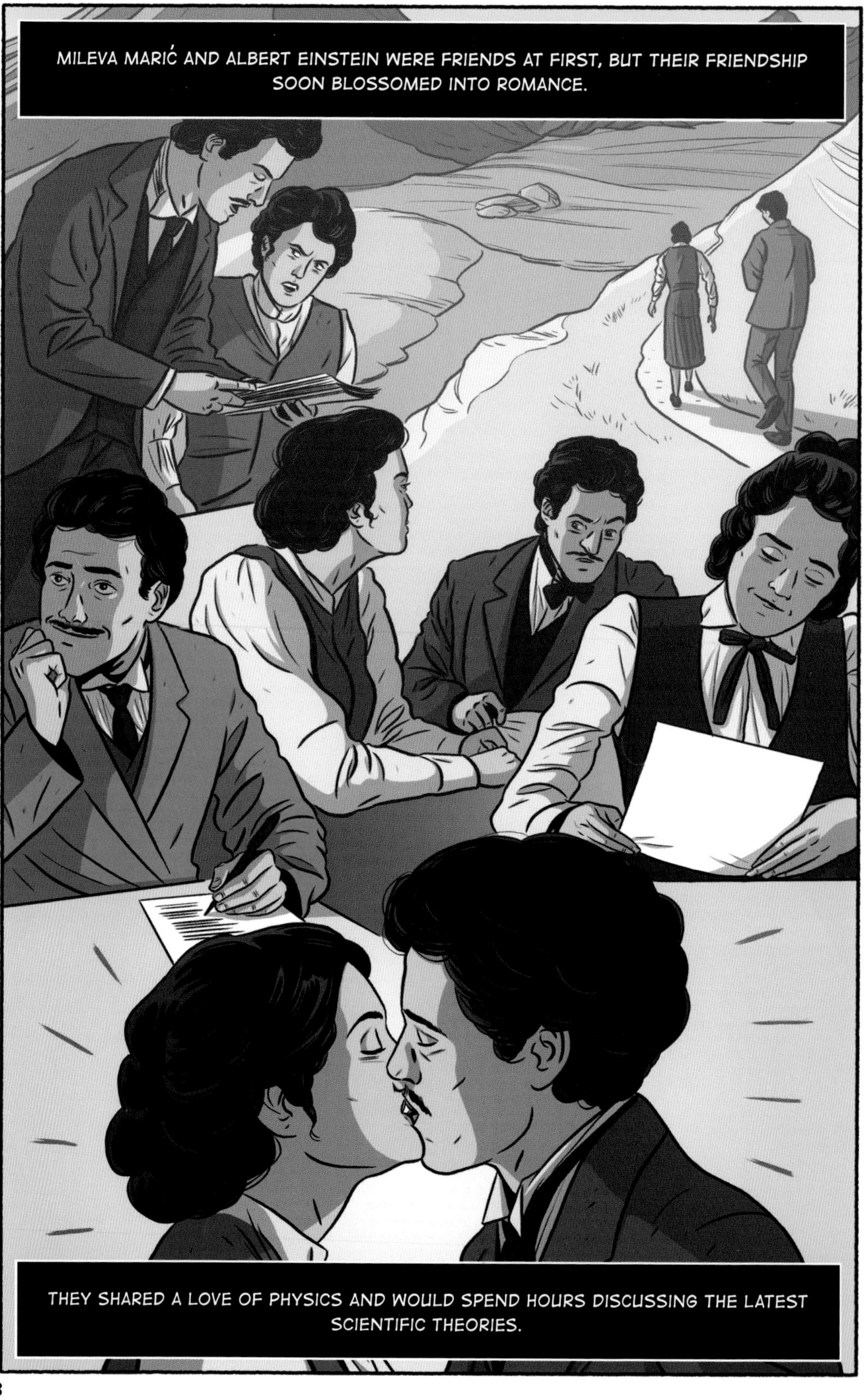
MILEVA MARIĆ AND ALBERT EINSTEIN WERE FRIENDS AT FIRST, BUT THEIR FRIENDSHIP SOON BLOSSOMED INTO ROMANCE.
THEY SHARED A LOVE OF PHYSICS AND WOULD SPEND HOURS DISCUSSING THE LATEST SCIENTIFIC THEORIES.

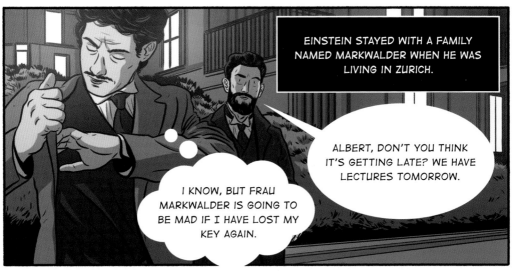

EINSTEIN STAYED WITH A FAMILY NAMED MARKWALDER WHEN HE WAS LIVING IN ZURICH.

ALBERT, DON'T YOU THINK IT'S GETTING LATE? WE HAVE LECTURES TOMORROW.

I KNOW, BUT FRAU MARKWALDER IS GOING TO BE MAD IF I HAVE LOST MY KEY AGAIN.

BUZZ!

WHY GO TO LECTURES WHEN I CAN COPY YOUR NOTES?

BESIDES, I LEARN FAR MORE STAYING AT HOME AND READING THE LATEST RESEARCH!

FRAU MARKWALDER! I'VE FORGOTTEN MY KEY AGAIN!

ALBERT, YOU CAN'T JUST MAKE UP YOUR OWN RULES, YOU KNOW.

MAYBE...

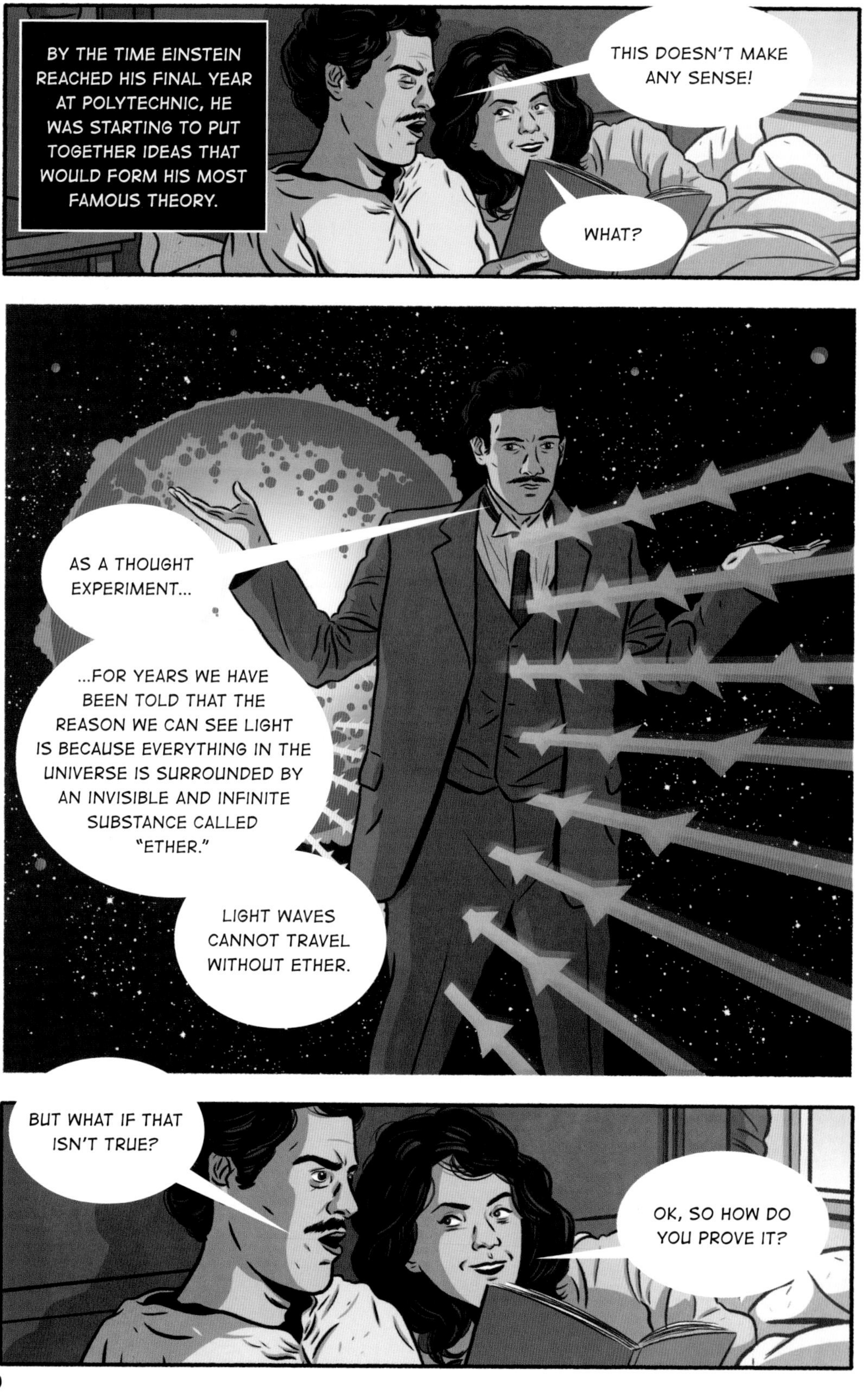
BY THE TIME EINSTEIN REACHED HIS FINAL YEAR AT POLYTECHNIC, HE WAS STARTING TO PUT TOGETHER IDEAS THAT WOULD FORM HIS MOST FAMOUS THEORY.
THIS DOESN'T MAKE ANY SENSE!
WHAT?
AS A THOUGHT EXPERIMENT...
...FOR YEARS WE HAVE BEEN TOLD THAT THE REASON WE CAN SEE LIGHT IS BECAUSE EVERYTHING IN THE UNIVERSE IS SURROUNDED BY AN INVISIBLE AND INFINITE SUBSTANCE CALLED "ETHER."
LIGHT WAVES CANNOT TRAVEL WITHOUT ETHER.
BUT WHAT IF THAT ISN'T TRUE?
OK, SO HOW DO YOU PROVE IT?

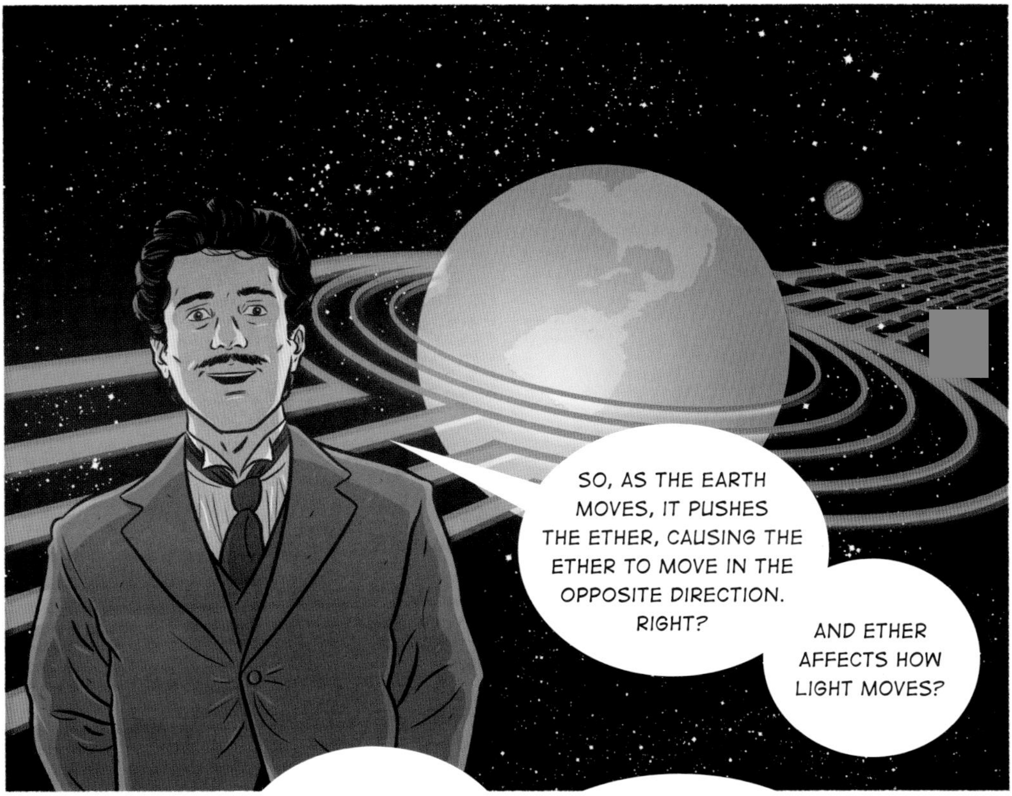
SO, AS THE EARTH MOVES, IT PUSHES THE ETHER, CAUSING THE ETHER TO MOVE IN THE OPPOSITE DIRECTION. RIGHT?
AND ETHER AFFECTS HOW LIGHT MOVES?

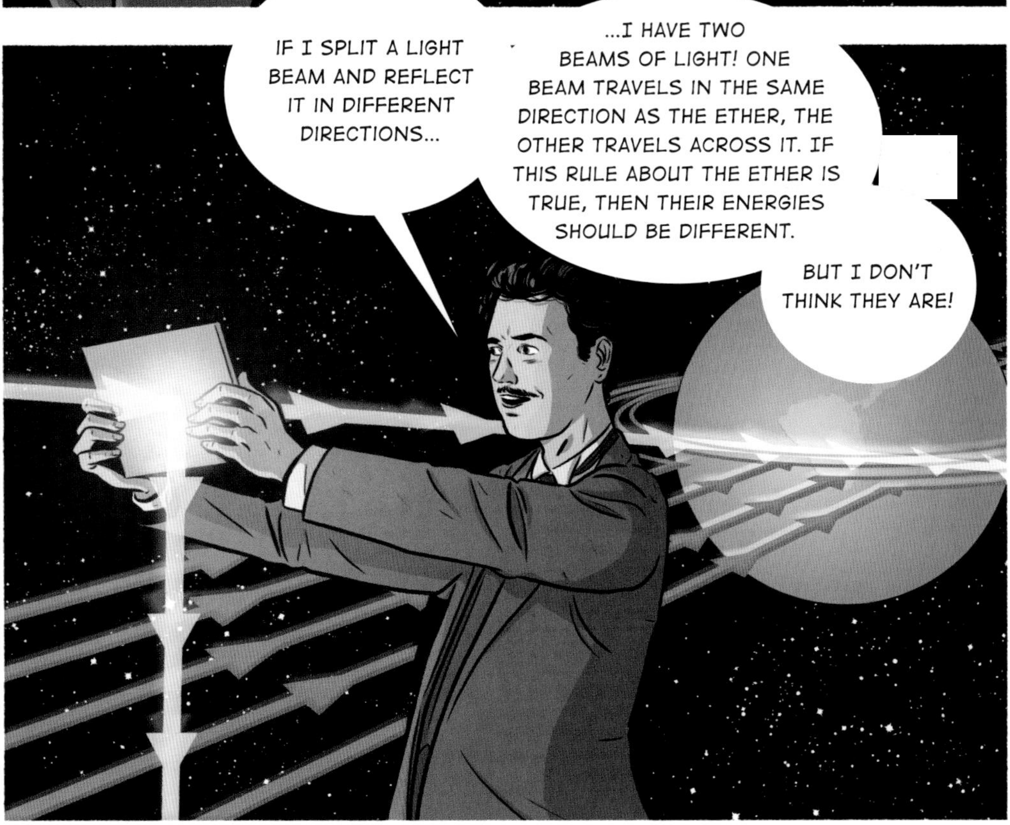
IF I SPLIT A LIGHT BEAM AND REFLECT IT IN DIFFERENT DIRECTIONS...
...I HAVE TWO BEAMS OF LIGHT! ONE BEAM TRAVELS IN THE SAME DIRECTION AS THE ETHER, THE OTHER TRAVELS ACROSS IT. IF THIS RULE ABOUT THE ETHER IS TRUE, THEN THEIR ENERGIES SHOULD BE DIFFERENT.
BUT I DON'T THINK THEY ARE!

BEFORE WRITING HIS PAPER, EINSTEIN HAD TO GET THE TOPIC APPROVED BY WEBER.

MMMM.

I DON'T THINK THAT'S A GOOD IDEA. COME UP WITH SOMETHING ELSE.

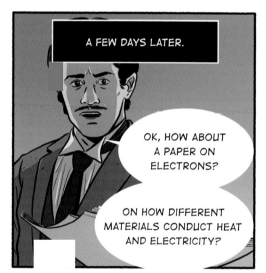

A FEW DAYS LATER.

OK, HOW ABOUT A PAPER ON ELECTRONS?

ON HOW DIFFERENT MATERIALS CONDUCT HEAT AND ELECTRICITY?

DOESN'T SOUND VERY INTERESTING.

A FEW DAYS LATER.

HEAT CONDUCTION?

AH! MY SPECIALTY! WHAT A GOOD IDEA!

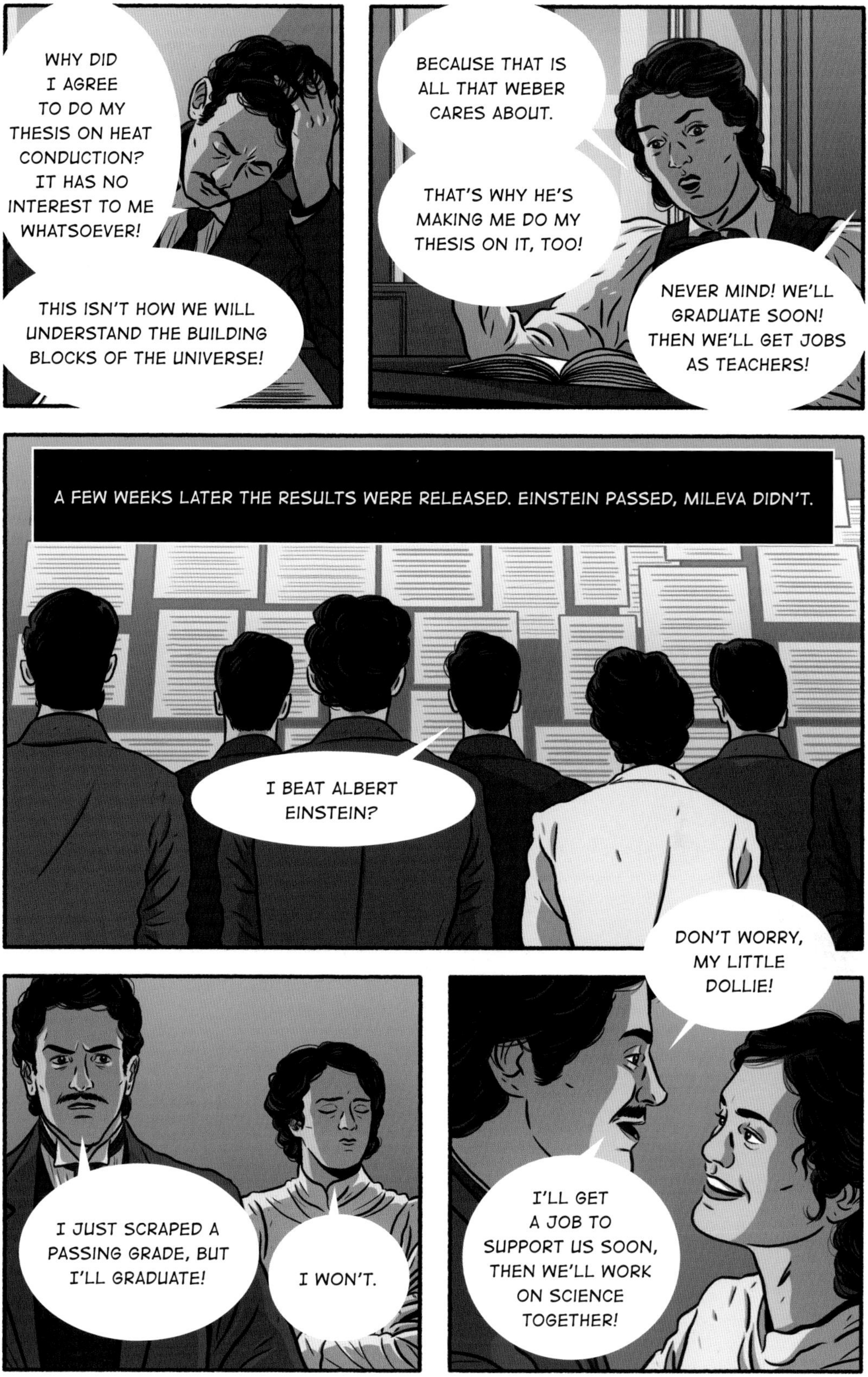
WHY DID I AGREE TO DO MY THESIS ON HEAT CONDUCTION? IT HAS NO INTEREST TO ME WHATSOEVER!
THIS ISN'T HOW WE WILL UNDERSTAND THE BUILDING BLOCKS OF THE UNIVERSE!
BECAUSE THAT IS ALL THAT WEBER CARES ABOUT.
THAT'S WHY HE'S MAKING ME DO MY THESIS ON IT, TOO!
NEVER MIND! WE'LL GRADUATE SOON! THEN WE'LL GET JOBS AS TEACHERS!
A FEW WEEKS LATER THE RESULTS WERE RELEASED. EINSTEIN PASSED, MILEVA DIDN'T.
I BEAT ALBERT EINSTEIN?
I JUST SCRAPED A PASSING GRADE, BUT I'LL GRADUATE!
I WON'T.
DON'T WORRY, MY LITTLE DOLLIE!
I'LL GET A JOB TO SUPPORT US SOON, THEN WE'LL WORK ON SCIENCE TOGETHER!

CHAPTER 3

Einstein's First Job

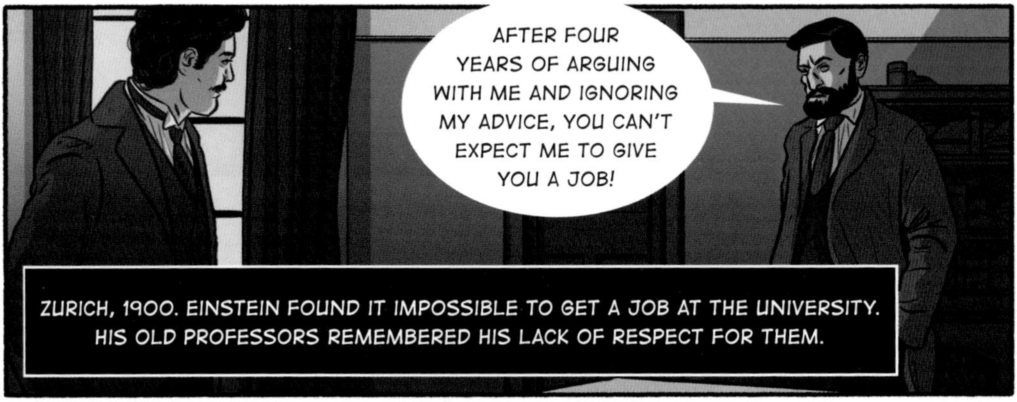
AFTER FOUR YEARS OF ARGUING WITH ME AND IGNORING MY ADVICE, YOU CAN'T EXPECT ME TO GIVE YOU A JOB!
ZURICH, 1900. EINSTEIN FOUND IT IMPOSSIBLE TO GET A JOB AT THE UNIVERSITY. HIS OLD PROFESSORS REMEMBERED HIS LACK OF RESPECT FOR THEM.

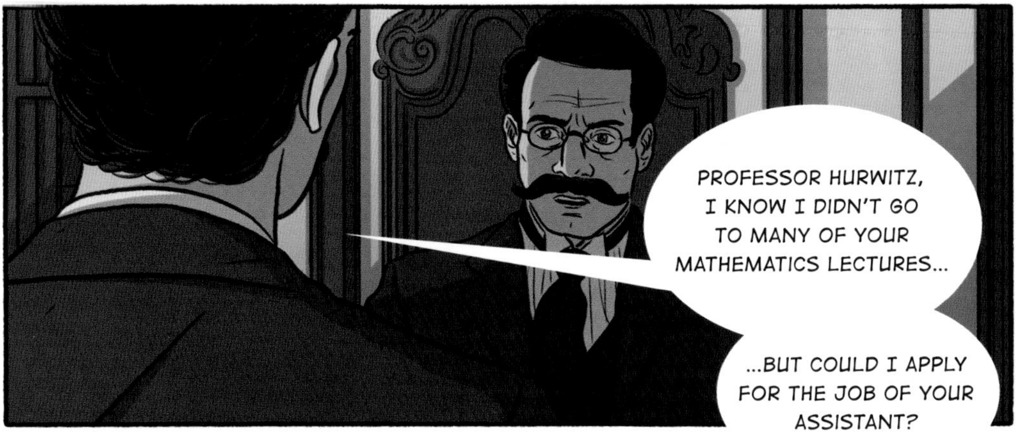
PROFESSOR HURWITZ, I KNOW I DIDN'T GO TO MANY OF YOUR MATHEMATICS LECTURES...
...BUT COULD I APPLY FOR THE JOB OF YOUR ASSISTANT?

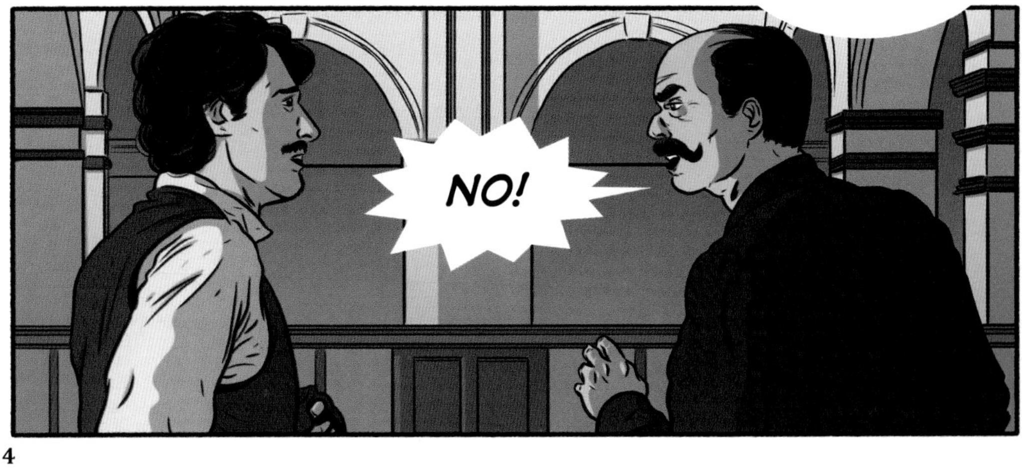
NO!

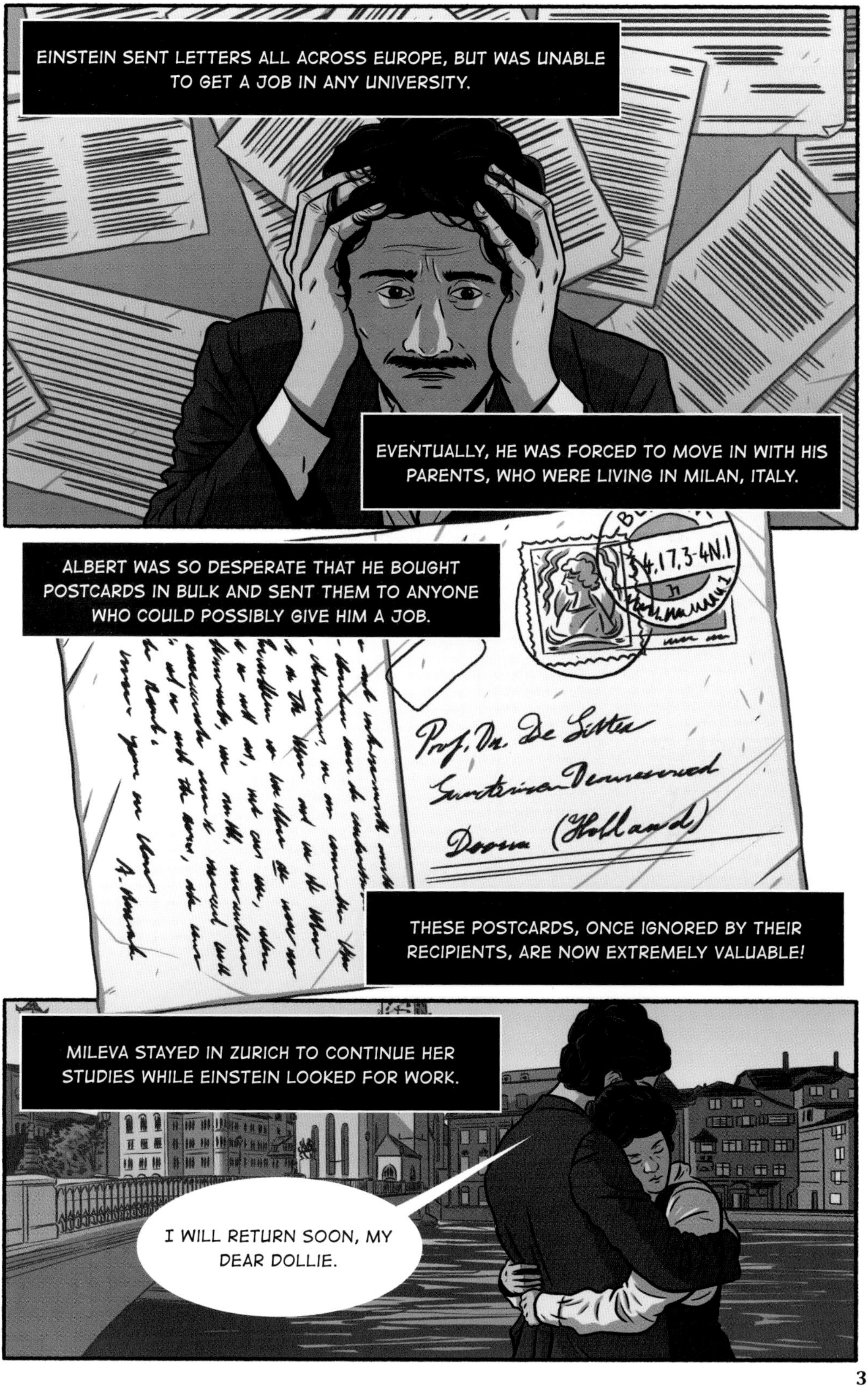
EINSTEIN SENT LETTERS ALL ACROSS EUROPE, BUT WAS UNABLE TO GET A JOB IN ANY UNIVERSITY.
EVENTUALLY, HE WAS FORCED TO MOVE IN WITH HIS PARENTS, WHO WERE LIVING IN MILAN, ITALY.
ALBERT WAS SO DESPERATE THAT HE BOUGHT POSTCARDS IN BULK AND SENT THEM TO ANYONE WHO COULD POSSIBLY GIVE HIM A JOB.
Prof. Dr. De Sitter
Doorn (Holland)
THESE POSTCARDS, ONCE IGNORED BY THEIR RECIPIENTS, ARE NOW EXTREMELY VALUABLE!
MILEVA STAYED IN ZURICH TO CONTINUE HER STUDIES WHILE EINSTEIN LOOKED FOR WORK.
I WILL RETURN SOON, MY DEAR DOLLIE.

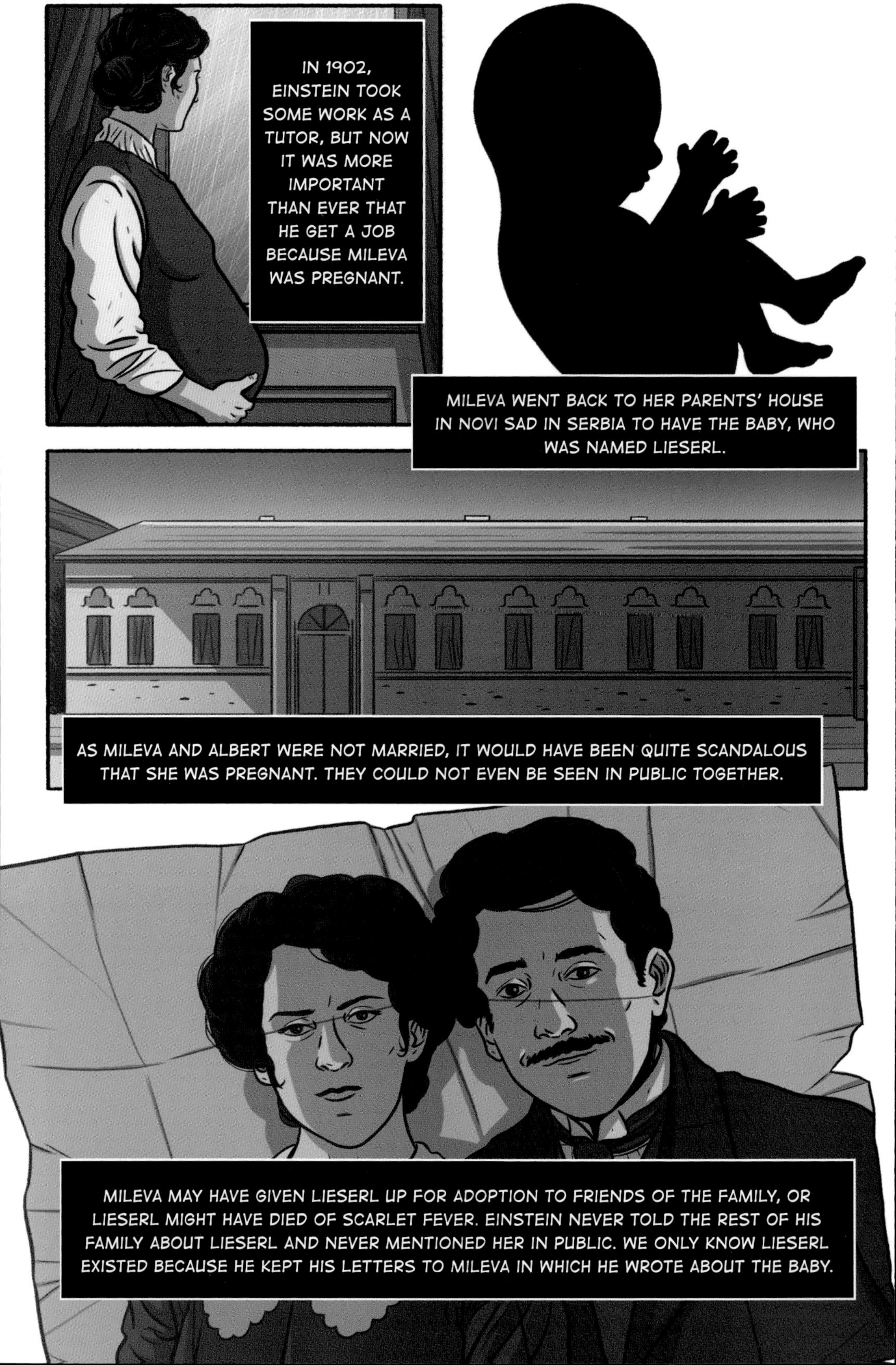
IN 1902, EINSTEIN TOOK SOME WORK AS A TUTOR, BUT NOW IT WAS MORE IMPORTANT THAN EVER THAT HE GET A JOB BECAUSE MILEVA WAS PREGNANT.
MILEVA WENT BACK TO HER PARENTS' HOUSE IN NOVI SAD IN SERBIA TO HAVE THE BABY, WHO WAS NAMED LIESERL.
AS MILEVA AND ALBERT WERE NOT MARRIED, IT WOULD HAVE BEEN QUITE SCANDALOUS THAT SHE WAS PREGNANT. THEY COULD NOT EVEN BE SEEN IN PUBLIC TOGETHER.
MILEVA MAY HAVE GIVEN LIESERL UP FOR ADOPTION TO FRIENDS OF THE FAMILY, OR LIESERL MIGHT HAVE DIED OF SCARLET FEVER. EINSTEIN NEVER TOLD THE REST OF HIS FAMILY ABOUT LIESERL AND NEVER MENTIONED HER IN PUBLIC. WE ONLY KNOW LIESERL EXISTED BECAUSE HE KEPT HIS LETTERS TO MILEVA IN WHICH HE WROTE ABOUT THE BABY.

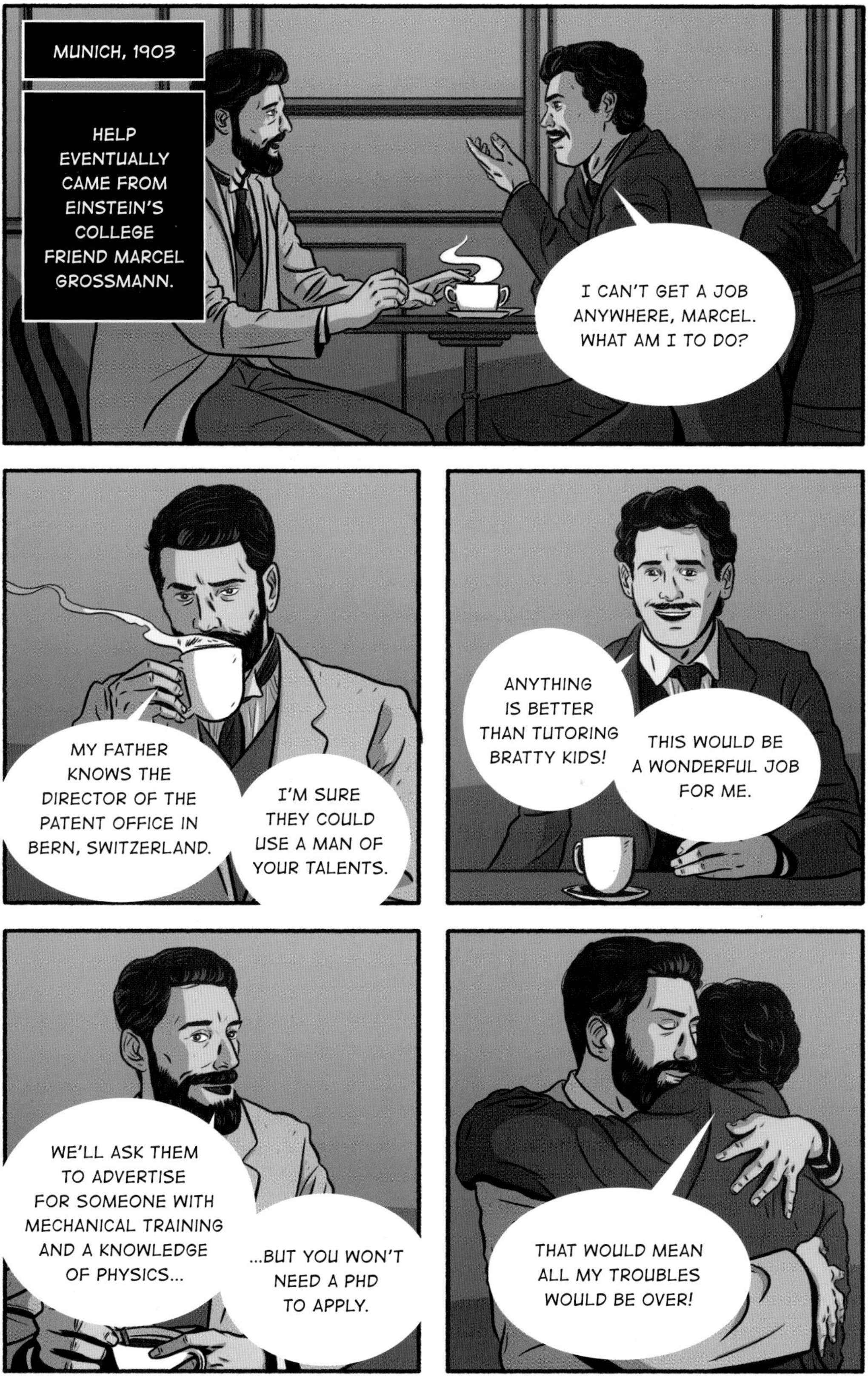
MUNICH, 1903
HELP EVENTUALLY CAME FROM EINSTEIN'S COLLEGE FRIEND MARCEL GROSSMANN.
I CAN'T GET A JOB ANYWHERE, MARCEL. WHAT AM I TO DO?
MY FATHER KNOWS THE DIRECTOR OF THE PATENT OFFICE IN BERN, SWITZERLAND.
I'M SURE THEY COULD USE A MAN OF YOUR TALENTS.
ANYTHING IS BETTER THAN TUTORING BRATTY KIDS!
THIS WOULD BE A WONDERFUL JOB FOR ME.
WE'LL ASK THEM TO ADVERTISE FOR SOMEONE WITH MECHANICAL TRAINING AND A KNOWLEDGE OF PHYSICS...
...BUT YOU WON'T NEED A PHD TO APPLY.
THAT WOULD MEAN ALL MY TROUBLES WOULD BE OVER!

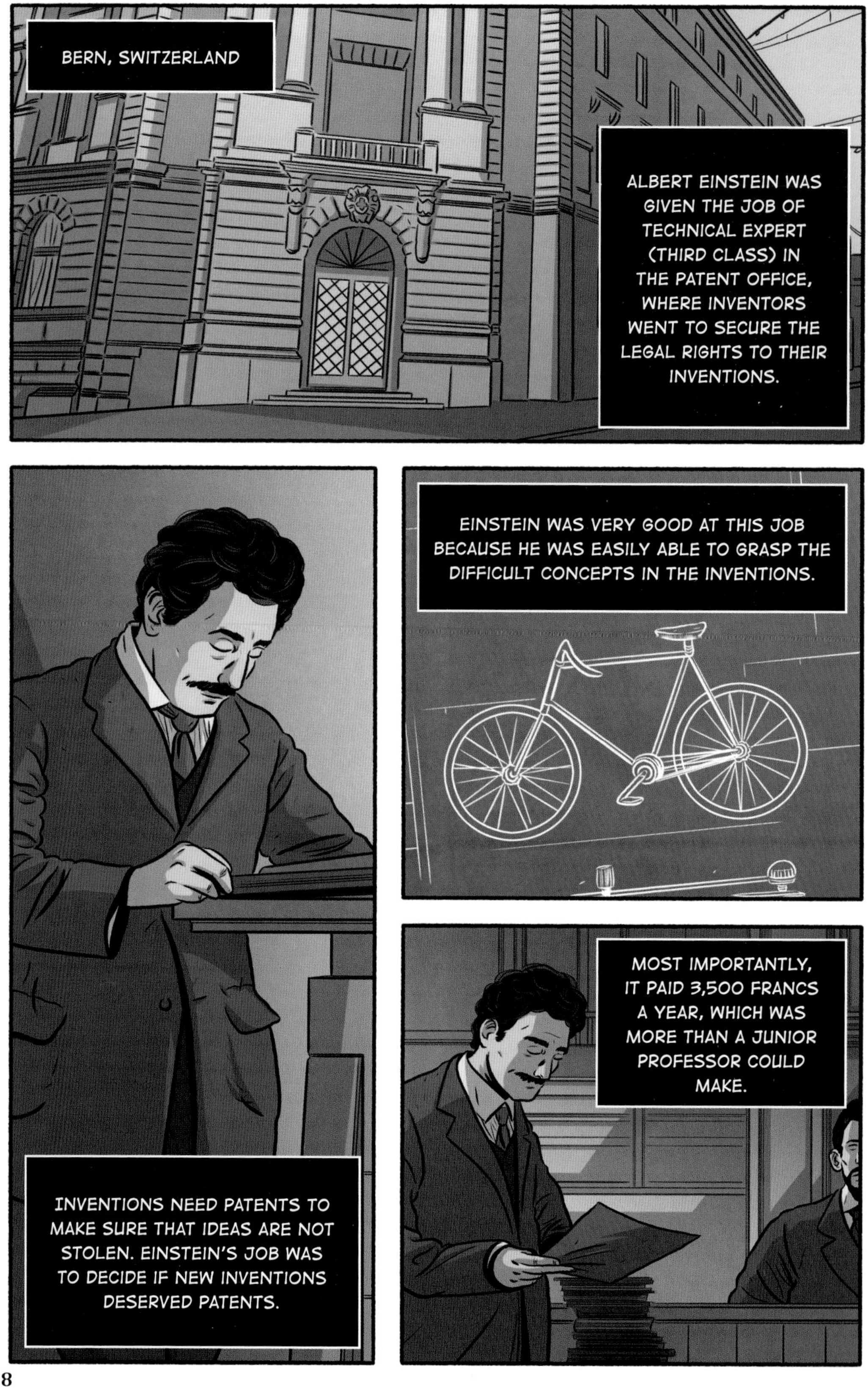
BERN, SWITZERLAND
ALBERT EINSTEIN WAS GIVEN THE JOB OF TECHNICAL EXPERT (THIRD CLASS) IN THE PATENT OFFICE, WHERE INVENTORS WENT TO SECURE THE LEGAL RIGHTS TO THEIR INVENTIONS.
INVENTIONS NEED PATENTS TO MAKE SURE THAT IDEAS ARE NOT STOLEN. EINSTEIN'S JOB WAS TO DECIDE IF NEW INVENTIONS DESERVED PATENTS.
EINSTEIN WAS VERY GOOD AT THIS JOB BECAUSE HE WAS EASILY ABLE TO GRASP THE DIFFICULT CONCEPTS IN THE INVENTIONS.
MOST IMPORTANTLY, IT PAID 3,500 FRANCS A YEAR, WHICH WAS MORE THAN A JUNIOR PROFESSOR COULD MAKE.

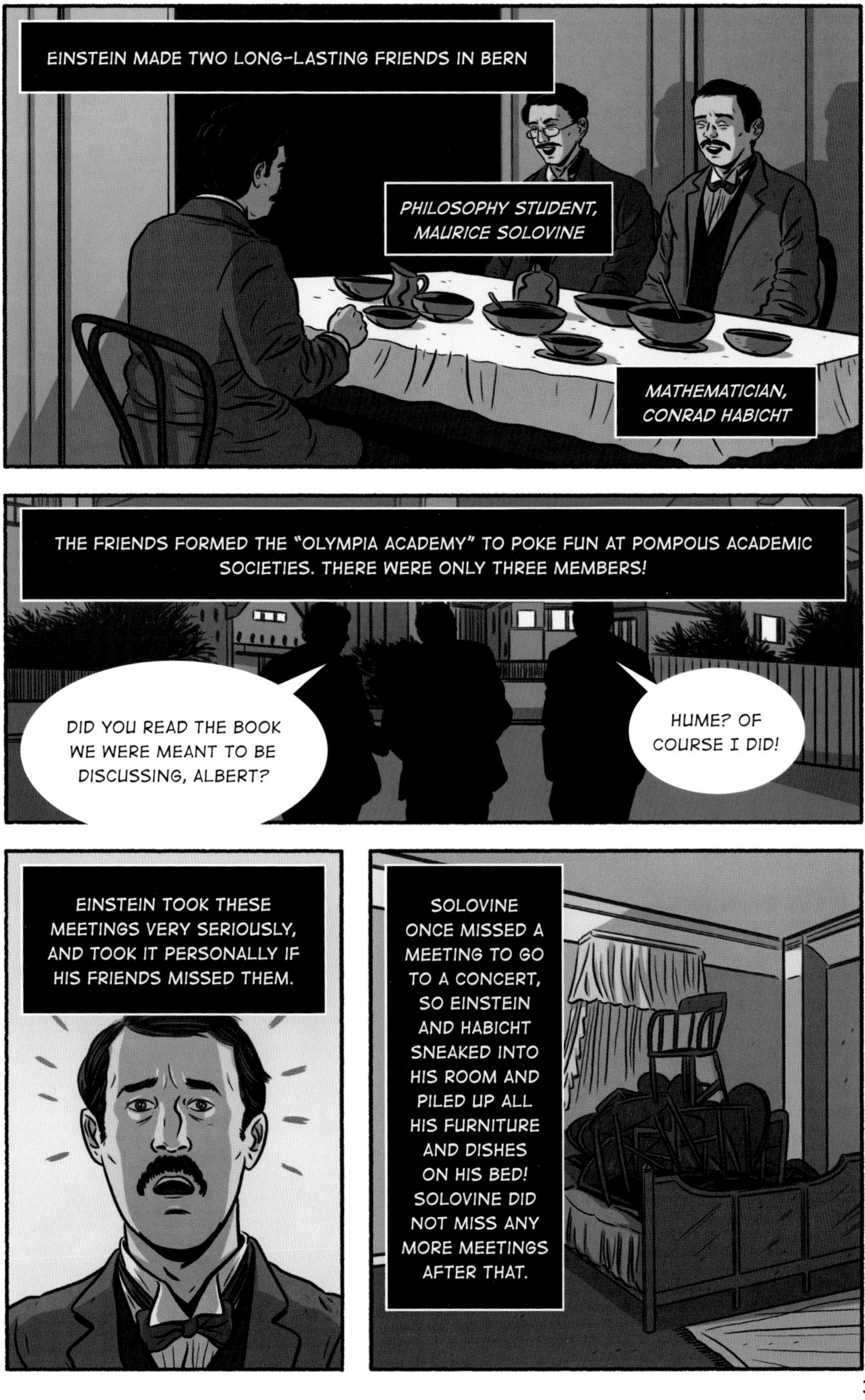
EINSTEIN MADE TWO LONG-LASTING FRIENDS IN BERN
PHILOSOPHY STUDENT, MAURICE SOLOVINE
MATHEMATICIAN, CONRAD HABICHT
THE FRIENDS FORMED THE "OLYMPIA ACADEMY" TO POKE FUN AT POMPOUS ACADEMIC SOCIETIES. THERE WERE ONLY THREE MEMBERS!
DID YOU READ THE BOOK WE WERE MEANT TO BE DISCUSSING, ALBERT?
HUME? OF COURSE I DID!
EINSTEIN TOOK THESE MEETINGS VERY SERIOUSLY, AND TOOK IT PERSONALLY IF HIS FRIENDS MISSED THEM.
SOLOVINE ONCE MISSED A MEETING TO GO TO A CONCERT, SO EINSTEIN AND HABICHT SNEAKED INTO HIS ROOM AND PILED UP ALL HIS FURNITURE AND DISHES ON HIS BED! SOLOVINE DID NOT MISS ANY MORE MEETINGS AFTER THAT.

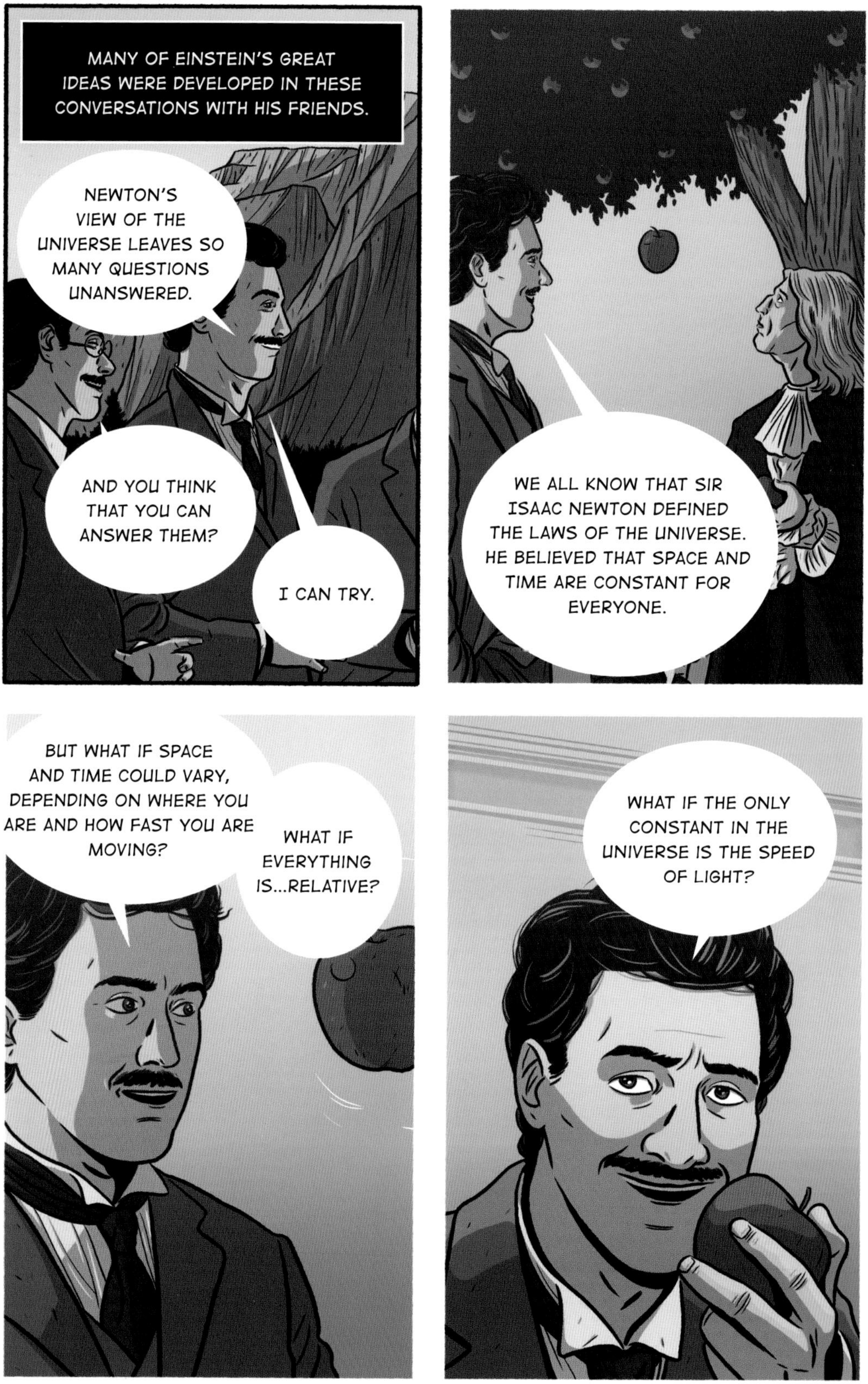
MANY OF EINSTEIN'S GREAT IDEAS WERE DEVELOPED IN THESE CONVERSATIONS WITH HIS FRIENDS.
NEWTON'S VIEW OF THE UNIVERSE LEAVES SO MANY QUESTIONS UNANSWERED.
AND YOU THINK THAT YOU CAN ANSWER THEM?
I CAN TRY.
WE ALL KNOW THAT SIR ISAAC NEWTON DEFINED THE LAWS OF THE UNIVERSE. HE BELIEVED THAT SPACE AND TIME ARE CONSTANT FOR EVERYONE.
BUT WHAT IF SPACE AND TIME COULD VARY, DEPENDING ON WHERE YOU ARE AND HOW FAST YOU ARE MOVING?
WHAT IF EVERYTHING IS...RELATIVE?
WHAT IF THE ONLY CONSTANT IN THE UNIVERSE IS THE SPEED OF LIGHT?

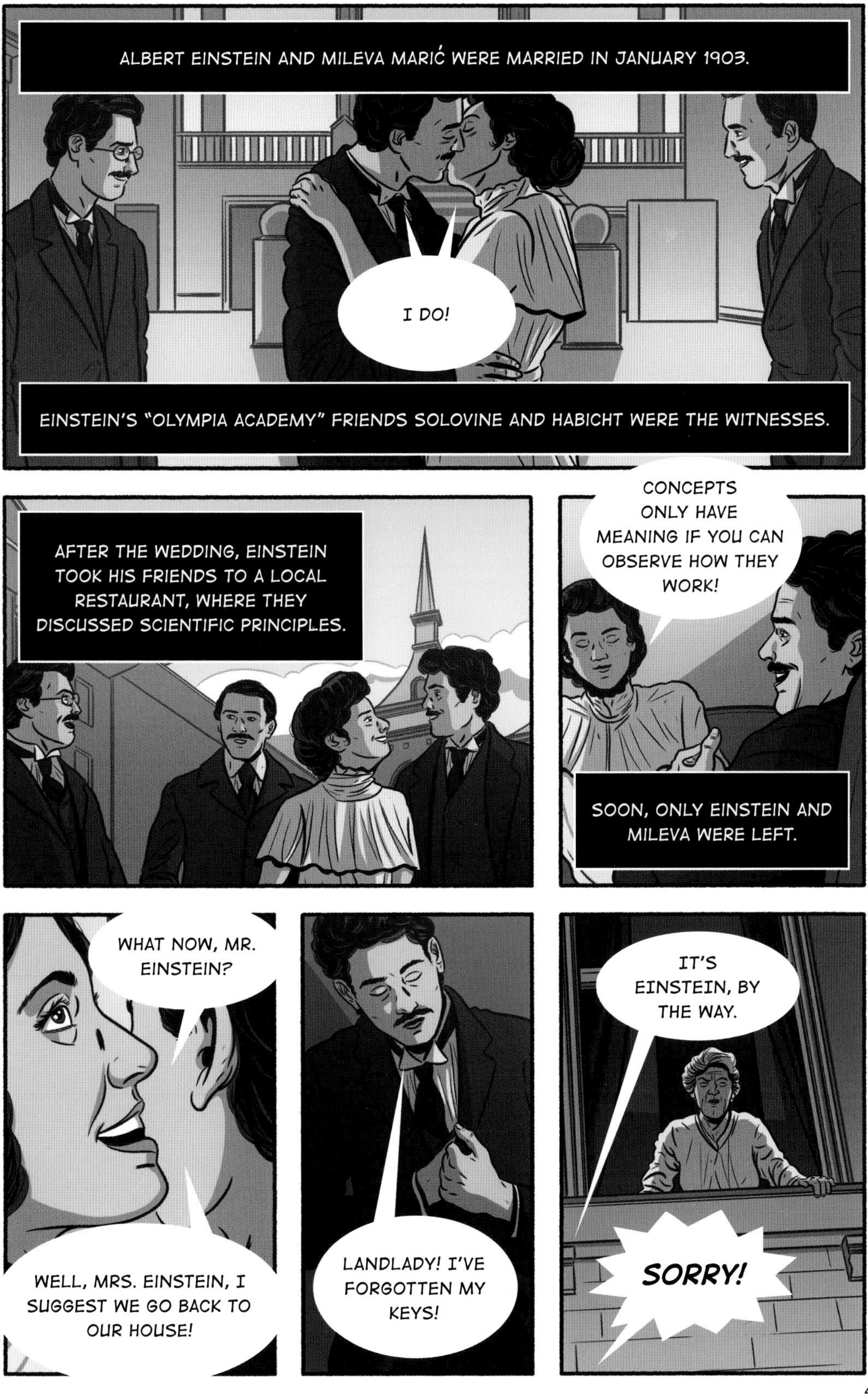
ALBERT EINSTEIN AND MILEVA MARIĆ WERE MARRIED IN JANUARY 1903.
I DO!
EINSTEIN'S "OLYMPIA ACADEMY" FRIENDS SOLOVINE AND HABICHT WERE THE WITNESSES.
AFTER THE WEDDING, EINSTEIN TOOK HIS FRIENDS TO A LOCAL RESTAURANT, WHERE THEY DISCUSSED SCIENTIFIC PRINCIPLES.
CONCEPTS ONLY HAVE MEANING IF YOU CAN OBSERVE HOW THEY WORK!
SOON, ONLY EINSTEIN AND MILEVA WERE LEFT.
WHAT NOW, MR. EINSTEIN?
WELL, MRS. EINSTEIN, I SUGGEST WE GO BACK TO OUR HOUSE!
LANDLADY! I'VE FORGOTTEN MY KEYS!
IT'S EINSTEIN, BY THE WAY.
SORRY!

ALBERT AND MILEVA'S FIRST SON, HANS ALBERT EINSTEIN, WAS BORN IN MAY 1904.

HE IS SO BEAUTIFUL! HE HAS YOUR NOSE!

HE HAS YOUR EYES!

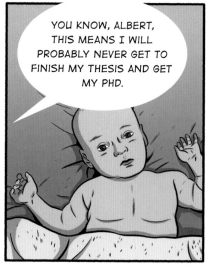

YOU KNOW, ALBERT, THIS MEANS I WILL PROBABLY NEVER GET TO FINISH MY THESIS AND GET MY PHD.

WE DON'T NEED UNIVERSITIES AND ACADEMIA! I'M DOING SOME OF MY BEST THINKING RIGHT NOW, AWAY FROM THE STIFLING PRESSURES OF UNIVERSITIES.

AND WHAT ABOUT ME?! WHEN IS IT MY TIME TO THINK?!

WAAAH! WAAH!

OH, LOOK! NOW THE BABY IS CRYING.

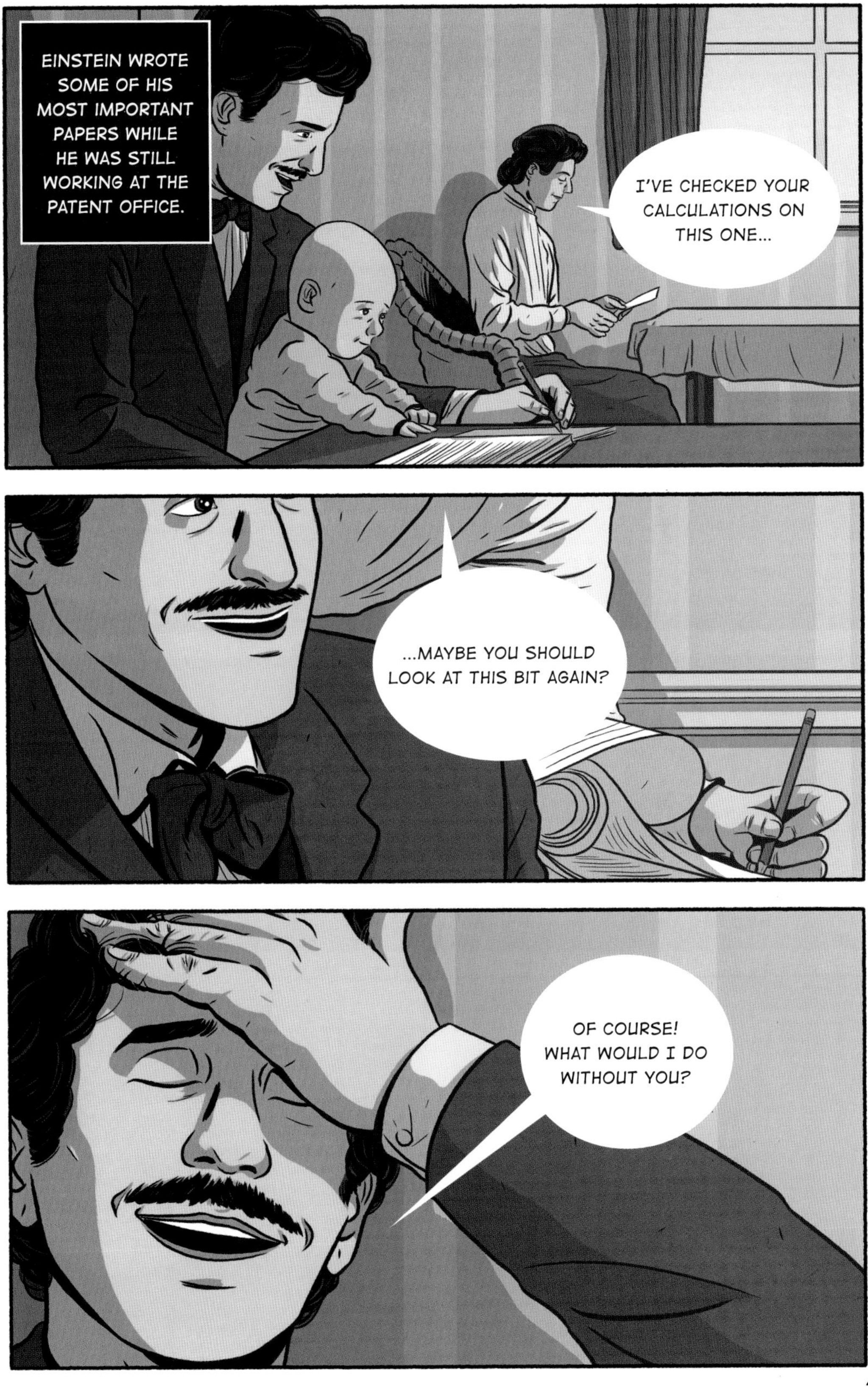
EINSTEIN WROTE SOME OF HIS MOST IMPORTANT PAPERS WHILE HE WAS STILL WORKING AT THE PATENT OFFICE.
I'VE CHECKED YOUR CALCULATIONS ON THIS ONE...
...MAYBE YOU SHOULD LOOK AT THIS BIT AGAIN?
OF COURSE! WHAT WOULD I DO WITHOUT YOU?

CHAPTER 4

A Miracle Year for Einstein

BERN, 1905

THE YEAR 1905 IS OFTEN CALLED EINSTEIN'S *ANNUS MIRABILIS*, WHICH MEANS "MIRACLE YEAR," BECAUSE OF THE IMPORTANCE OF THE PAPERS THAT HE PRODUCED.

HABICHT, YOU BIG FROZEN WHALE, THIS YEAR I PROMISE YOU THAT I WILL PUBLISH FOUR PAPERS!

WHAT WILL THEY BE ABOUT?

THE FIRST WILL DESCRIBE THE PROPERTIES OF LIGHT AND HOW IT BEHAVES.

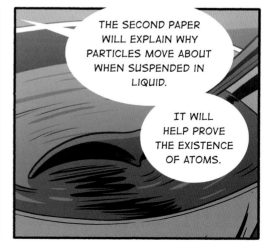

THE SECOND PAPER WILL EXPLAIN WHY PARTICLES MOVE ABOUT WHEN SUSPENDED IN LIQUID.

IT WILL HELP PROVE THE EXISTENCE OF ATOMS.

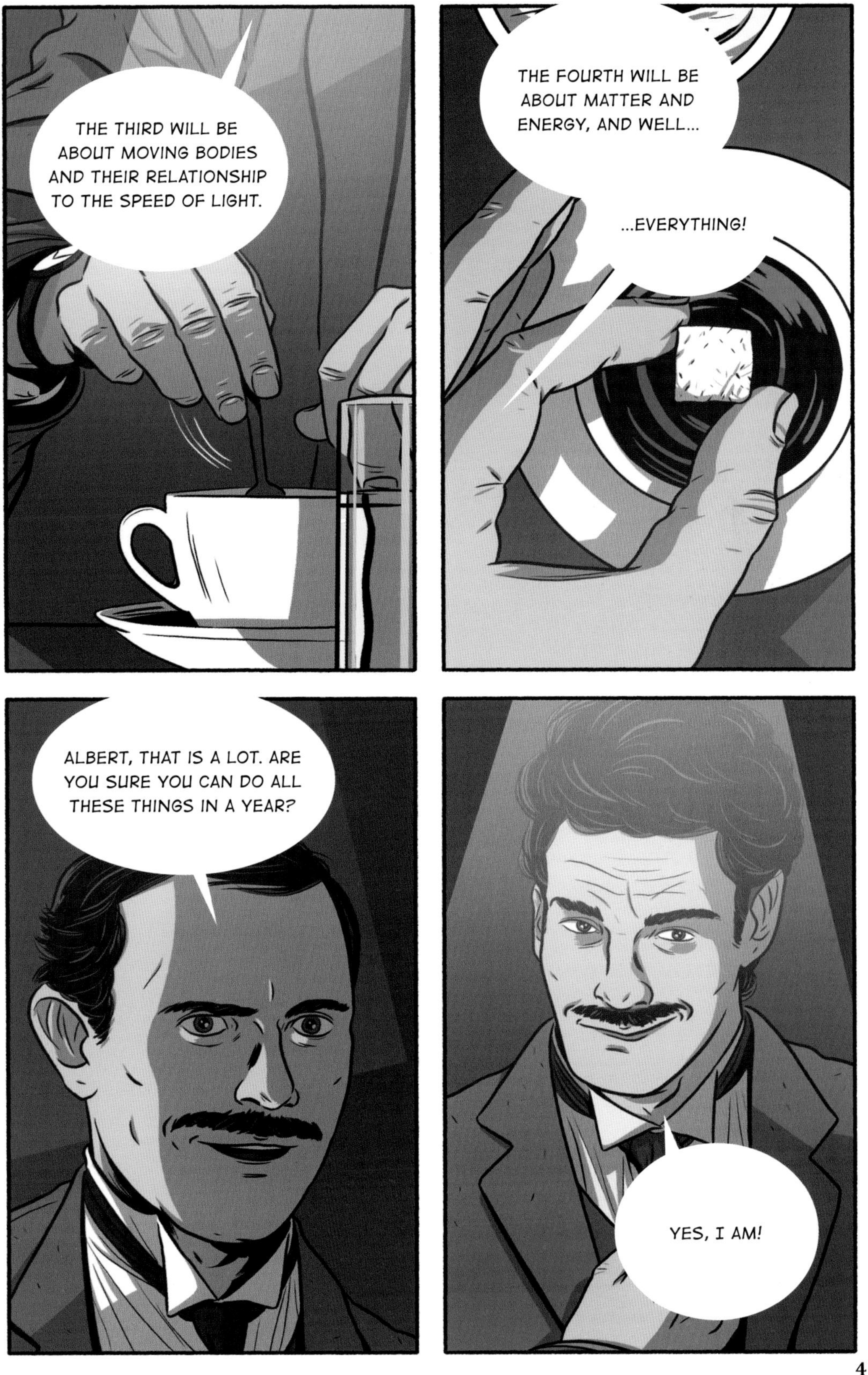
THE THIRD WILL BE ABOUT MOVING BODIES AND THEIR RELATIONSHIP TO THE SPEED OF LIGHT.
THE FOURTH WILL BE ABOUT MATTER AND ENERGY, AND WELL...
...EVERYTHING!
ALBERT, THAT IS A LOT. ARE YOU SURE YOU CAN DO ALL THESE THINGS IN A YEAR?
YES, I AM!

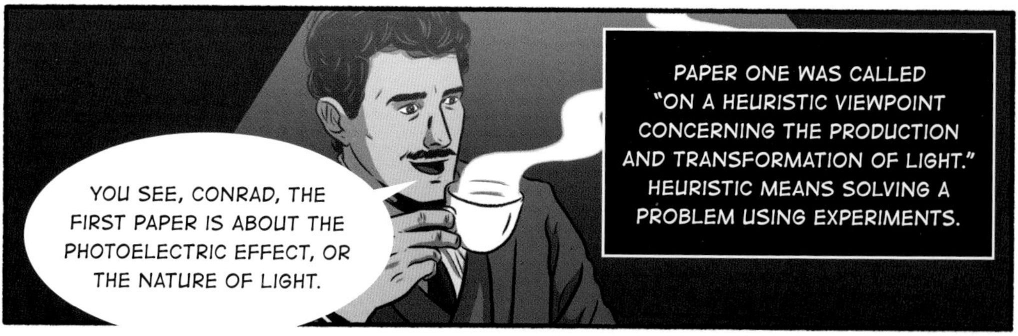
PAPER ONE WAS CALLED "ON A HEURISTIC VIEWPOINT CONCERNING THE PRODUCTION AND TRANSFORMATION OF LIGHT." HEURISTIC MEANS SOLVING A PROBLEM USING EXPERIMENTS.
YOU SEE, CONRAD, THE FIRST PAPER IS ABOUT THE PHOTOELECTRIC EFFECT, OR THE NATURE OF LIGHT.

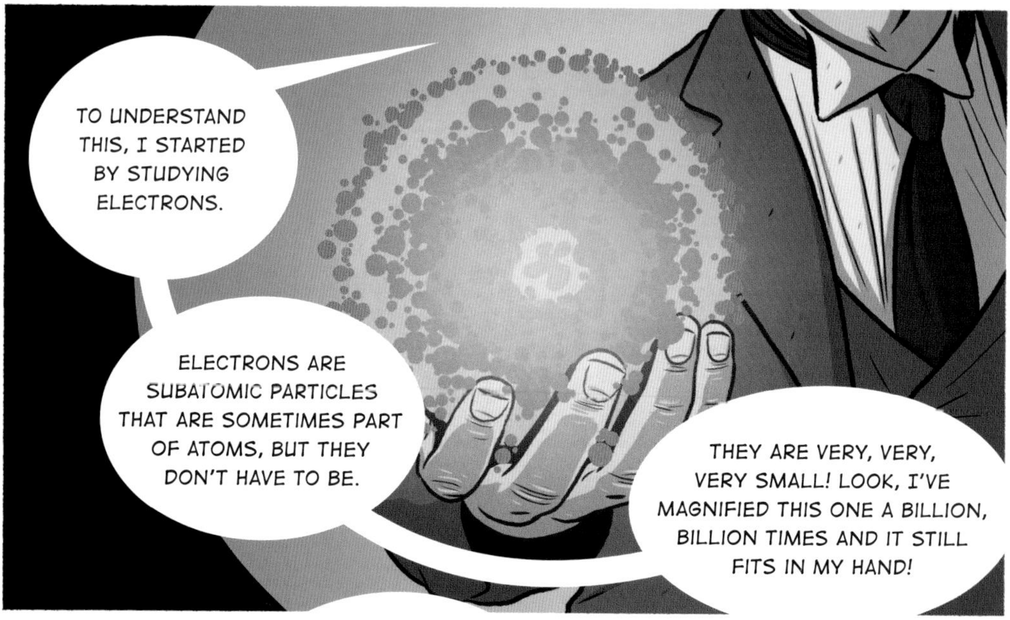
TO UNDERSTAND THIS, I STARTED BY STUDYING ELECTRONS.
ELECTRONS ARE SUBATOMIC PARTICLES THAT ARE SOMETIMES PART OF ATOMS, BUT THEY DON'T HAVE TO BE.
THEY ARE VERY, VERY, VERY SMALL! LOOK, I'VE MAGNIFIED THIS ONE A BILLION, BILLION TIMES AND IT STILL FITS IN MY HAND!

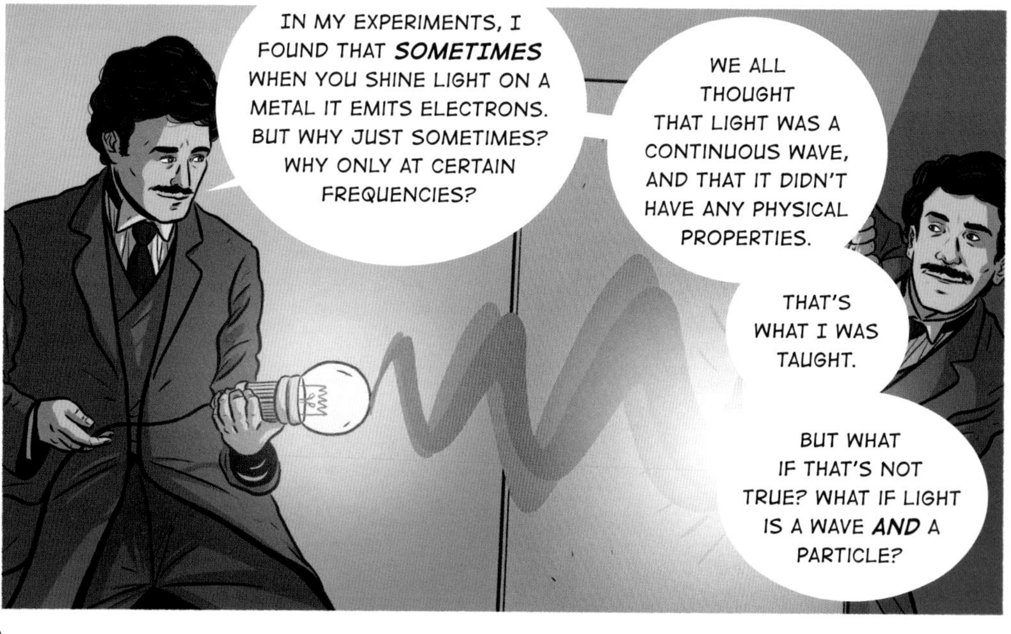
IN MY EXPERIMENTS, I FOUND THAT ***SOMETIMES*** WHEN YOU SHINE LIGHT ON A METAL IT EMITS ELECTRONS. BUT WHY JUST SOMETIMES? WHY ONLY AT CERTAIN FREQUENCIES?
WE ALL THOUGHT THAT LIGHT WAS A CONTINUOUS WAVE, AND THAT IT DIDN'T HAVE ANY PHYSICAL PROPERTIES.
THAT'S WHAT I WAS TAUGHT.
BUT WHAT IF THAT'S NOT TRUE? WHAT IF LIGHT IS A WAVE ***AND*** A PARTICLE?

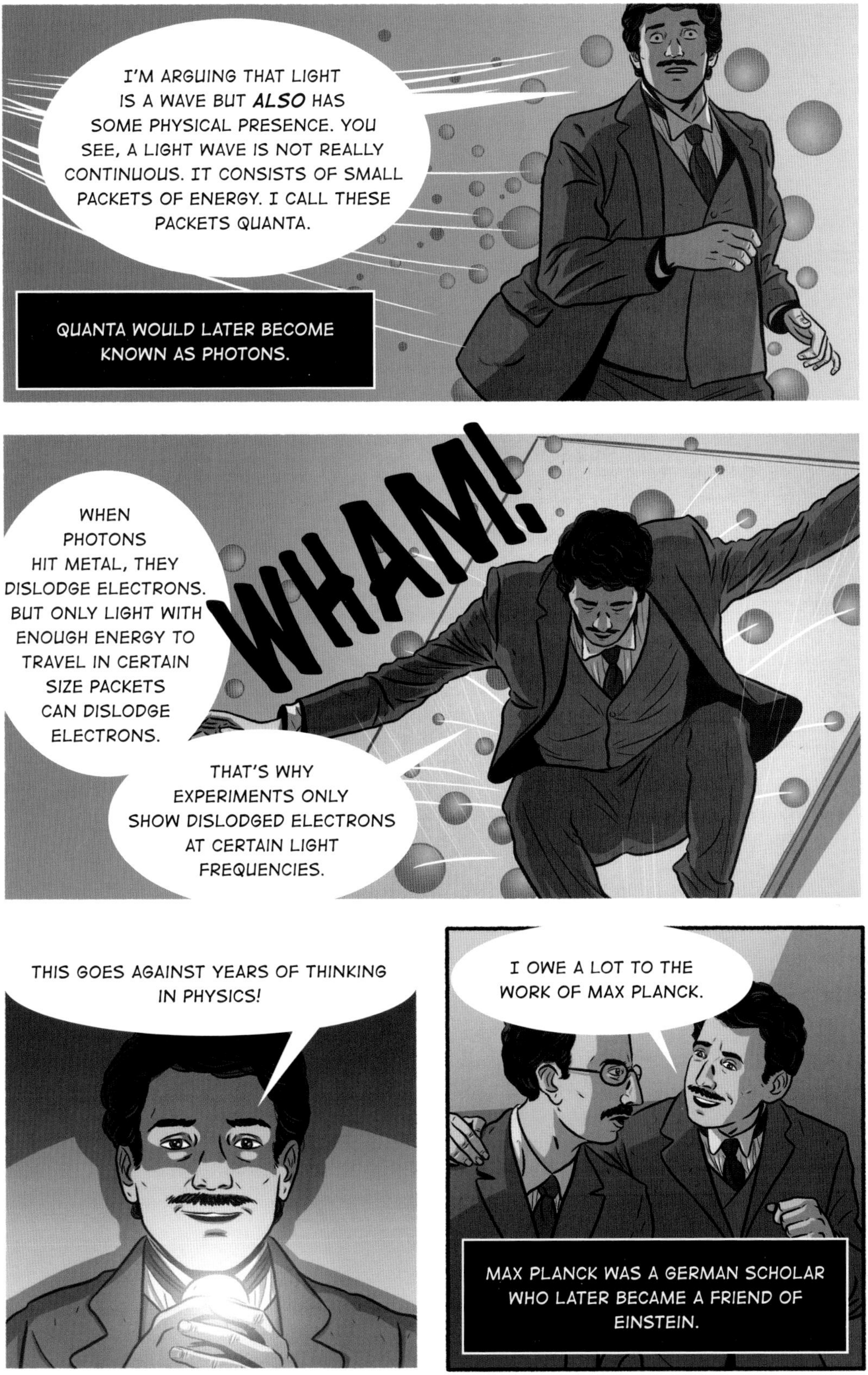
I'M ARGUING THAT LIGHT IS A WAVE BUT *ALSO* HAS SOME PHYSICAL PRESENCE. YOU SEE, A LIGHT WAVE IS NOT REALLY CONTINUOUS. IT CONSISTS OF SMALL PACKETS OF ENERGY. I CALL THESE PACKETS QUANTA.
QUANTA WOULD LATER BECOME KNOWN AS PHOTONS.
WHAM!
WHEN PHOTONS HIT METAL, THEY DISLODGE ELECTRONS. BUT ONLY LIGHT WITH ENOUGH ENERGY TO TRAVEL IN CERTAIN SIZE PACKETS CAN DISLODGE ELECTRONS.
THAT'S WHY EXPERIMENTS ONLY SHOW DISLODGED ELECTRONS AT CERTAIN LIGHT FREQUENCIES.
THIS GOES AGAINST YEARS OF THINKING IN PHYSICS!
I OWE A LOT TO THE WORK OF MAX PLANCK.
MAX PLANCK WAS A GERMAN SCHOLAR WHO LATER BECAME A FRIEND OF EINSTEIN.

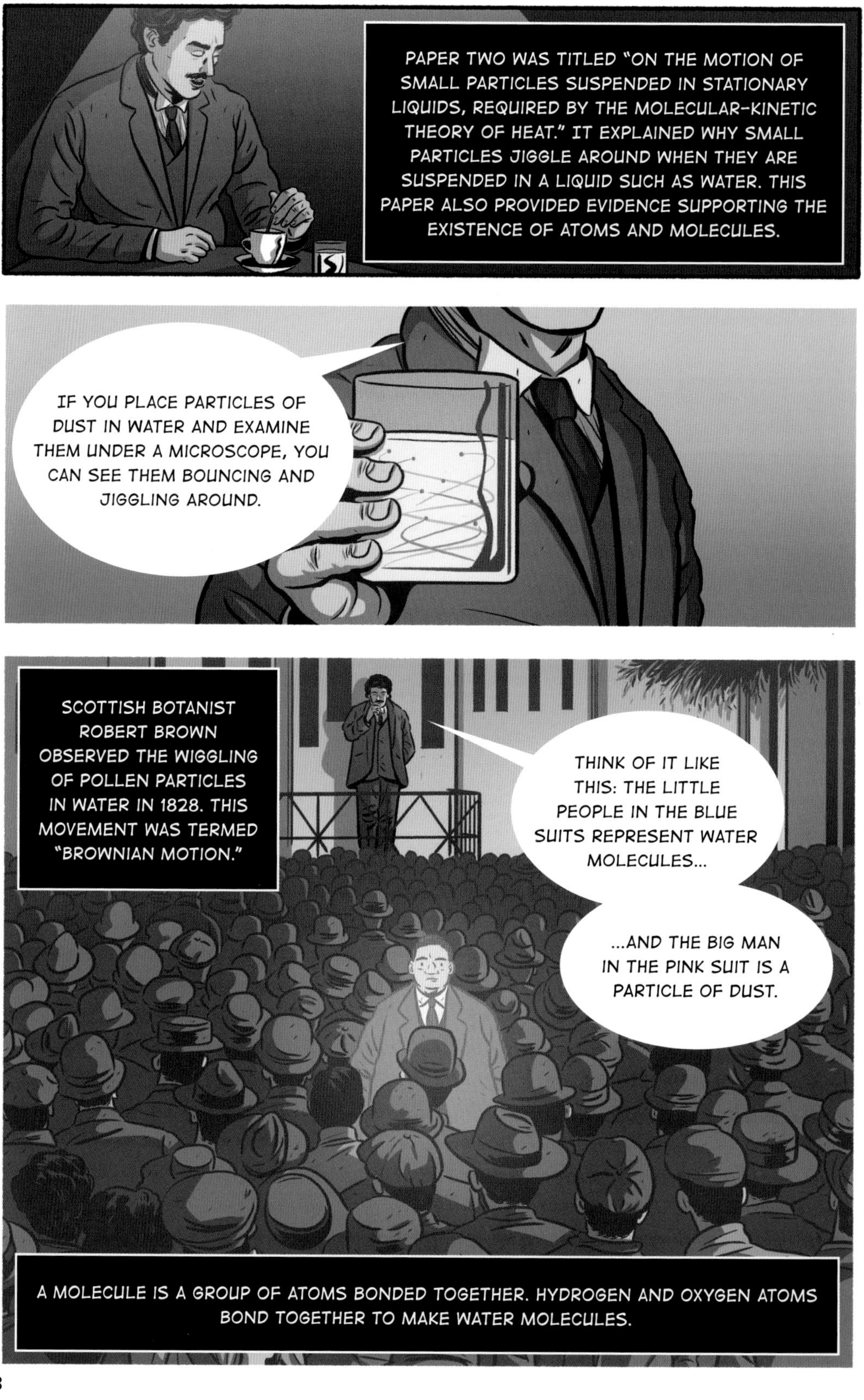
PAPER TWO WAS TITLED "ON THE MOTION OF SMALL PARTICLES SUSPENDED IN STATIONARY LIQUIDS, REQUIRED BY THE MOLECULAR-KINETIC THEORY OF HEAT." IT EXPLAINED WHY SMALL PARTICLES JIGGLE AROUND WHEN THEY ARE SUSPENDED IN A LIQUID SUCH AS WATER. THIS PAPER ALSO PROVIDED EVIDENCE SUPPORTING THE EXISTENCE OF ATOMS AND MOLECULES.
IF YOU PLACE PARTICLES OF DUST IN WATER AND EXAMINE THEM UNDER A MICROSCOPE, YOU CAN SEE THEM BOUNCING AND JIGGLING AROUND.
SCOTTISH BOTANIST ROBERT BROWN OBSERVED THE WIGGLING OF POLLEN PARTICLES IN WATER IN 1828. THIS MOVEMENT WAS TERMED "BROWNIAN MOTION."
THINK OF IT LIKE THIS: THE LITTLE PEOPLE IN THE BLUE SUITS REPRESENT WATER MOLECULES...
...AND THE BIG MAN IN THE PINK SUIT IS A PARTICLE OF DUST.
A MOLECULE IS A GROUP OF ATOMS BONDED TOGETHER. HYDROGEN AND OXYGEN ATOMS BOND TOGETHER TO MAKE WATER MOLECULES.

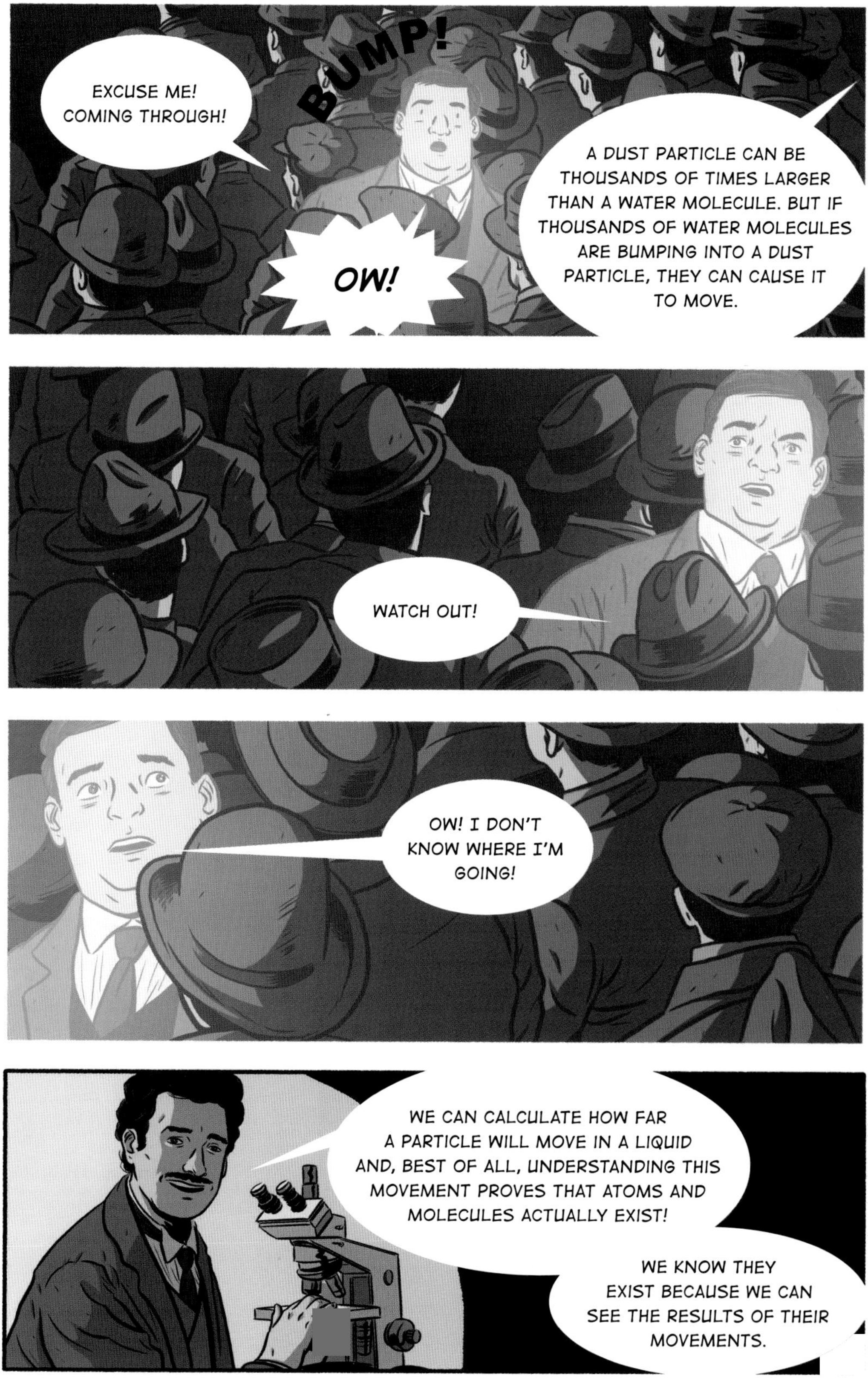
EXCUSE ME! COMING THROUGH!
BUMP!
OW!
A DUST PARTICLE CAN BE THOUSANDS OF TIMES LARGER THAN A WATER MOLECULE. BUT IF THOUSANDS OF WATER MOLECULES ARE BUMPING INTO A DUST PARTICLE, THEY CAN CAUSE IT TO MOVE.
WATCH OUT!
OW! I DON'T KNOW WHERE I'M GOING!
WE CAN CALCULATE HOW FAR A PARTICLE WILL MOVE IN A LIQUID AND, BEST OF ALL, UNDERSTANDING THIS MOVEMENT PROVES THAT ATOMS AND MOLECULES ACTUALLY EXIST!
WE KNOW THEY EXIST BECAUSE WE CAN SEE THE RESULTS OF THEIR MOVEMENTS.

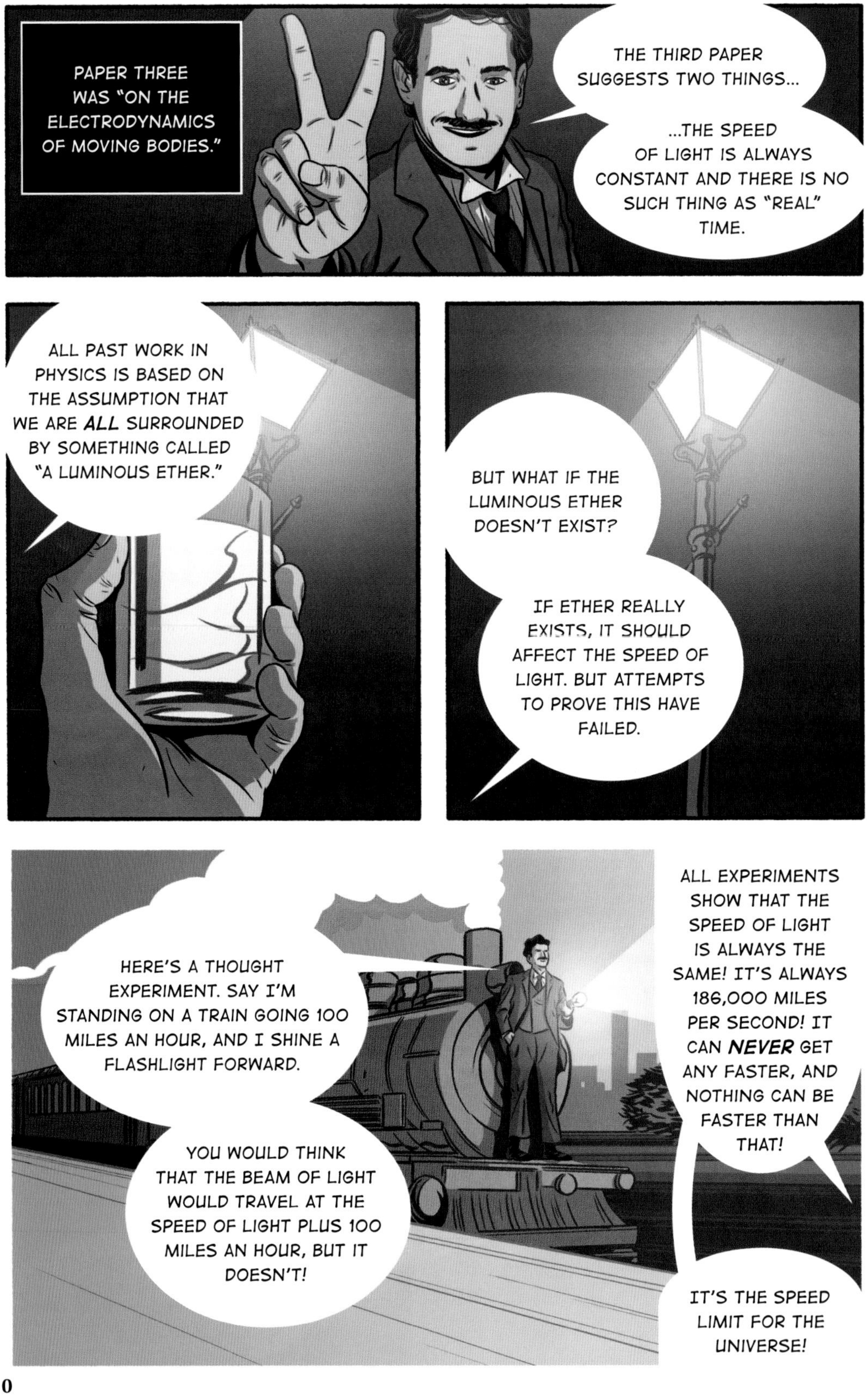
PAPER THREE WAS "ON THE ELECTRODYNAMICS OF MOVING BODIES."
THE THIRD PAPER SUGGESTS TWO THINGS...
...THE SPEED OF LIGHT IS ALWAYS CONSTANT AND THERE IS NO SUCH THING AS "REAL" TIME.
ALL PAST WORK IN PHYSICS IS BASED ON THE ASSUMPTION THAT WE ARE ALL SURROUNDED BY SOMETHING CALLED "A LUMINOUS ETHER."
BUT WHAT IF THE LUMINOUS ETHER DOESN'T EXIST?
IF ETHER REALLY EXISTS, IT SHOULD AFFECT THE SPEED OF LIGHT. BUT ATTEMPTS TO PROVE THIS HAVE FAILED.
HERE'S A THOUGHT EXPERIMENT. SAY I'M STANDING ON A TRAIN GOING 100 MILES AN HOUR, AND I SHINE A FLASHLIGHT FORWARD.
YOU WOULD THINK THAT THE BEAM OF LIGHT WOULD TRAVEL AT THE SPEED OF LIGHT PLUS 100 MILES AN HOUR, BUT IT DOESN'T!
ALL EXPERIMENTS SHOW THAT THE SPEED OF LIGHT IS ALWAYS THE SAME! IT'S ALWAYS 186,000 MILES PER SECOND! IT CAN NEVER GET ANY FASTER, AND NOTHING CAN BE FASTER THAN THAT!
IT'S THE SPEED LIMIT FOR THE UNIVERSE!

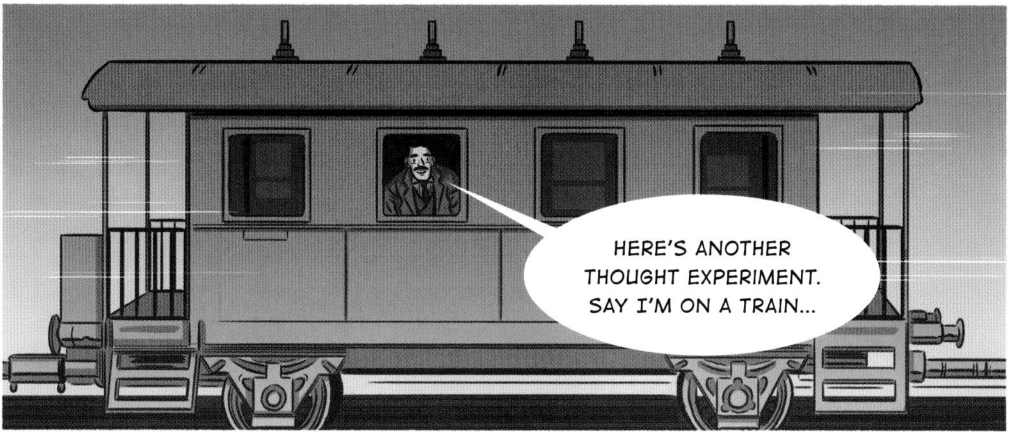
HERE'S ANOTHER THOUGHT EXPERIMENT. SAY I'M ON A TRAIN...

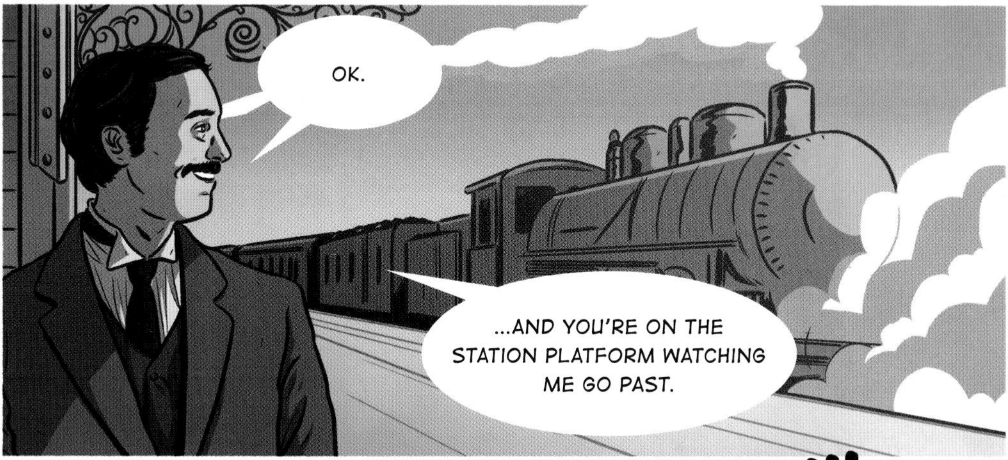
OK.
...AND YOU'RE ON THE STATION PLATFORM WATCHING ME GO PAST.

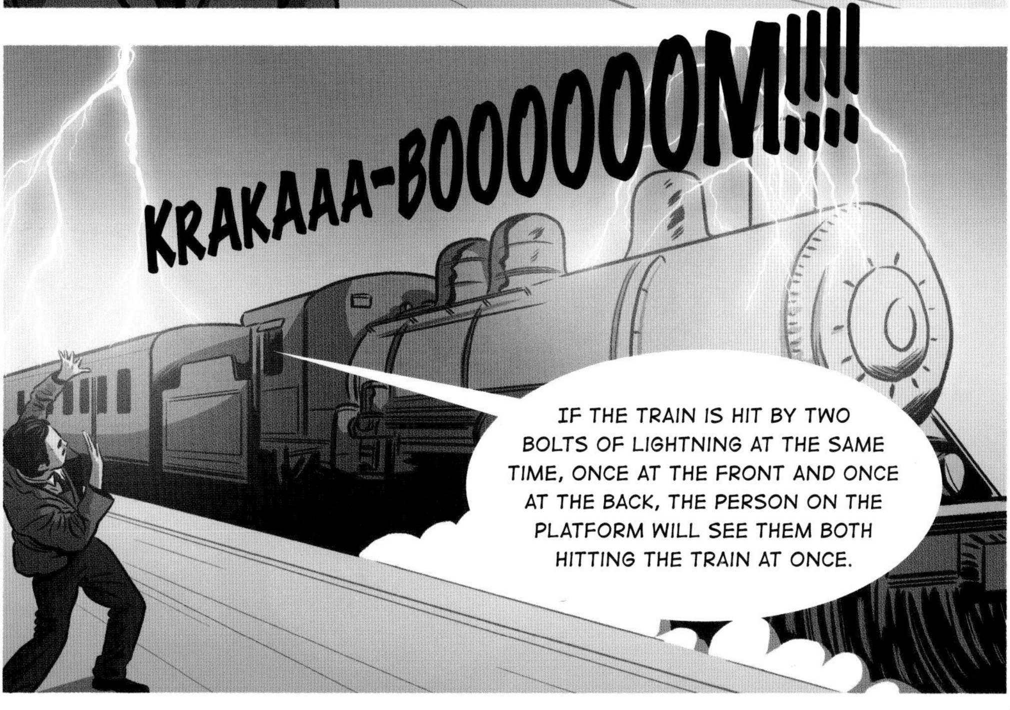
KRAKAAA-BOOOOOOM!!!!
IF THE TRAIN IS HIT BY TWO BOLTS OF LIGHTNING AT THE SAME TIME, ONCE AT THE FRONT AND ONCE AT THE BACK, THE PERSON ON THE PLATFORM WILL SEE THEM BOTH HITTING THE TRAIN AT ONCE.

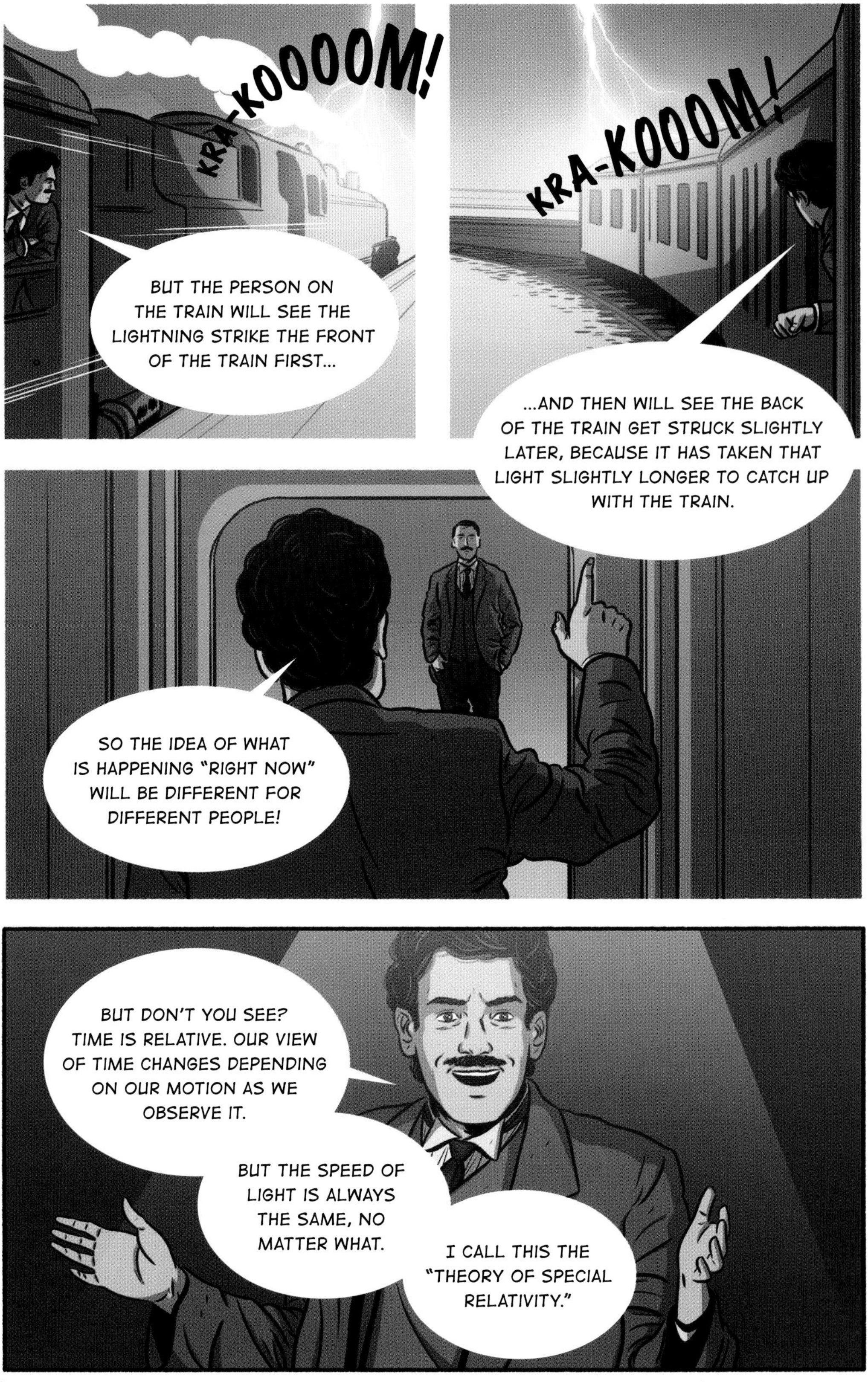
KRA-KOOOOM!
BUT THE PERSON ON THE TRAIN WILL SEE THE LIGHTNING STRIKE THE FRONT OF THE TRAIN FIRST...
KRA-KOOOM!
...AND THEN WILL SEE THE BACK OF THE TRAIN GET STRUCK SLIGHTLY LATER, BECAUSE IT HAS TAKEN THAT LIGHT SLIGHTLY LONGER TO CATCH UP WITH THE TRAIN.
SO THE IDEA OF WHAT IS HAPPENING "RIGHT NOW" WILL BE DIFFERENT FOR DIFFERENT PEOPLE!
BUT DON'T YOU SEE? TIME IS RELATIVE. OUR VIEW OF TIME CHANGES DEPENDING ON OUR MOTION AS WE OBSERVE IT.
BUT THE SPEED OF LIGHT IS ALWAYS THE SAME, NO MATTER WHAT.
I CALL THIS THE "THEORY OF SPECIAL RELATIVITY."

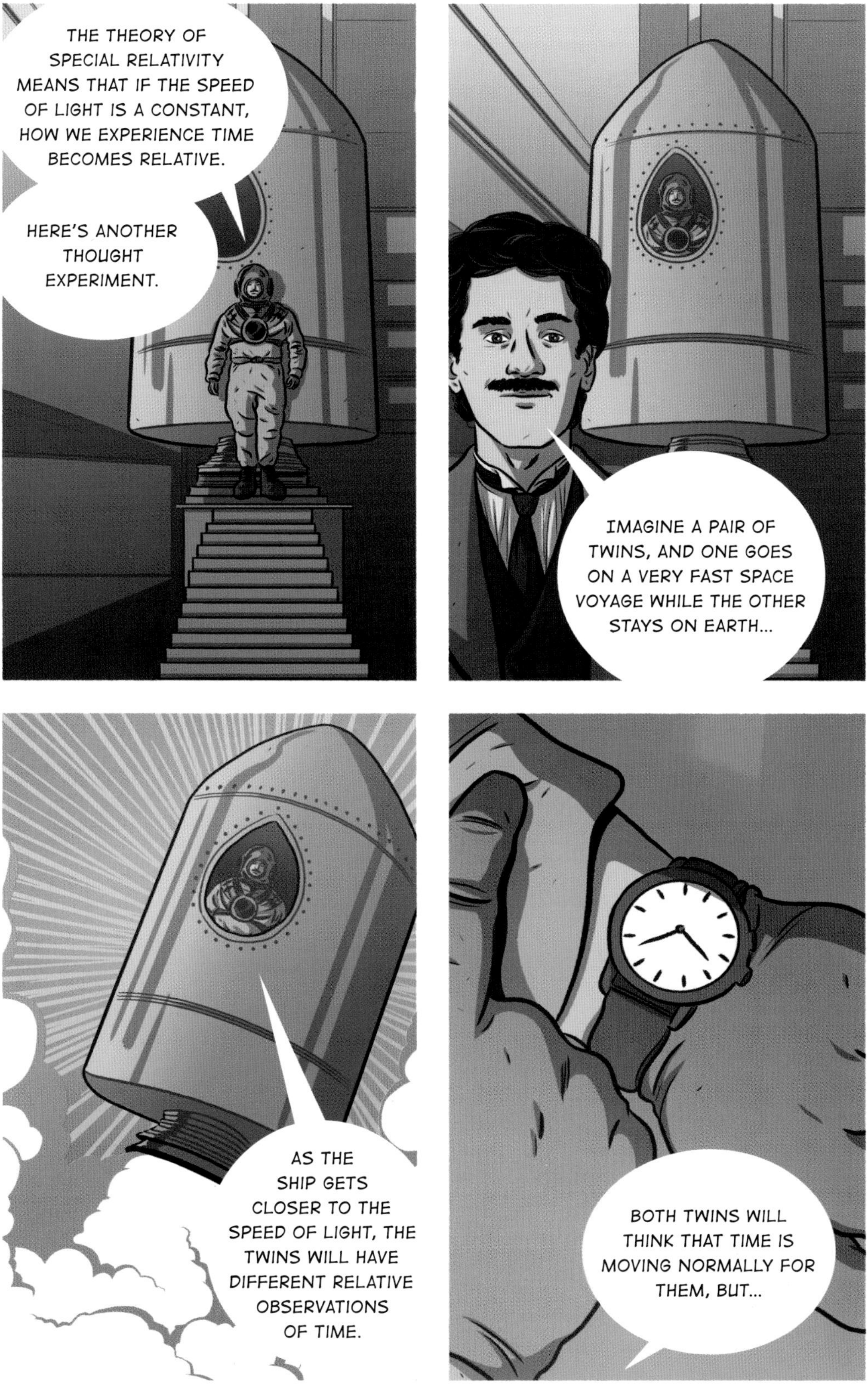
THE THEORY OF SPECIAL RELATIVITY MEANS THAT IF THE SPEED OF LIGHT IS A CONSTANT, HOW WE EXPERIENCE TIME BECOMES RELATIVE.
HERE'S ANOTHER THOUGHT EXPERIMENT.
IMAGINE A PAIR OF TWINS, AND ONE GOES ON A VERY FAST SPACE VOYAGE WHILE THE OTHER STAYS ON EARTH...
AS THE SHIP GETS CLOSER TO THE SPEED OF LIGHT, THE TWINS WILL HAVE DIFFERENT RELATIVE OBSERVATIONS OF TIME.
BOTH TWINS WILL THINK THAT TIME IS MOVING NORMALLY FOR THEM, BUT...

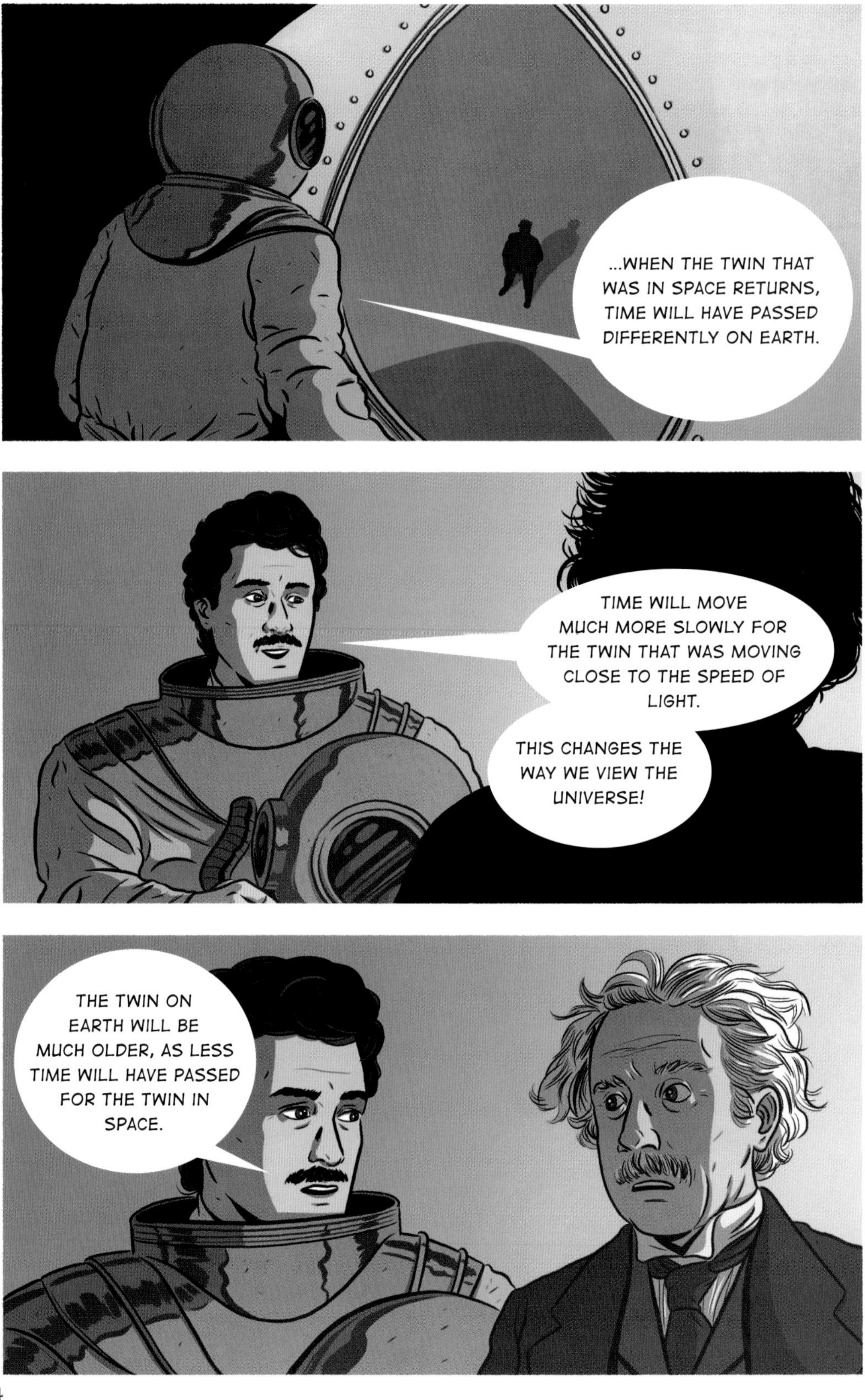
...WHEN THE TWIN THAT WAS IN SPACE RETURNS, TIME WILL HAVE PASSED DIFFERENTLY ON EARTH.
TIME WILL MOVE MUCH MORE SLOWLY FOR THE TWIN THAT WAS MOVING CLOSE TO THE SPEED OF LIGHT.
THIS CHANGES THE WAY WE VIEW THE UNIVERSE!
THE TWIN ON EARTH WILL BE MUCH OLDER, AS LESS TIME WILL HAVE PASSED FOR THE TWIN IN SPACE.

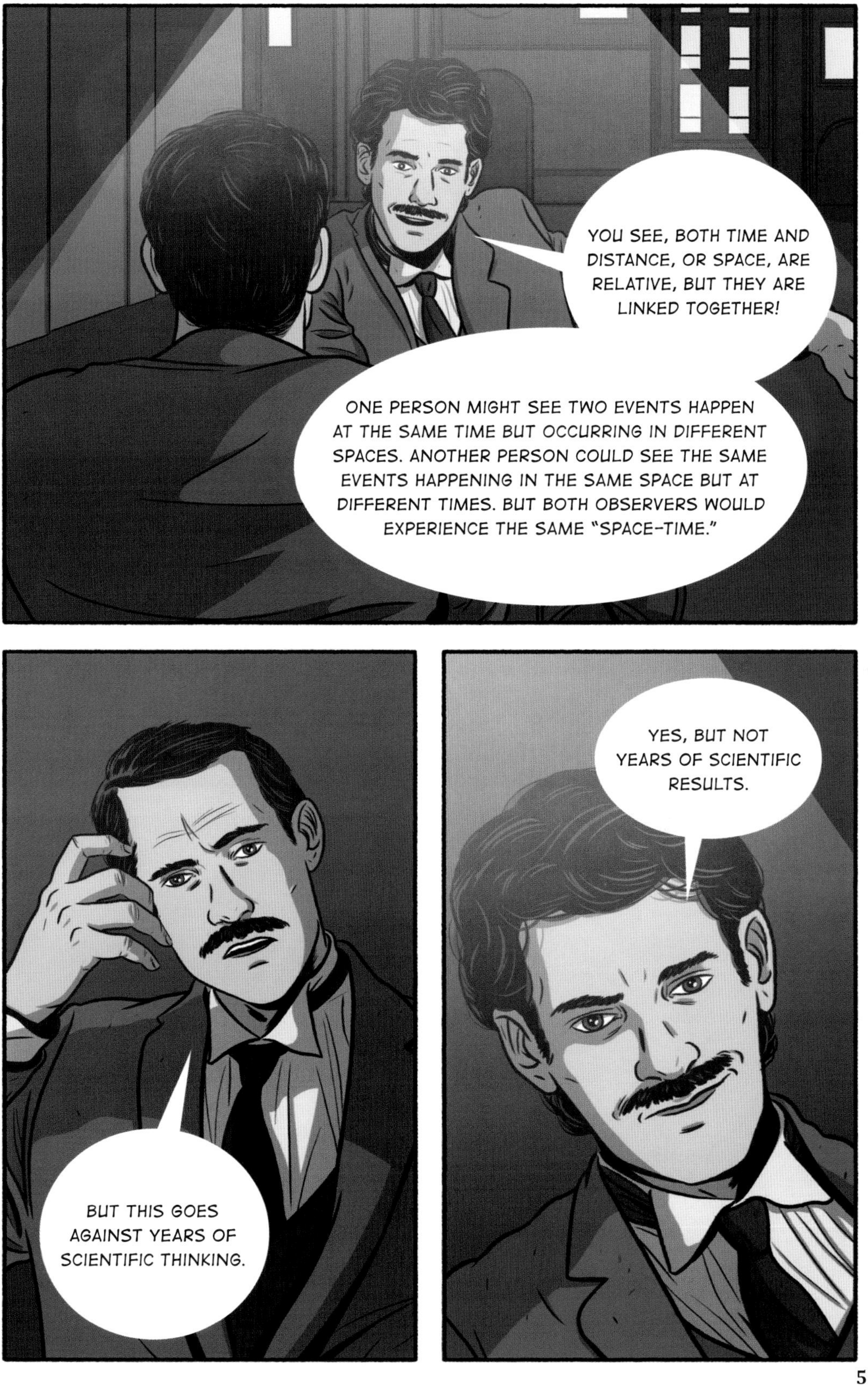
YOU SEE, BOTH TIME AND DISTANCE, OR SPACE, ARE RELATIVE, BUT THEY ARE LINKED TOGETHER!
ONE PERSON MIGHT SEE TWO EVENTS HAPPEN AT THE SAME TIME BUT OCCURRING IN DIFFERENT SPACES. ANOTHER PERSON COULD SEE THE SAME EVENTS HAPPENING IN THE SAME SPACE BUT AT DIFFERENT TIMES. BUT BOTH OBSERVERS WOULD EXPERIENCE THE SAME "SPACE-TIME."
BUT THIS GOES AGAINST YEARS OF SCIENTIFIC THINKING.
YES, BUT NOT YEARS OF SCIENTIFIC RESULTS.

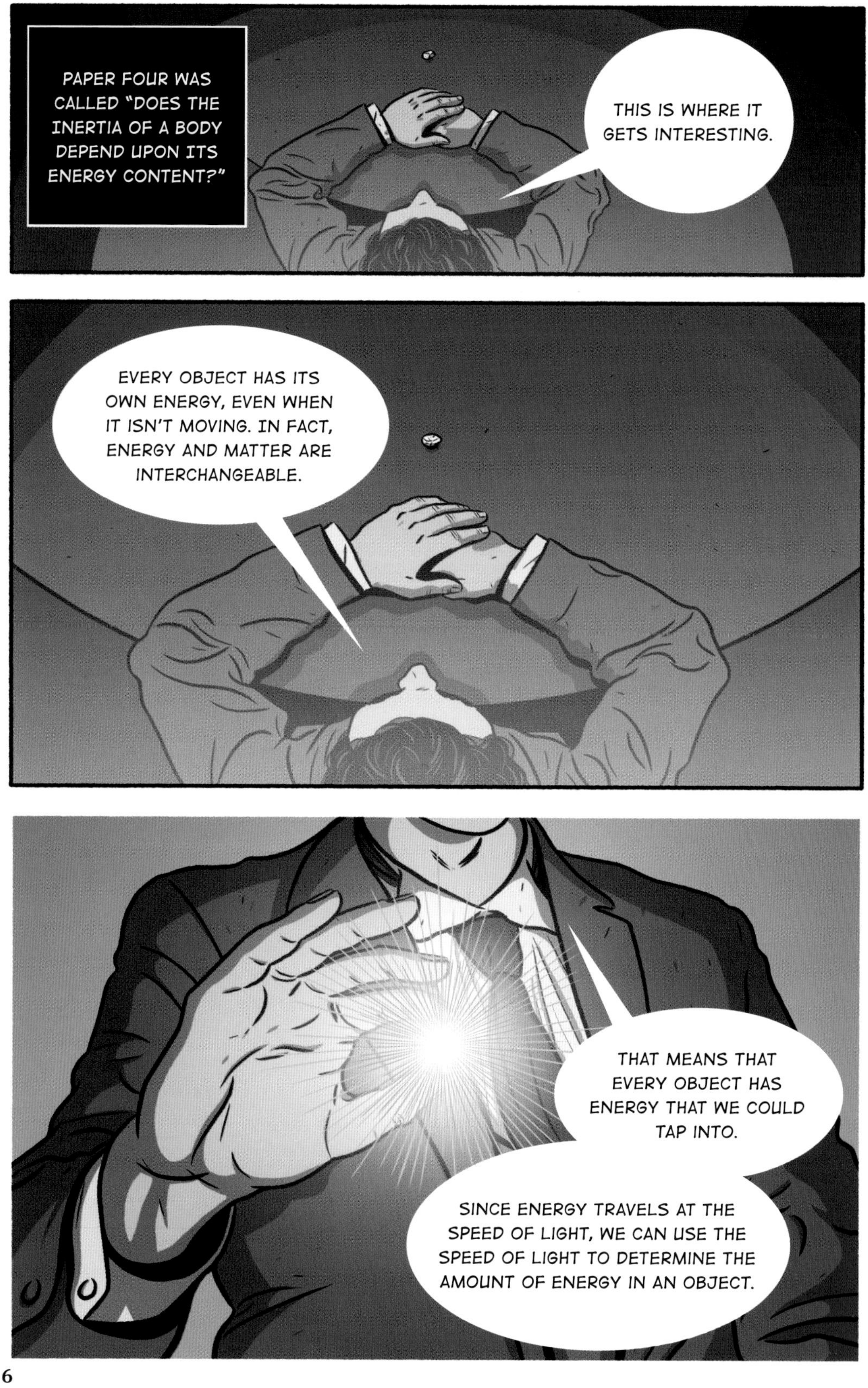
PAPER FOUR WAS CALLED "DOES THE INERTIA OF A BODY DEPEND UPON ITS ENERGY CONTENT?"
THIS IS WHERE IT GETS INTERESTING.
EVERY OBJECT HAS ITS OWN ENERGY, EVEN WHEN IT ISN'T MOVING. IN FACT, ENERGY AND MATTER ARE INTERCHANGEABLE.
THAT MEANS THAT EVERY OBJECT HAS ENERGY THAT WE COULD TAP INTO.
SINCE ENERGY TRAVELS AT THE SPEED OF LIGHT, WE CAN USE THE SPEED OF LIGHT TO DETERMINE THE AMOUNT OF ENERGY IN AN OBJECT.

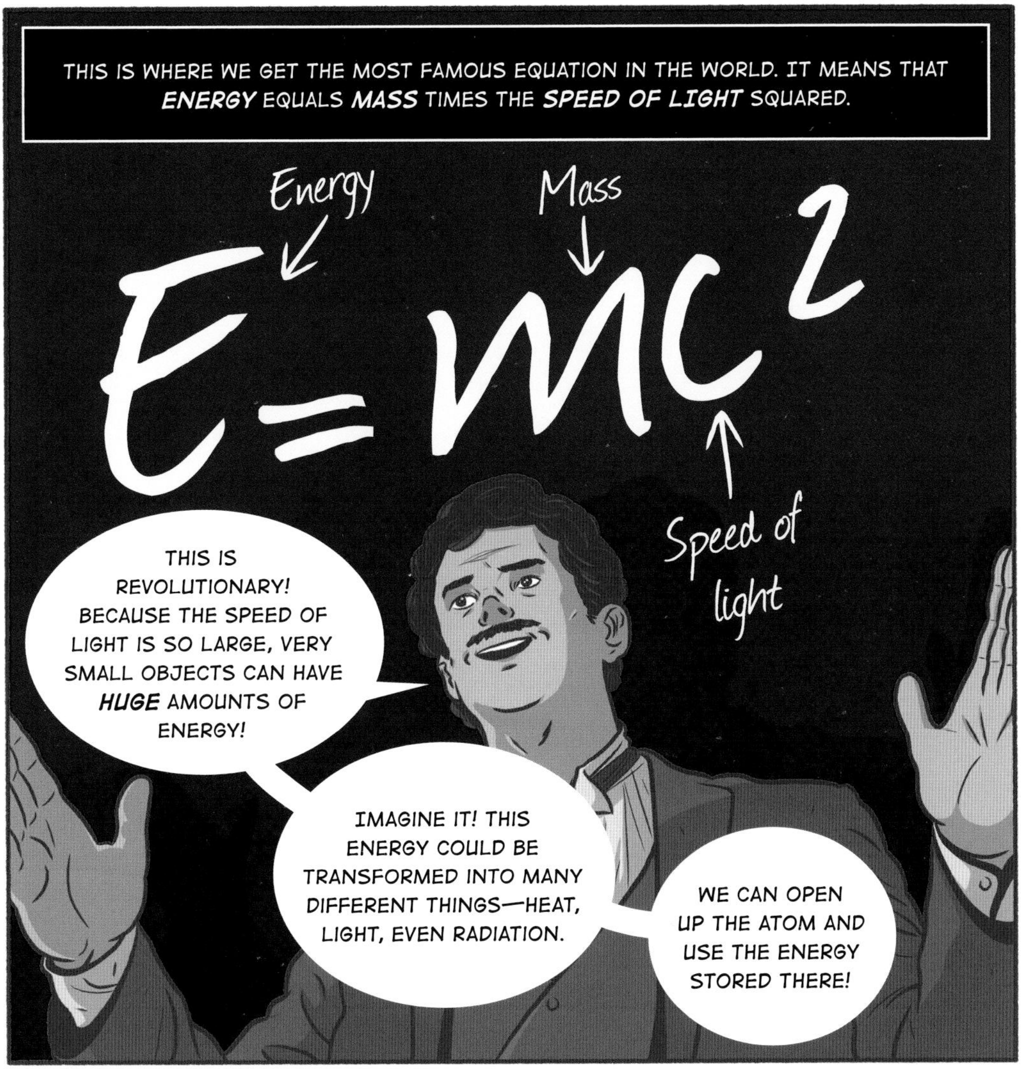
THIS IS WHERE WE GET THE MOST FAMOUS EQUATION IN THE WORLD. IT MEANS THAT ENERGY EQUALS MASS TIMES THE SPEED OF LIGHT SQUARED.
Energy
Mass
$E = mc^2$
Speed of light
THIS IS REVOLUTIONARY! BECAUSE THE SPEED OF LIGHT IS SO LARGE, VERY SMALL OBJECTS CAN HAVE HUGE AMOUNTS OF ENERGY!
IMAGINE IT! THIS ENERGY COULD BE TRANSFORMED INTO MANY DIFFERENT THINGS—HEAT, LIGHT, EVEN RADIATION.
WE CAN OPEN UP THE ATOM AND USE THE ENERGY STORED THERE!

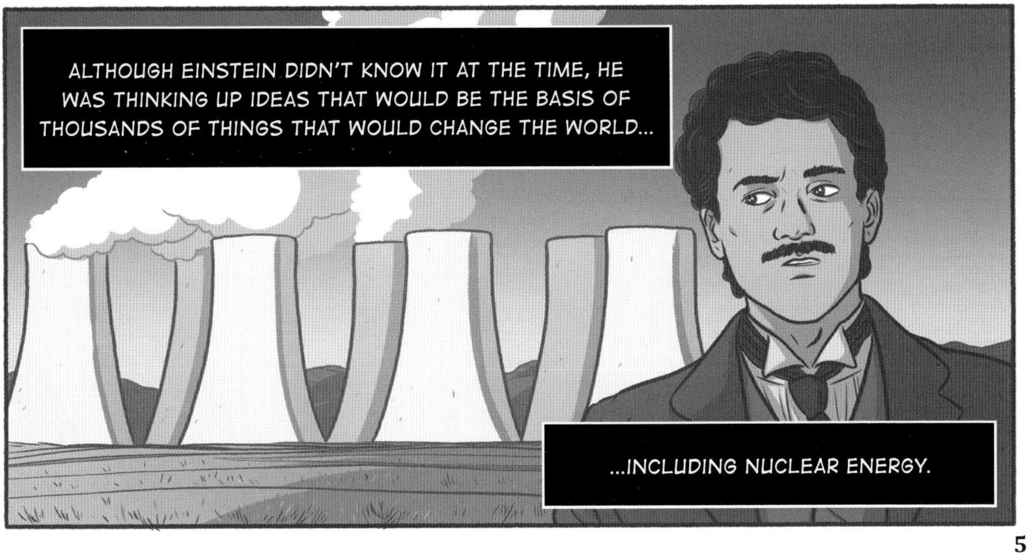
ALTHOUGH EINSTEIN DIDN'T KNOW IT AT THE TIME, HE WAS THINKING UP IDEAS THAT WOULD BE THE BASIS OF THOUSANDS OF THINGS THAT WOULD CHANGE THE WORLD...
...INCLUDING NUCLEAR ENERGY.

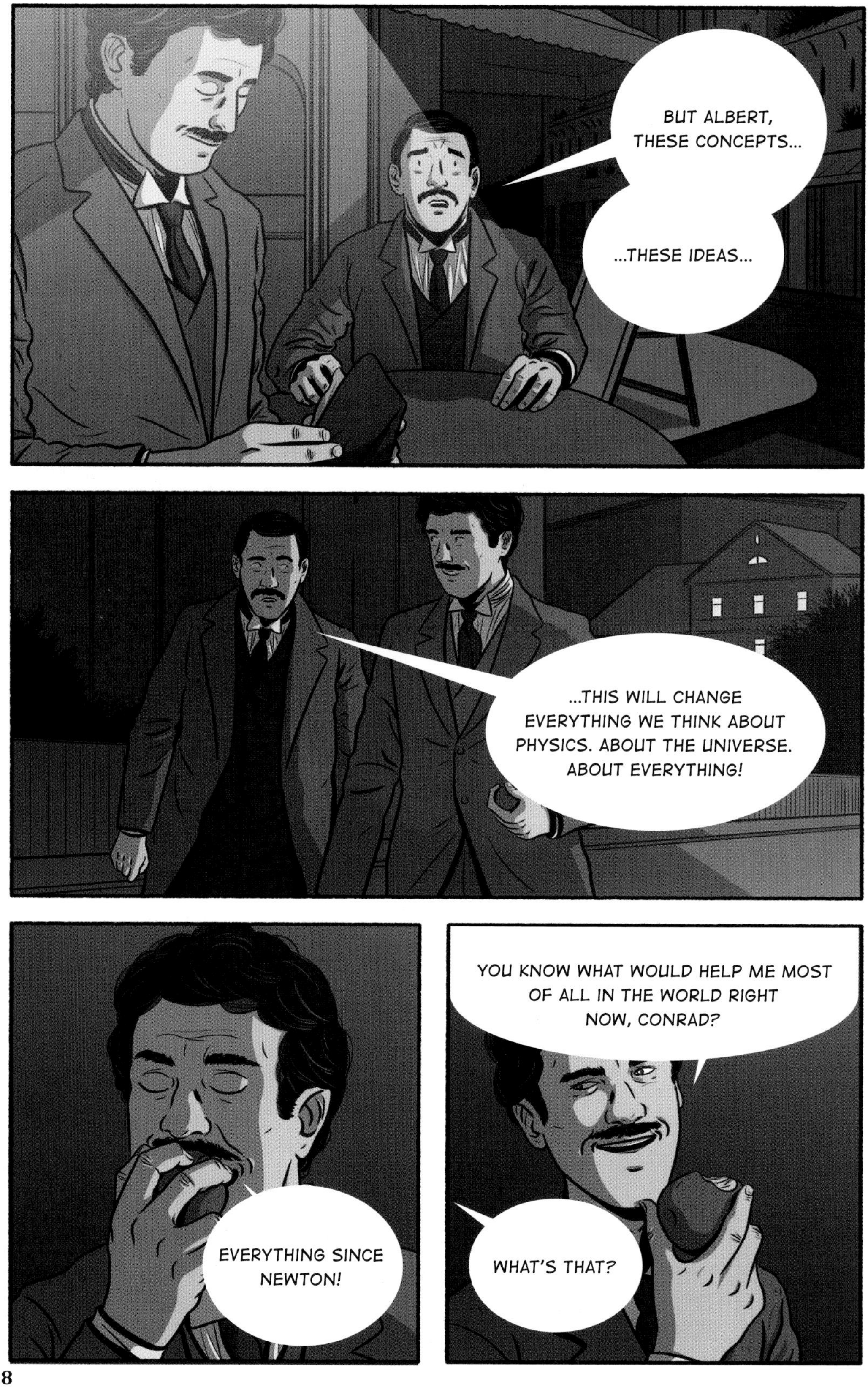
BUT ALBERT, THESE CONCEPTS...
...THESE IDEAS...
...THIS WILL CHANGE EVERYTHING WE THINK ABOUT PHYSICS. ABOUT THE UNIVERSE. ABOUT EVERYTHING!
EVERYTHING SINCE NEWTON!
YOU KNOW WHAT WOULD HELP ME MOST OF ALL IN THE WORLD RIGHT NOW, CONRAD?
WHAT'S THAT?

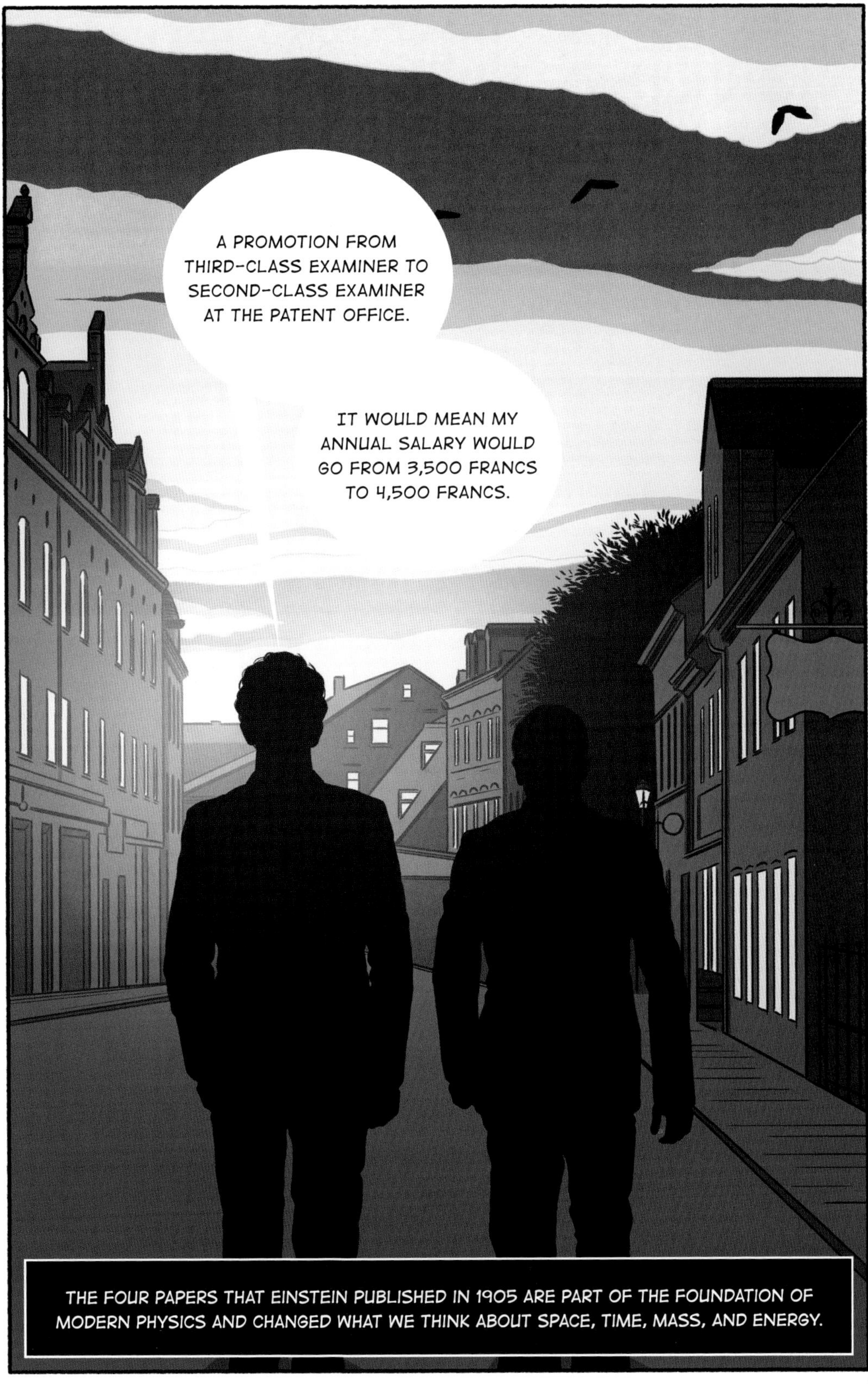
A PROMOTION FROM THIRD-CLASS EXAMINER TO SECOND-CLASS EXAMINER AT THE PATENT OFFICE.
IT WOULD MEAN MY ANNUAL SALARY WOULD GO FROM 3,500 FRANCS TO 4,500 FRANCS.
THE FOUR PAPERS THAT EINSTEIN PUBLISHED IN 1905 ARE PART OF THE FOUNDATION OF MODERN PHYSICS AND CHANGED WHAT WE THINK ABOUT SPACE, TIME, MASS, AND ENERGY.

CHAPTER 5

Linking Space and Time

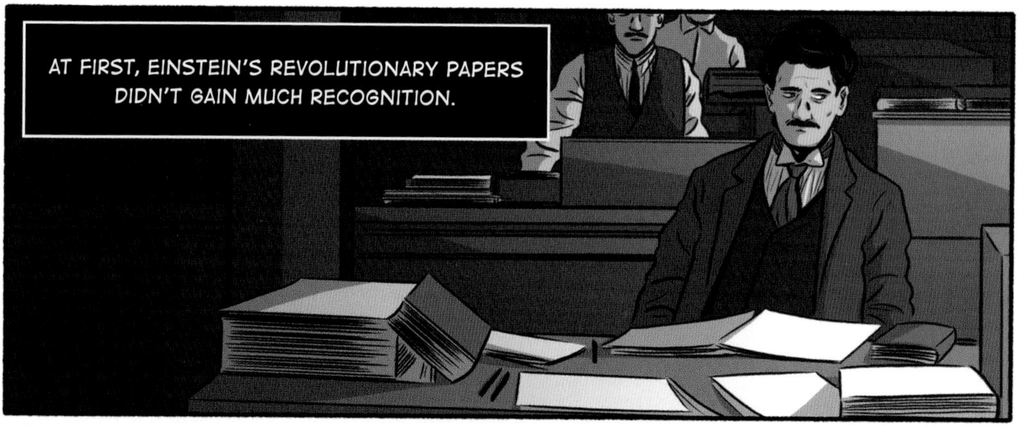
AT FIRST, EINSTEIN'S REVOLUTIONARY PAPERS DIDN'T GAIN MUCH RECOGNITION.

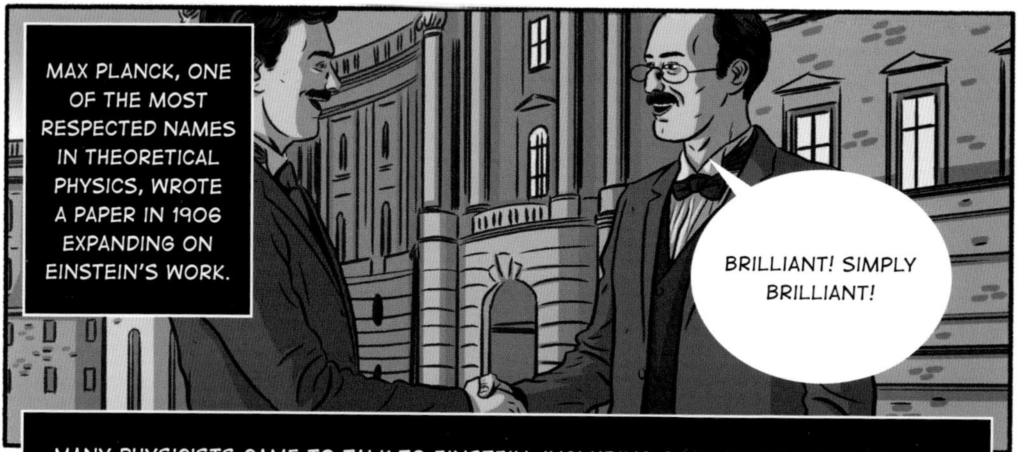
MAX PLANCK, ONE OF THE MOST RESPECTED NAMES IN THEORETICAL PHYSICS, WROTE A PAPER IN 1906 EXPANDING ON EINSTEIN'S WORK.
BRILLIANT! SIMPLY BRILLIANT!

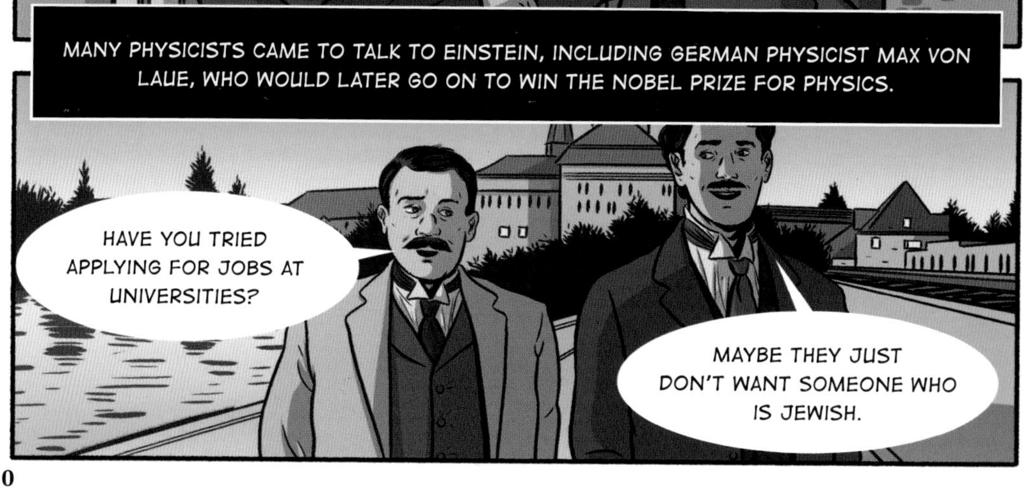
MANY PHYSICISTS CAME TO TALK TO EINSTEIN, INCLUDING GERMAN PHYSICIST MAX VON LAUE, WHO WOULD LATER GO ON TO WIN THE NOBEL PRIZE FOR PHYSICS.
HAVE YOU TRIED APPLYING FOR JOBS AT UNIVERSITIES?
MAYBE THEY JUST DON'T WANT SOMEONE WHO IS JEWISH.

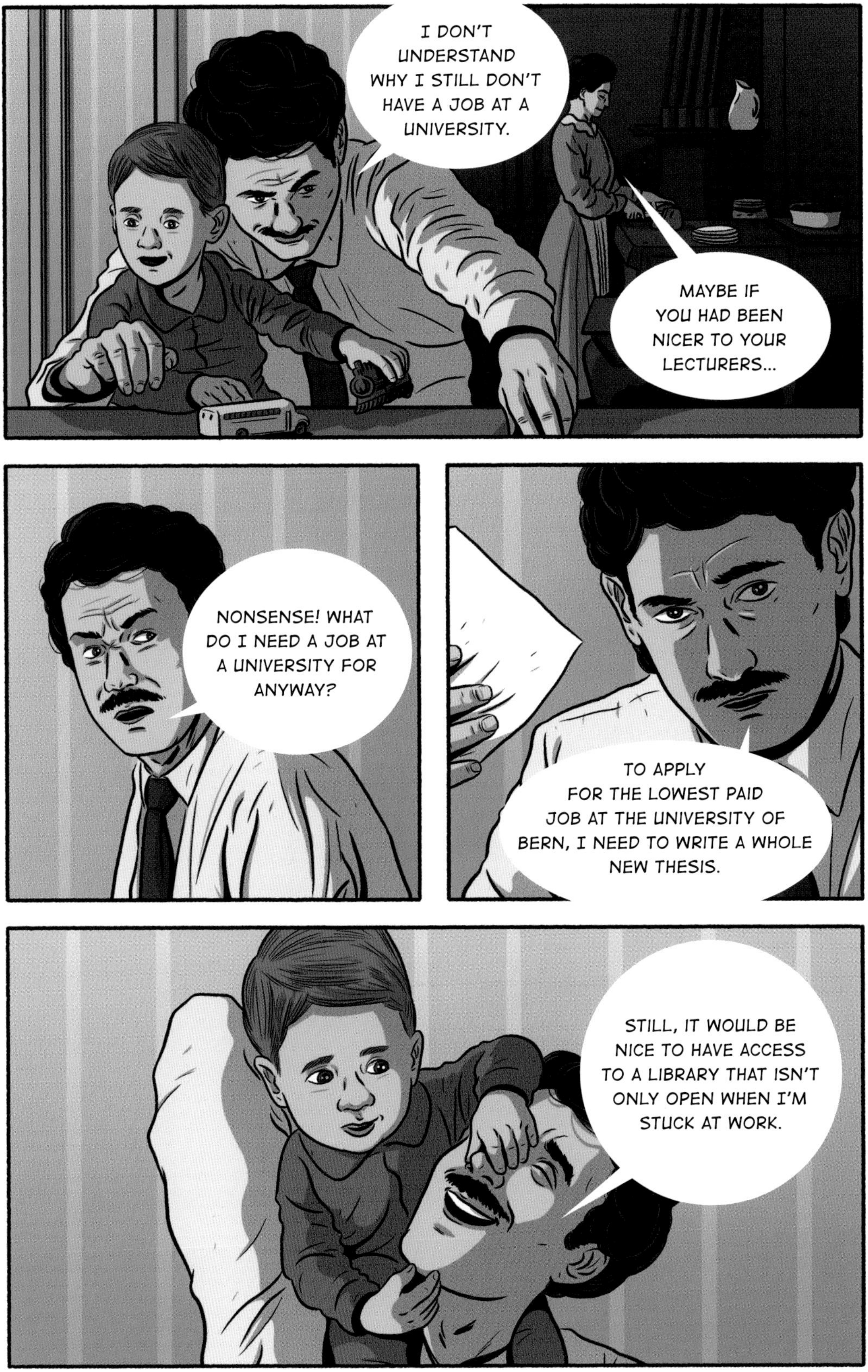
I DON'T UNDERSTAND WHY I STILL DON'T HAVE A JOB AT A UNIVERSITY.
MAYBE IF YOU HAD BEEN NICER TO YOUR LECTURERS...
NONSENSE! WHAT DO I NEED A JOB AT A UNIVERSITY FOR ANYWAY?
TO APPLY FOR THE LOWEST PAID JOB AT THE UNIVERSITY OF BERN, I NEED TO WRITE A WHOLE NEW THESIS.
STILL, IT WOULD BE NICE TO HAVE ACCESS TO A LIBRARY THAT ISN'T ONLY OPEN WHEN I'M STUCK AT WORK.

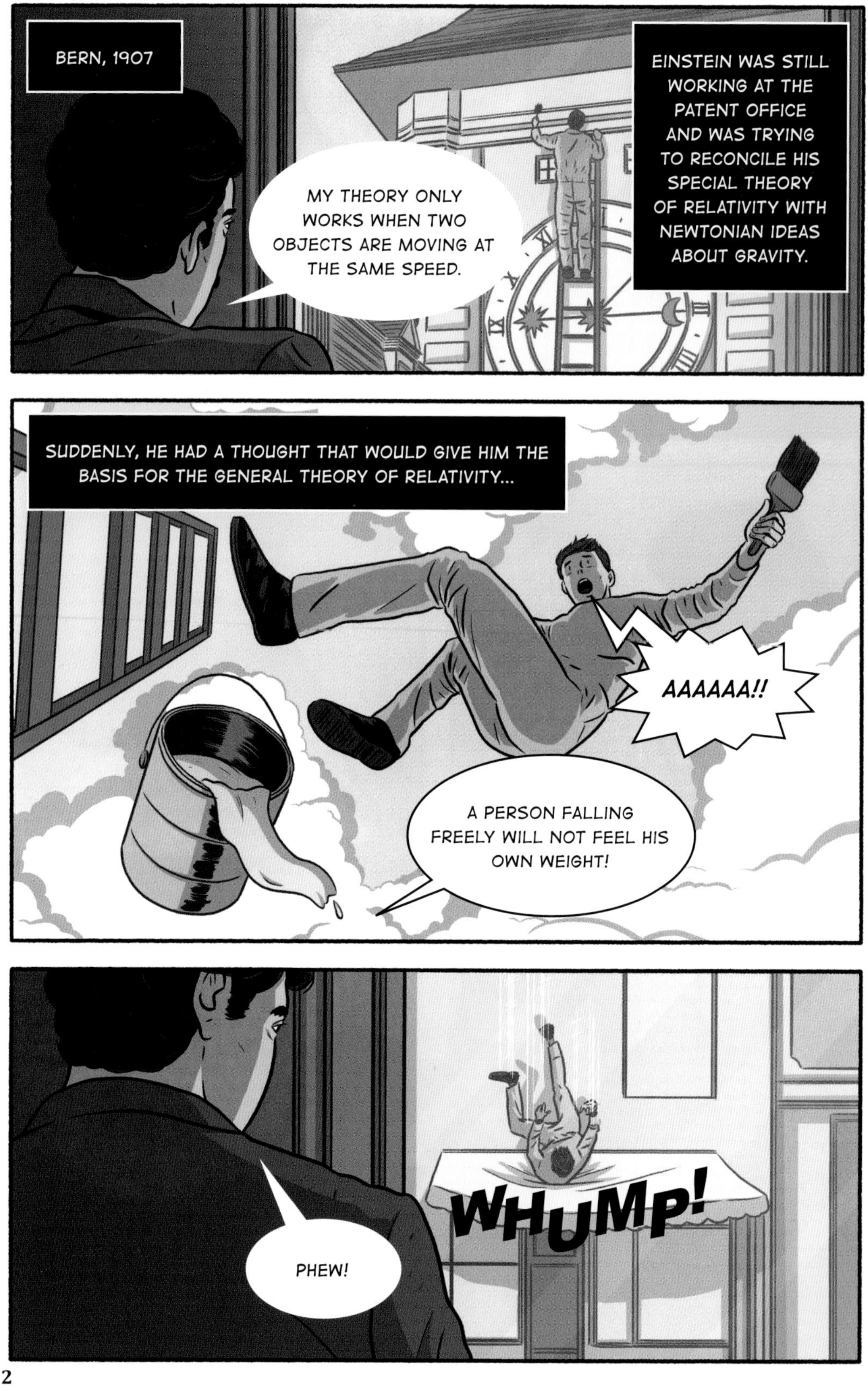
BERN, 1907
EINSTEIN WAS STILL WORKING AT THE PATENT OFFICE AND WAS TRYING TO RECONCILE HIS SPECIAL THEORY OF RELATIVITY WITH NEWTONIAN IDEAS ABOUT GRAVITY.
MY THEORY ONLY WORKS WHEN TWO OBJECTS ARE MOVING AT THE SAME SPEED.
SUDDENLY, HE HAD A THOUGHT THAT WOULD GIVE HIM THE BASIS FOR THE GENERAL THEORY OF RELATIVITY...
AAAAAA!!
A PERSON FALLING FREELY WILL NOT FEEL HIS OWN WEIGHT!
WHUMP!
PHEW!

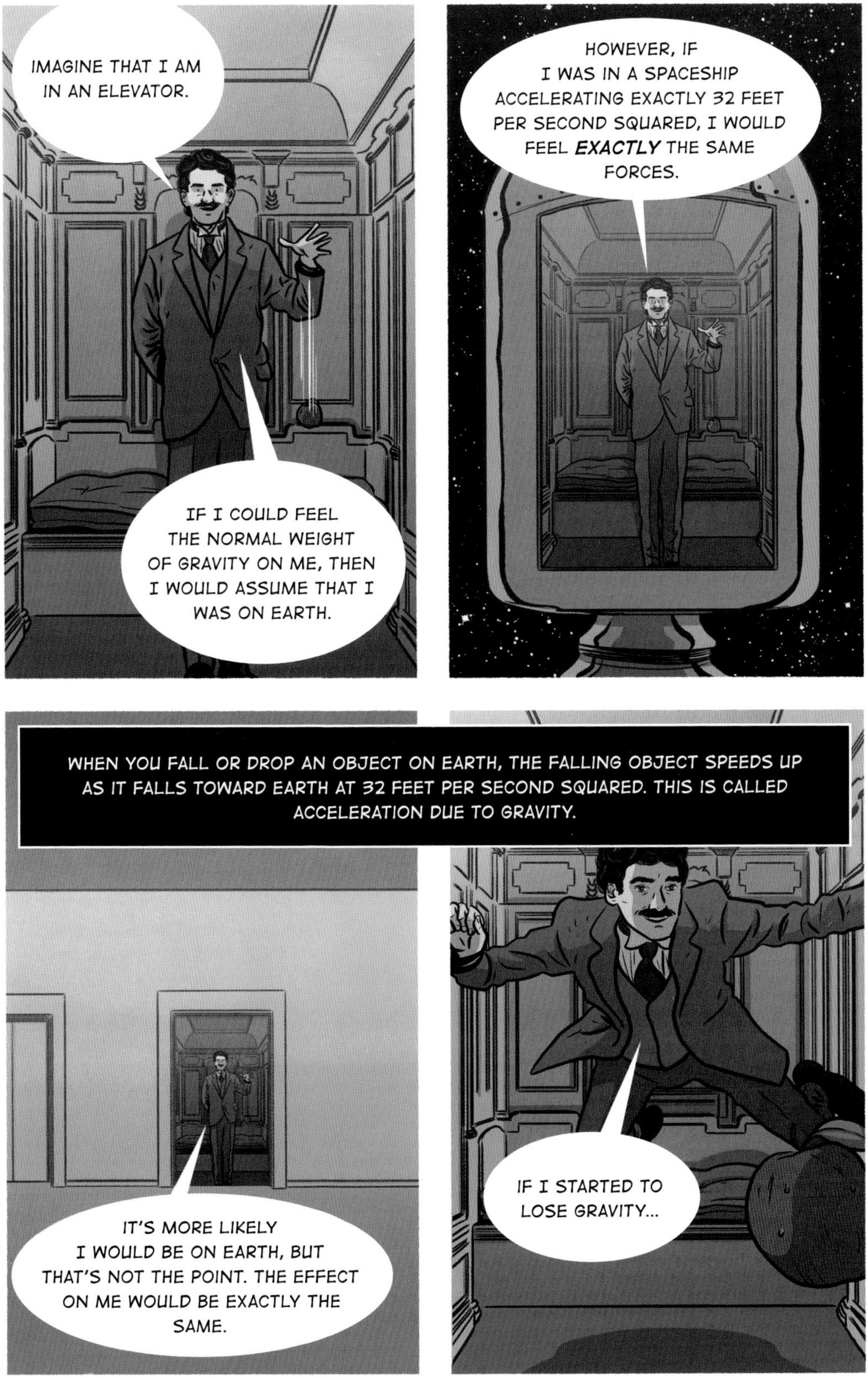
IMAGINE THAT I AM IN AN ELEVATOR.
IF I COULD FEEL THE NORMAL WEIGHT OF GRAVITY ON ME, THEN I WOULD ASSUME THAT I WAS ON EARTH.
HOWEVER, IF I WAS IN A SPACESHIP ACCELERATING EXACTLY 32 FEET PER SECOND SQUARED, I WOULD FEEL ***EXACTLY*** THE SAME FORCES.
WHEN YOU FALL OR DROP AN OBJECT ON EARTH, THE FALLING OBJECT SPEEDS UP AS IT FALLS TOWARD EARTH AT 32 FEET PER SECOND SQUARED. THIS IS CALLED ACCELERATION DUE TO GRAVITY.
IT'S MORE LIKELY I WOULD BE ON EARTH, BUT THAT'S NOT THE POINT. THE EFFECT ON ME WOULD BE EXACTLY THE SAME.
IF I STARTED TO LOSE GRAVITY...

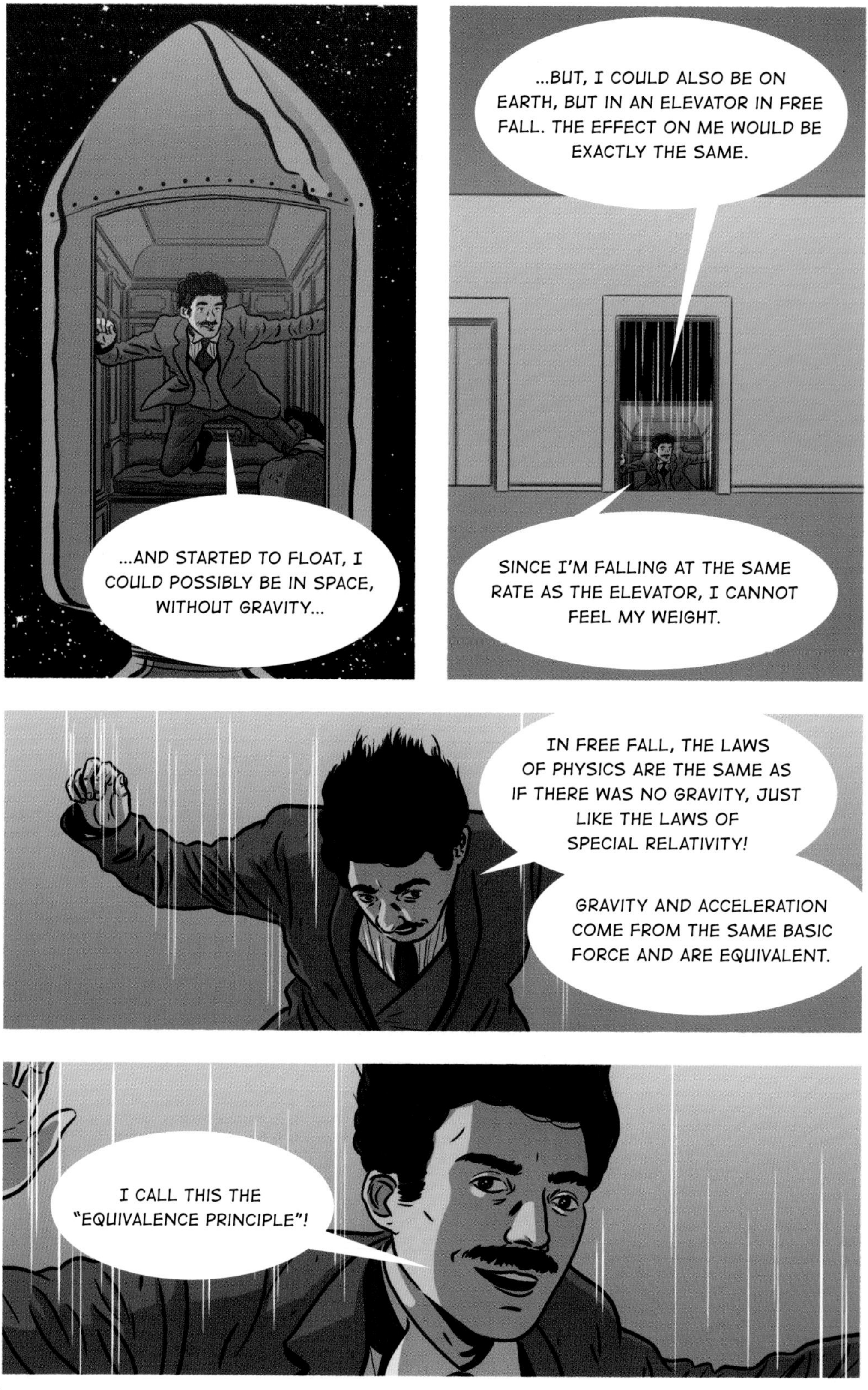
...AND STARTED TO FLOAT, I COULD POSSIBLY BE IN SPACE, WITHOUT GRAVITY...
...BUT, I COULD ALSO BE ON EARTH, BUT IN AN ELEVATOR IN FREE FALL. THE EFFECT ON ME WOULD BE EXACTLY THE SAME.
SINCE I'M FALLING AT THE SAME RATE AS THE ELEVATOR, I CANNOT FEEL MY WEIGHT.
IN FREE FALL, THE LAWS OF PHYSICS ARE THE SAME AS IF THERE WAS NO GRAVITY, JUST LIKE THE LAWS OF SPECIAL RELATIVITY!
GRAVITY AND ACCELERATION COME FROM THE SAME BASIC FORCE AND ARE EQUIVALENT.
I CALL THIS THE "EQUIVALENCE PRINCIPLE"!

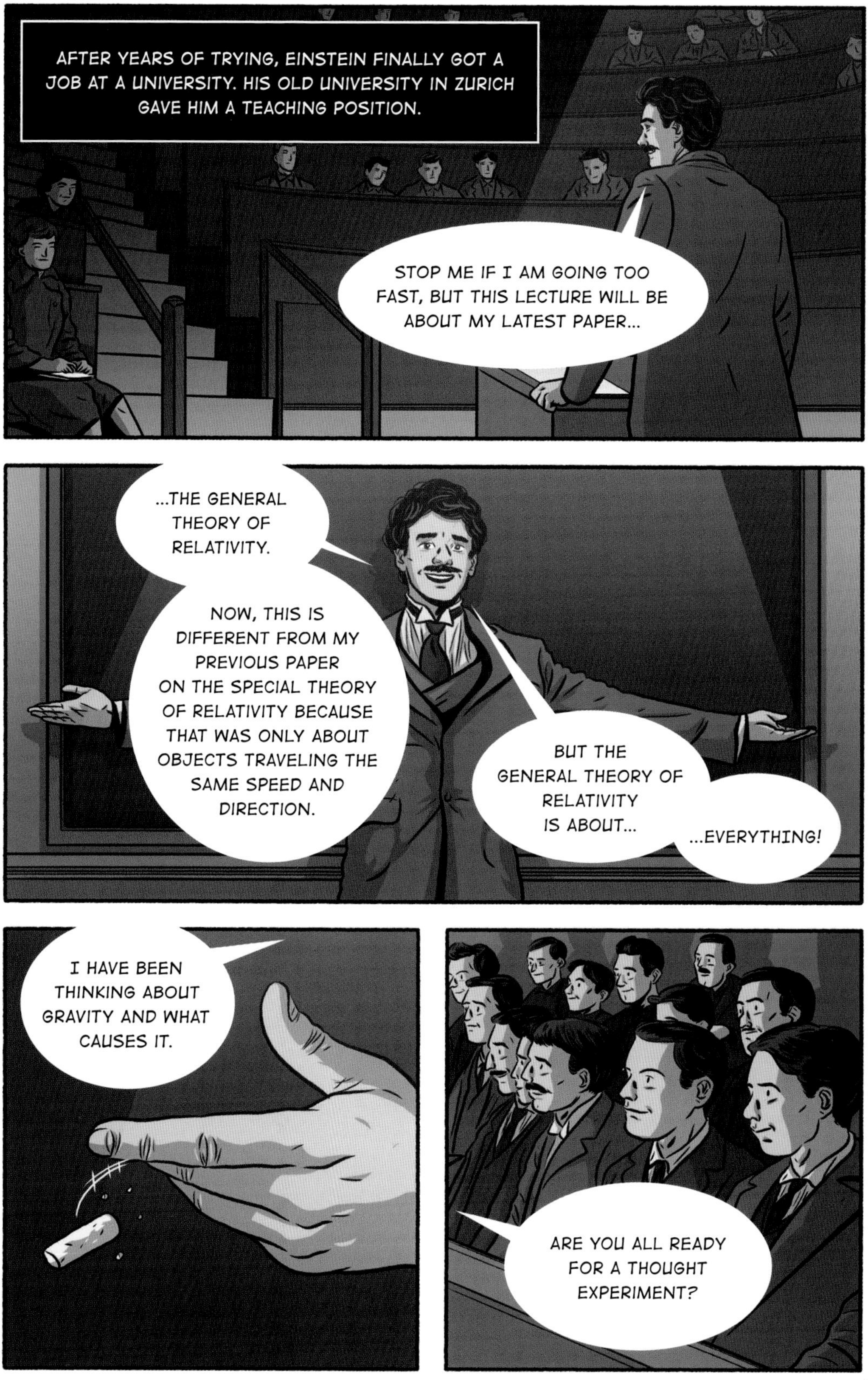
AFTER YEARS OF TRYING, EINSTEIN FINALLY GOT A JOB AT A UNIVERSITY. HIS OLD UNIVERSITY IN ZURICH GAVE HIM A TEACHING POSITION.
STOP ME IF I AM GOING TOO FAST, BUT THIS LECTURE WILL BE ABOUT MY LATEST PAPER...
...THE GENERAL THEORY OF RELATIVITY.
NOW, THIS IS DIFFERENT FROM MY PREVIOUS PAPER ON THE SPECIAL THEORY OF RELATIVITY BECAUSE THAT WAS ONLY ABOUT OBJECTS TRAVELING THE SAME SPEED AND DIRECTION.
BUT THE GENERAL THEORY OF RELATIVITY IS ABOUT...
...EVERYTHING!
I HAVE BEEN THINKING ABOUT GRAVITY AND WHAT CAUSES IT.
ARE YOU ALL READY FOR A THOUGHT EXPERIMENT?

REMEMBER HOW WE WERE TALKING ABOUT HOW SPACE AND TIME ARE LINKED? LET'S CALL IT SPACE-TIME!

IMAGINE THAT SPACE-TIME IS THIS RUBBER SHEET STRETCHED OVER THIS HOOP.

IMAGINE THAT THIS BOWLING BALL REPRESENTS SOMETHING *HUGE*, LIKE A STAR.

SEE THE WAY IT BENDS SPACE AND TIME A LITTLE BIT AROUND IT?

THE WEIGHT OF THE BOWLING BALL IS PULLING OTHER OBJECTS TOWARD IT.

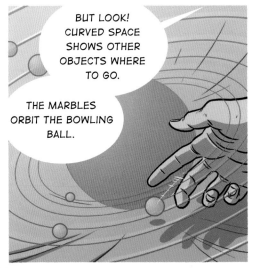

BUT LOOK! CURVED SPACE SHOWS OTHER OBJECTS WHERE TO GO.

THE MARBLES ORBIT THE BOWLING BALL.

THESE ARE THE FORCES THAT CONTROL THE UNIVERSE.

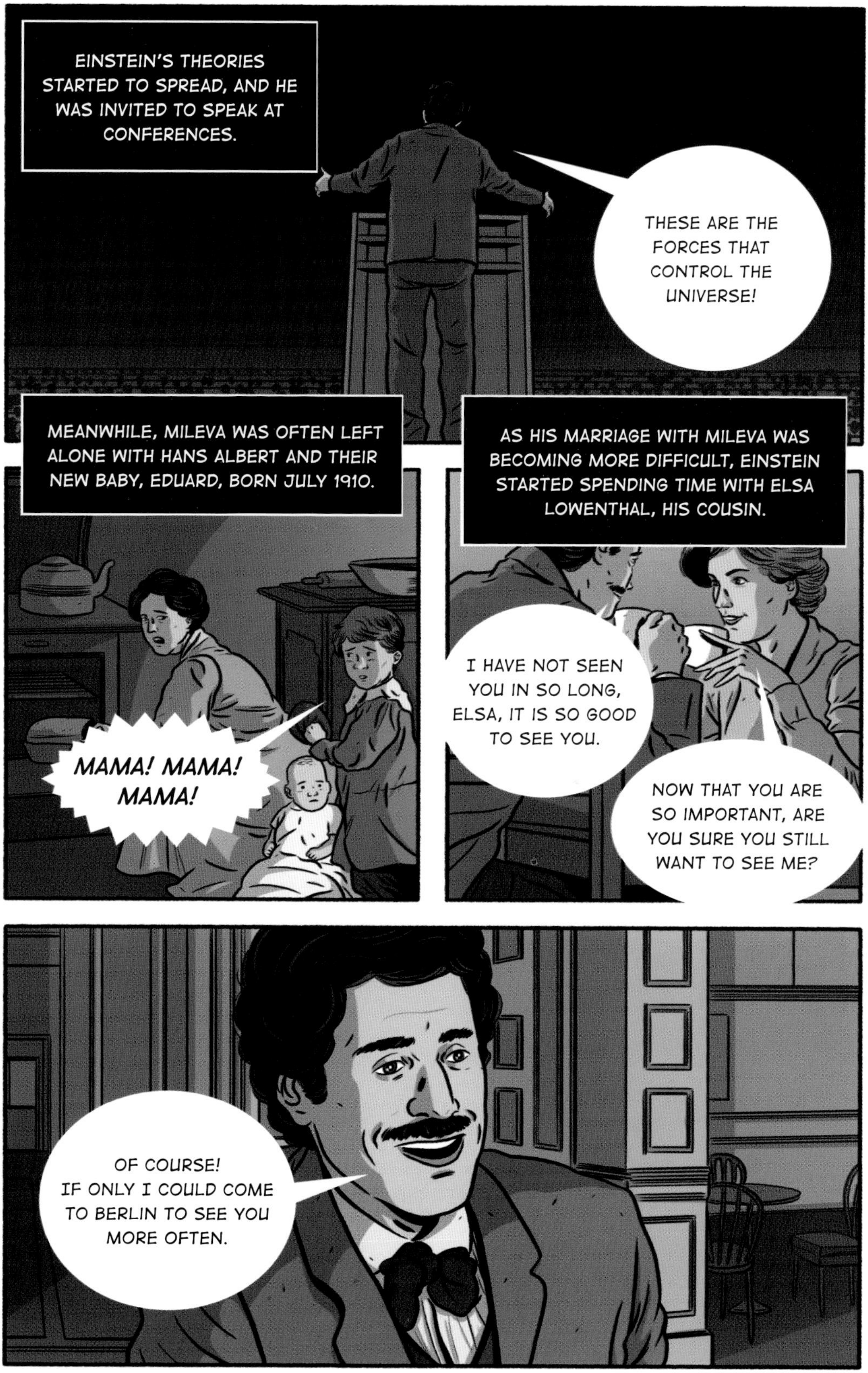
EINSTEIN'S THEORIES STARTED TO SPREAD, AND HE WAS INVITED TO SPEAK AT CONFERENCES.
THESE ARE THE FORCES THAT CONTROL THE UNIVERSE!
MEANWHILE, MILEVA WAS OFTEN LEFT ALONE WITH HANS ALBERT AND THEIR NEW BABY, EDUARD, BORN JULY 1910.
MAMA! MAMA! MAMA!
AS HIS MARRIAGE WITH MILEVA WAS BECOMING MORE DIFFICULT, EINSTEIN STARTED SPENDING TIME WITH ELSA LOWENTHAL, HIS COUSIN.
I HAVE NOT SEEN YOU IN SO LONG, ELSA, IT IS SO GOOD TO SEE YOU.
NOW THAT YOU ARE SO IMPORTANT, ARE YOU SURE YOU STILL WANT TO SEE ME?
OF COURSE! IF ONLY I COULD COME TO BERLIN TO SEE YOU MORE OFTEN.

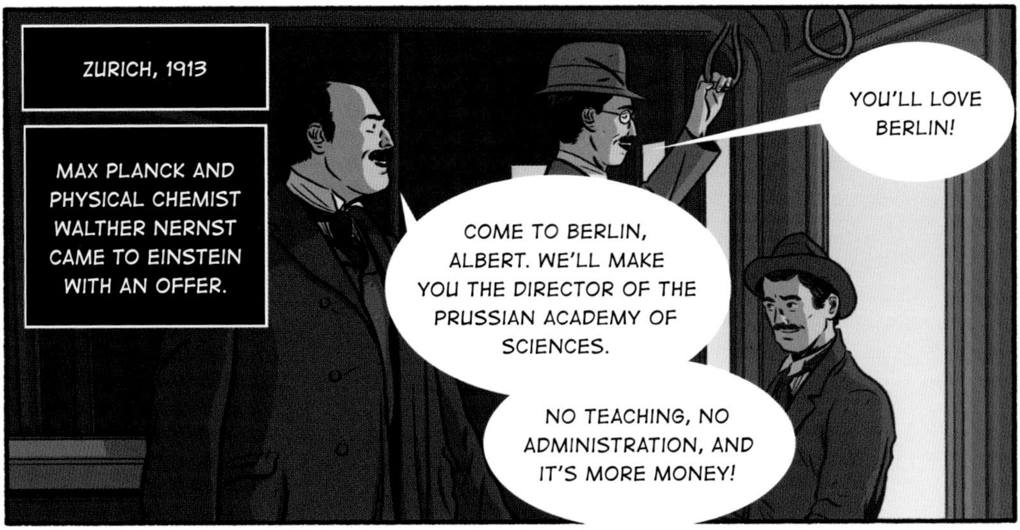
ZURICH, 1913
MAX PLANCK AND PHYSICAL CHEMIST WALTHER NERNST CAME TO EINSTEIN WITH AN OFFER.
YOU'LL LOVE BERLIN!
COME TO BERLIN, ALBERT. WE'LL MAKE YOU THE DIRECTOR OF THE PRUSSIAN ACADEMY OF SCIENCES.
NO TEACHING, NO ADMINISTRATION, AND IT'S MORE MONEY!

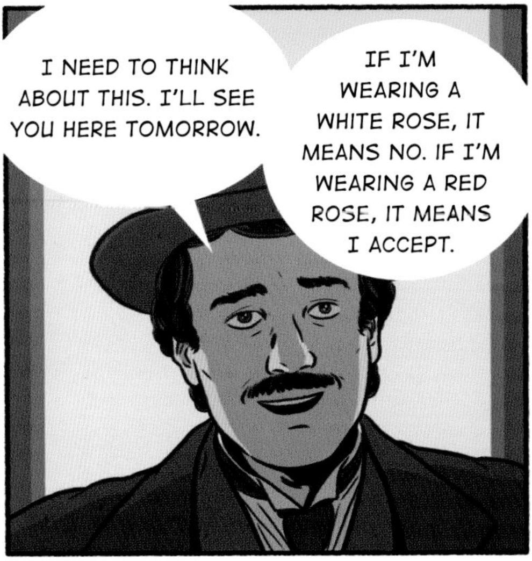
I NEED TO THINK ABOUT THIS. I'LL SEE YOU HERE TOMORROW.
IF I'M WEARING A WHITE ROSE, IT MEANS NO. IF I'M WEARING A RED ROSE, IT MEANS I ACCEPT.

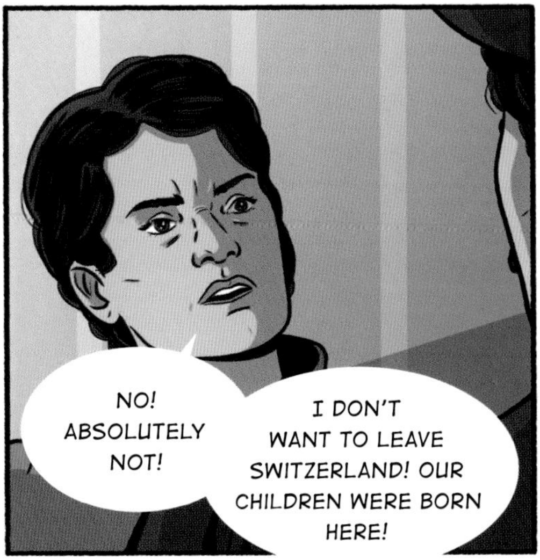
NO! ABSOLUTELY NOT!
I DON'T WANT TO LEAVE SWITZERLAND! OUR CHILDREN WERE BORN HERE!

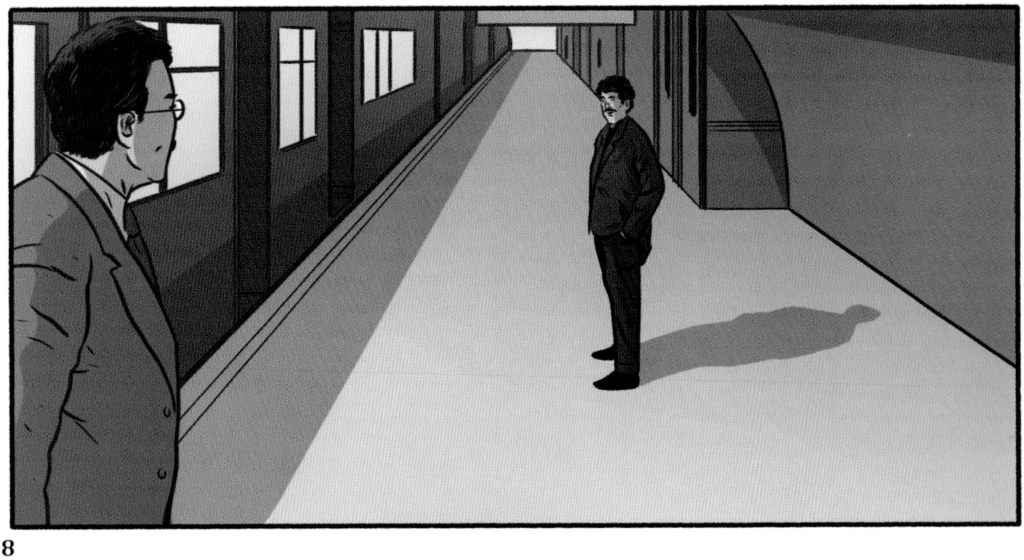

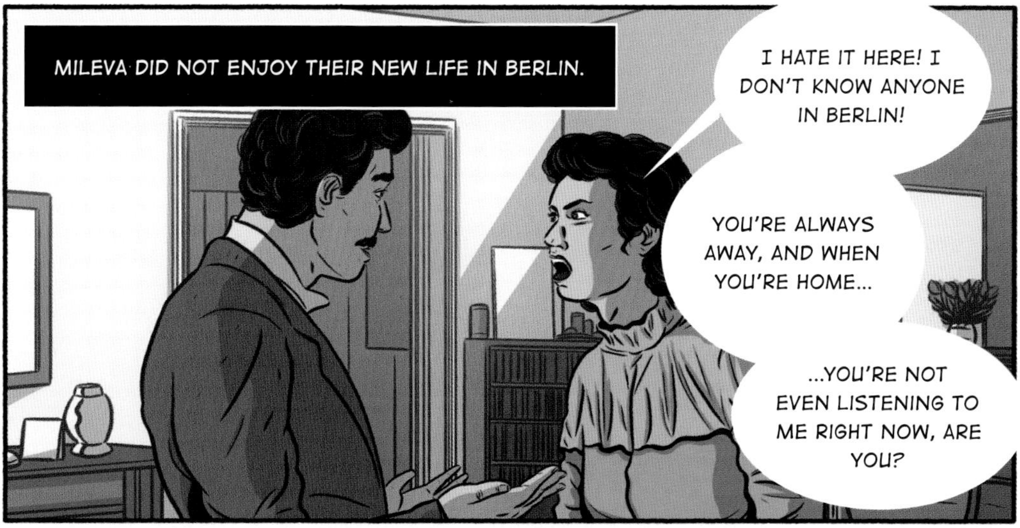
MILEVA DID NOT ENJOY THEIR NEW LIFE IN BERLIN.
I HATE IT HERE! I DON'T KNOW ANYONE IN BERLIN!
YOU'RE ALWAYS AWAY, AND WHEN YOU'RE HOME...
...YOU'RE NOT EVEN LISTENING TO ME RIGHT NOW, ARE YOU?

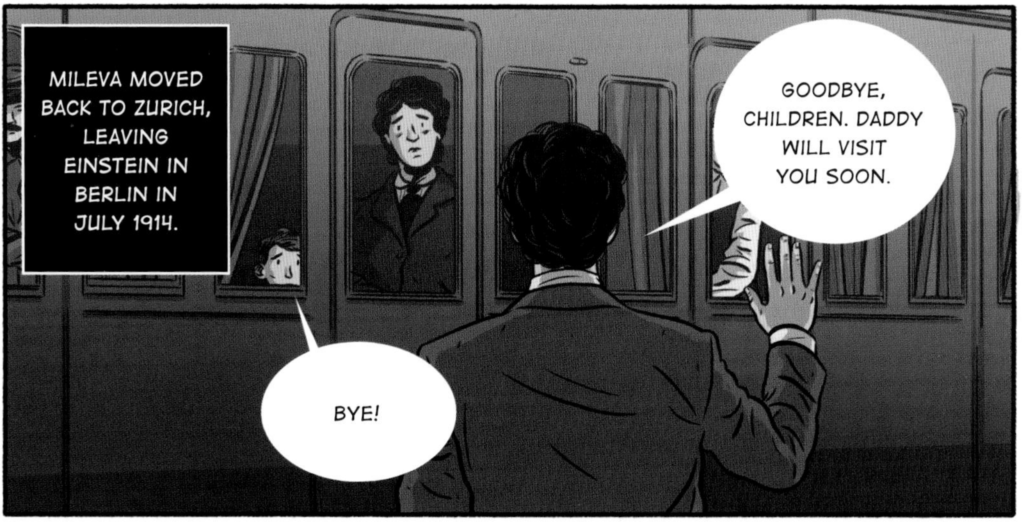
MILEVA MOVED BACK TO ZURICH, LEAVING EINSTEIN IN BERLIN IN JULY 1914.
GOODBYE, CHILDREN. DADDY WILL VISIT YOU SOON.
BYE!

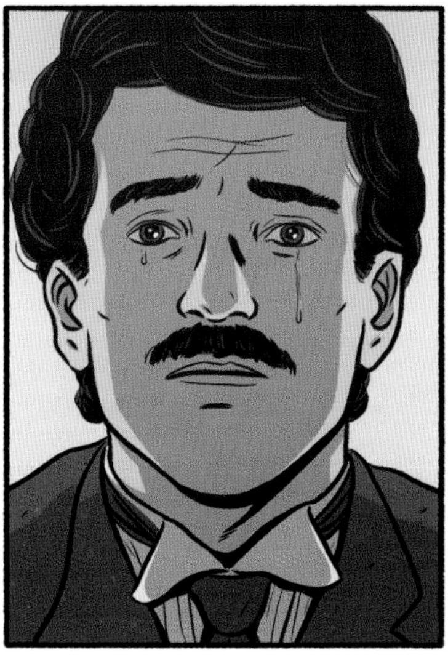

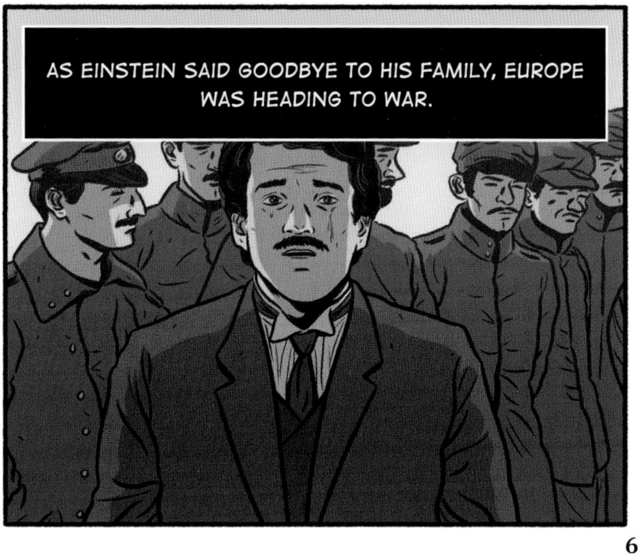
AS EINSTEIN SAID GOODBYE TO HIS FAMILY, EUROPE WAS HEADING TO WAR.

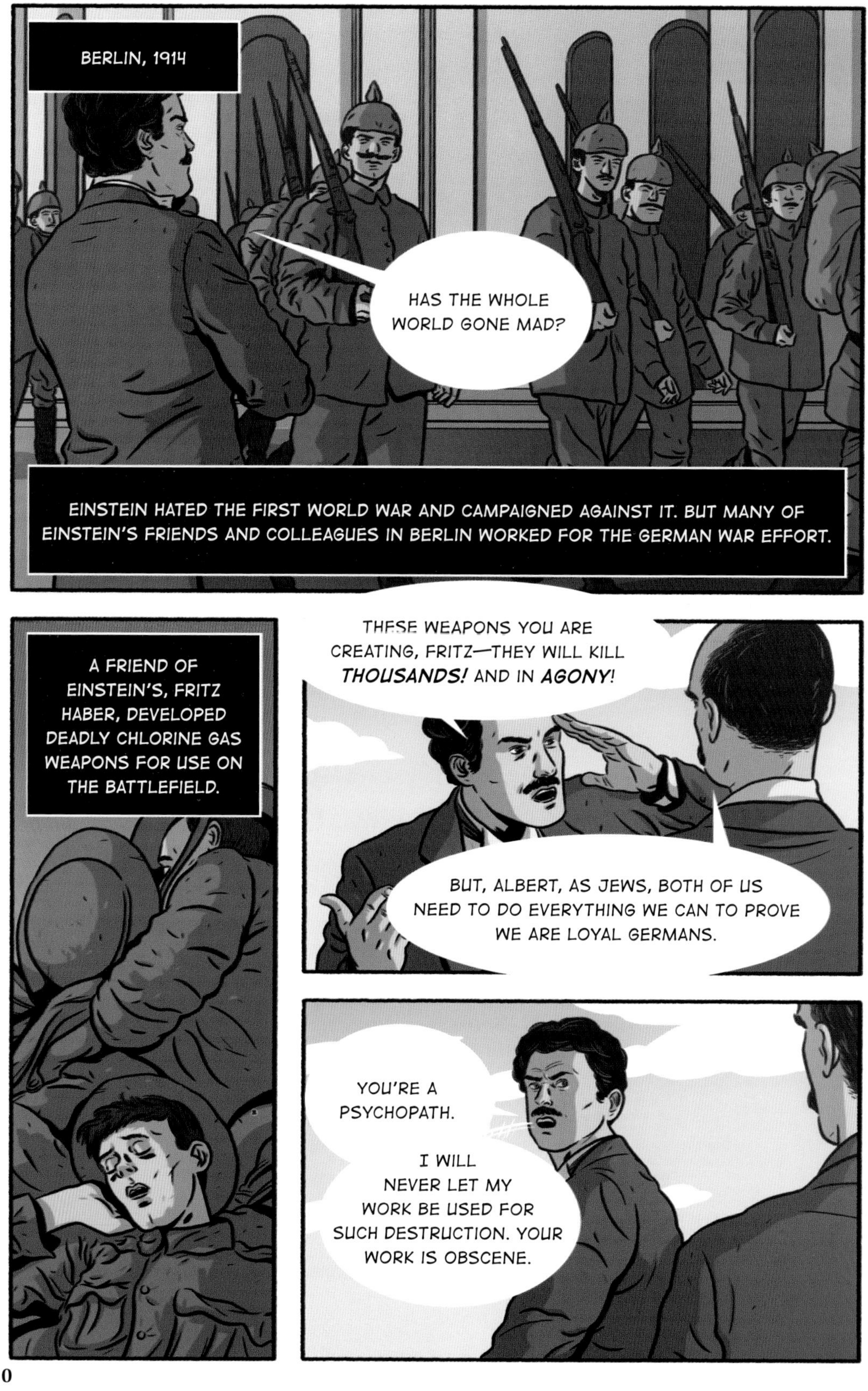
BERLIN, 1914
HAS THE WHOLE WORLD GONE MAD?
EINSTEIN HATED THE FIRST WORLD WAR AND CAMPAIGNED AGAINST IT. BUT MANY OF EINSTEIN'S FRIENDS AND COLLEAGUES IN BERLIN WORKED FOR THE GERMAN WAR EFFORT.
A FRIEND OF EINSTEIN'S, FRITZ HABER, DEVELOPED DEADLY CHLORINE GAS WEAPONS FOR USE ON THE BATTLEFIELD.
THESE WEAPONS YOU ARE CREATING, FRITZ—THEY WILL KILL ***THOUSANDS!*** AND IN ***AGONY***!
BUT, ALBERT, AS JEWS, BOTH OF US NEED TO DO EVERYTHING WE CAN TO PROVE WE ARE LOYAL GERMANS.
YOU'RE A PSYCHOPATH.
I WILL NEVER LET MY WORK BE USED FOR SUCH DESTRUCTION. YOUR WORK IS OBSCENE.

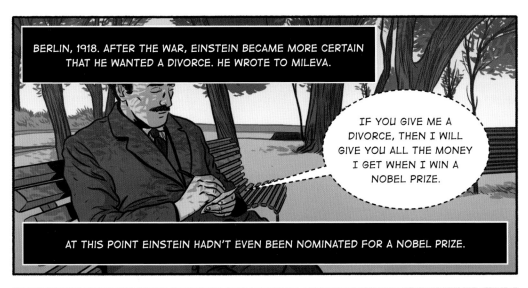

BERLIN, 1918. AFTER THE WAR, EINSTEIN BECAME MORE CERTAIN THAT HE WANTED A DIVORCE. HE WROTE TO MILEVA.

IF YOU GIVE ME A DIVORCE, THEN I WILL GIVE YOU ALL THE MONEY I GET WHEN I WIN A NOBEL PRIZE.

AT THIS POINT EINSTEIN HADN'T EVEN BEEN NOMINATED FOR A NOBEL PRIZE.

ALBERT AND ELSA WERE MARRIED IN JUNE 1919.

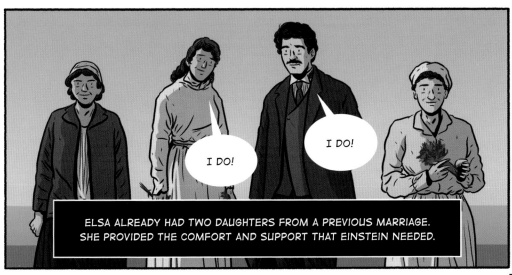

I DO!

I DO!

ELSA ALREADY HAD TWO DAUGHTERS FROM A PREVIOUS MARRIAGE. SHE PROVIDED THE COMFORT AND SUPPORT THAT EINSTEIN NEEDED.

FOR YEARS, EINSTEIN HAD BEEN EXPLAINING HIS THEORY OF RELATIVITY, BUT HE NEEDED SOMETHING BIG TO PROVE IT TO THE WORLD.

THE GENERAL THEORY OF RELATIVITY MEANS THAT LIGHT WILL CURVE AROUND THE GRAVITY OF A LARGE OBJECT LIKE A STAR.

SPACE-TIME IS DISTORTED, AND THE LIGHT IS SIMPLY FOLLOWING THAT.

DO YOU HAVE ANY EVIDENCE?

WELL, THE CALCULATIONS ARE CORRECT.

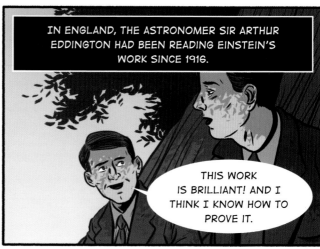

IN ENGLAND, THE ASTRONOMER SIR ARTHUR EDDINGTON HAD BEEN READING EINSTEIN'S WORK SINCE 1916.

THIS WORK IS BRILLIANT! AND I THINK I KNOW HOW TO PROVE IT.

THE ONLY WAY TO PROVE THAT EINSTEIN IS RIGHT IS TO SHOW THAT LIGHT FROM OTHER STARS IS BENDING AROUND THE SUN.

HOWEVER, THE SUN IS TOO BRIGHT FOR US TO SEE THE STARS AROUND IT DURING THE DAY.

THERE WILL BE A SOLAR ECLIPSE NEAR AFRICA IN MAY 1919.

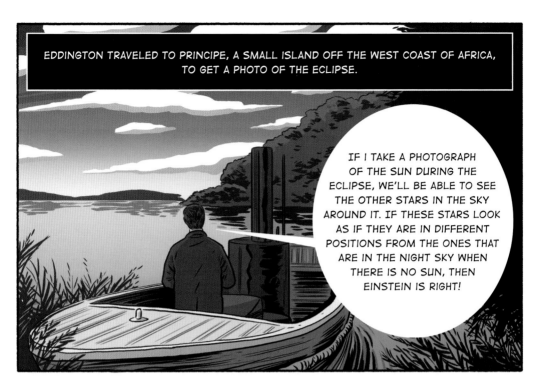

EDDINGTON TRAVELED TO PRINCIPE, A SMALL ISLAND OFF THE WEST COAST OF AFRICA, TO GET A PHOTO OF THE ECLIPSE.

IF I TAKE A PHOTOGRAPH OF THE SUN DURING THE ECLIPSE, WE'LL BE ABLE TO SEE THE OTHER STARS IN THE SKY AROUND IT. IF THESE STARS LOOK AS IF THEY ARE IN DIFFERENT POSITIONS FROM THE ONES THAT ARE IN THE NIGHT SKY WHEN THERE IS NO SUN, THEN EINSTEIN IS RIGHT!

NOW, I JUST HOPE THE CLOUDS CLEAR SO I CAN TAKE THE SHOT.

I THINK I HAVE IT!

THE POSITIONS OF THE STARS HAD MOVED, SHOWING THE LIGHT WAS "BENT" AS IT WENT AROUND THE SUN.

CHAPTER 6

Einstein Becomes a Celebrity

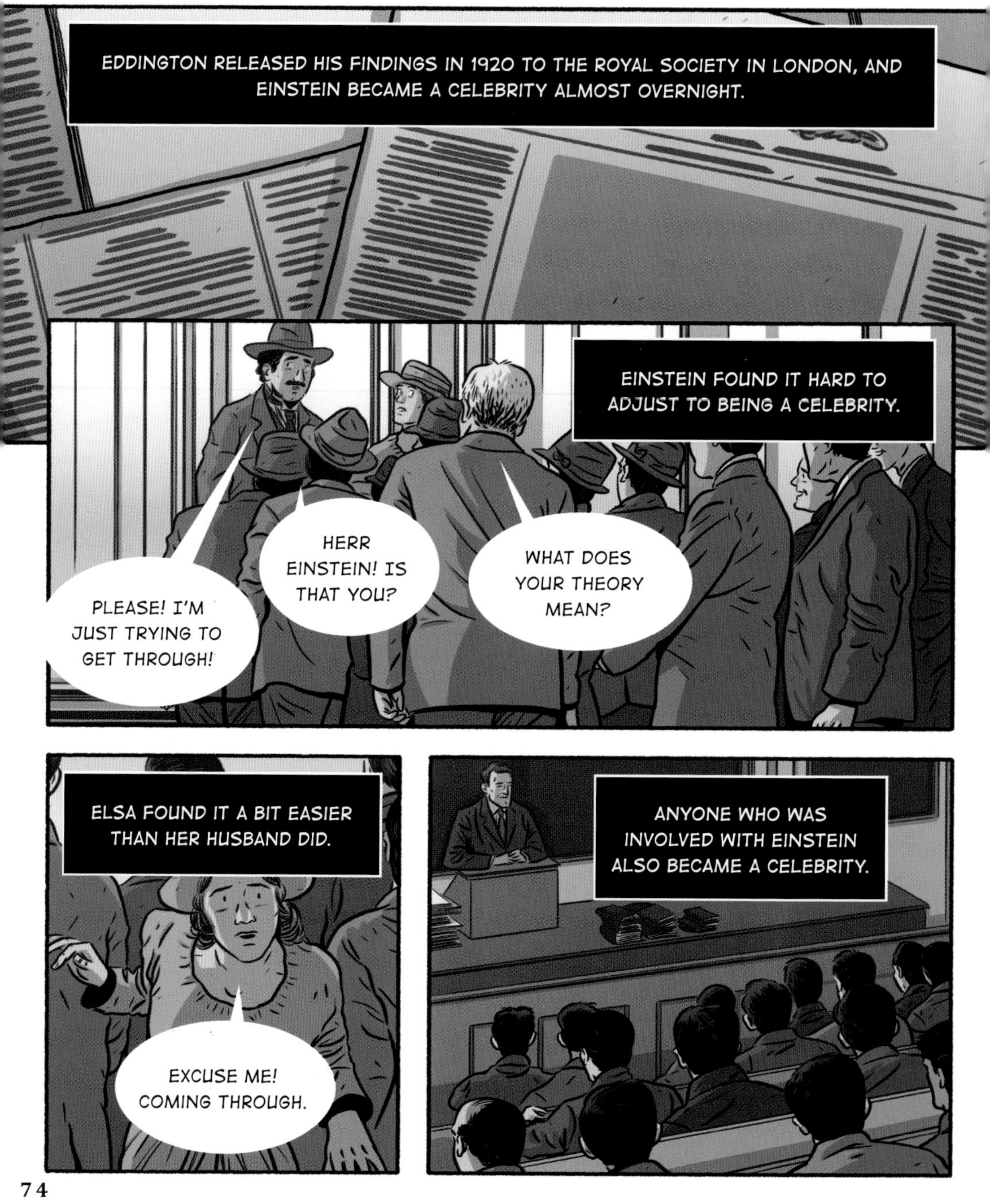
EDDINGTON RELEASED HIS FINDINGS IN 1920 TO THE ROYAL SOCIETY IN LONDON, AND EINSTEIN BECAME A CELEBRITY ALMOST OVERNIGHT.
EINSTEIN FOUND IT HARD TO ADJUST TO BEING A CELEBRITY.
PLEASE! I'M JUST TRYING TO GET THROUGH!
HERR EINSTEIN! IS THAT YOU?
WHAT DOES YOUR THEORY MEAN?
ELSA FOUND IT A BIT EASIER THAN HER HUSBAND DID.
EXCUSE ME! COMING THROUGH.
ANYONE WHO WAS INVOLVED WITH EINSTEIN ALSO BECAME A CELEBRITY.

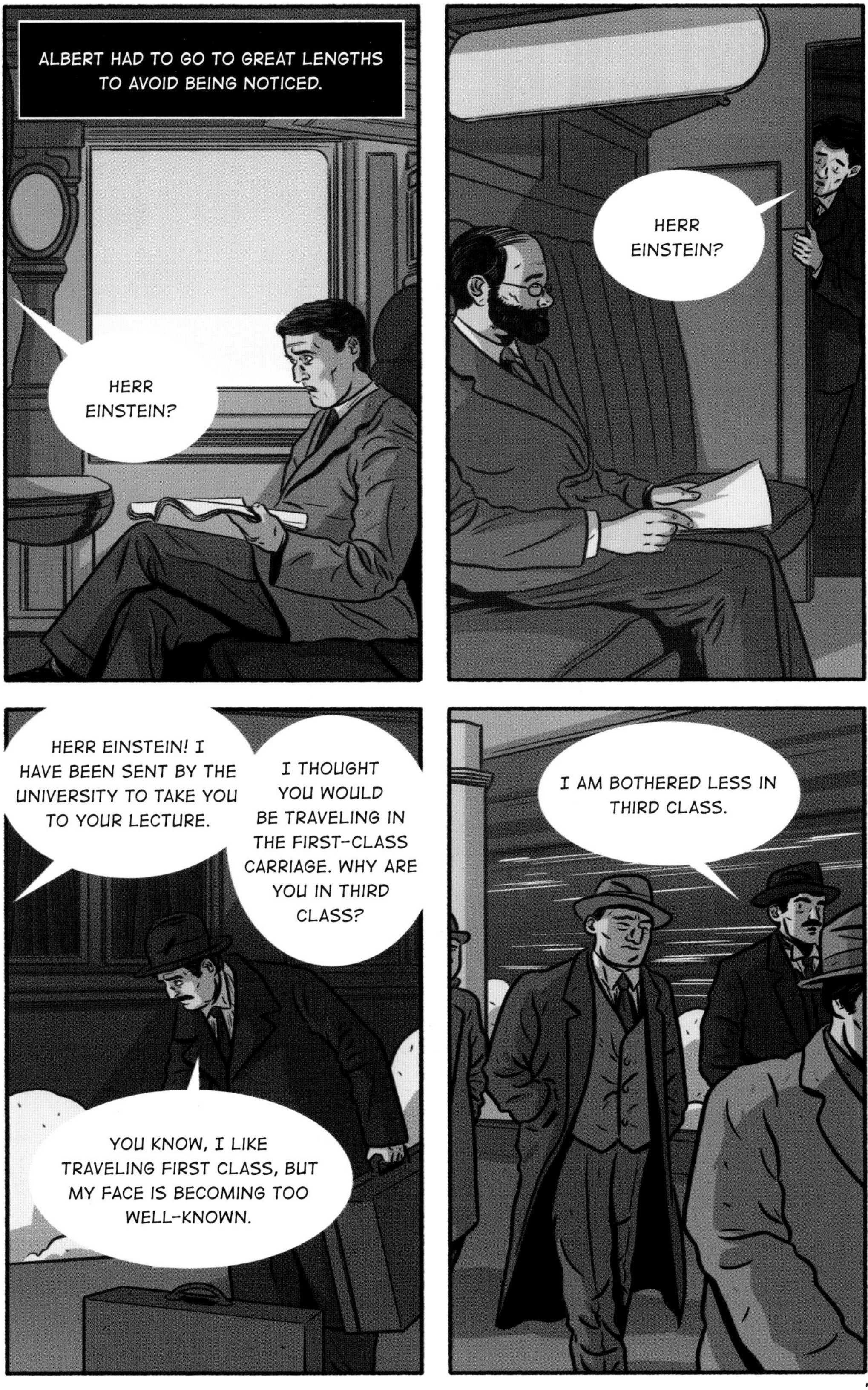
ALBERT HAD TO GO TO GREAT LENGTHS TO AVOID BEING NOTICED.
HERR EINSTEIN?
HERR EINSTEIN?
HERR EINSTEIN! I HAVE BEEN SENT BY THE UNIVERSITY TO TAKE YOU TO YOUR LECTURE.
I THOUGHT YOU WOULD BE TRAVELING IN THE FIRST-CLASS CARRIAGE. WHY ARE YOU IN THIRD CLASS?
YOU KNOW, I LIKE TRAVELING FIRST CLASS, BUT MY FACE IS BECOMING TOO WELL-KNOWN.
I AM BOTHERED LESS IN THIRD CLASS.

NEW YORK, USA, 1921

EINSTEIN EINSTEIN

BEEEEP!! BEEEEEP!!!

WHEN EINSTEIN VISITED THE UNITED STATES FOR THE FIRST TIME, THERE WAS A TICKER-TAPE PARADE!

THIS MUST SEEM AWFULLY VAIN OF ME, MY DEAR.

NOT AT ALL.

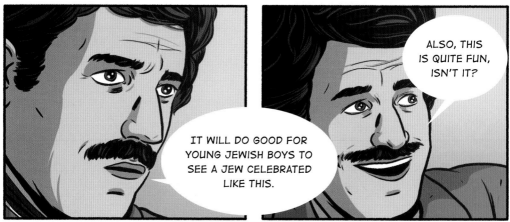

IT WILL DO GOOD FOR YOUNG JEWISH BOYS TO SEE A JEW CELEBRATED LIKE THIS.

ALSO, THIS IS QUITE FUN, ISN'T IT?

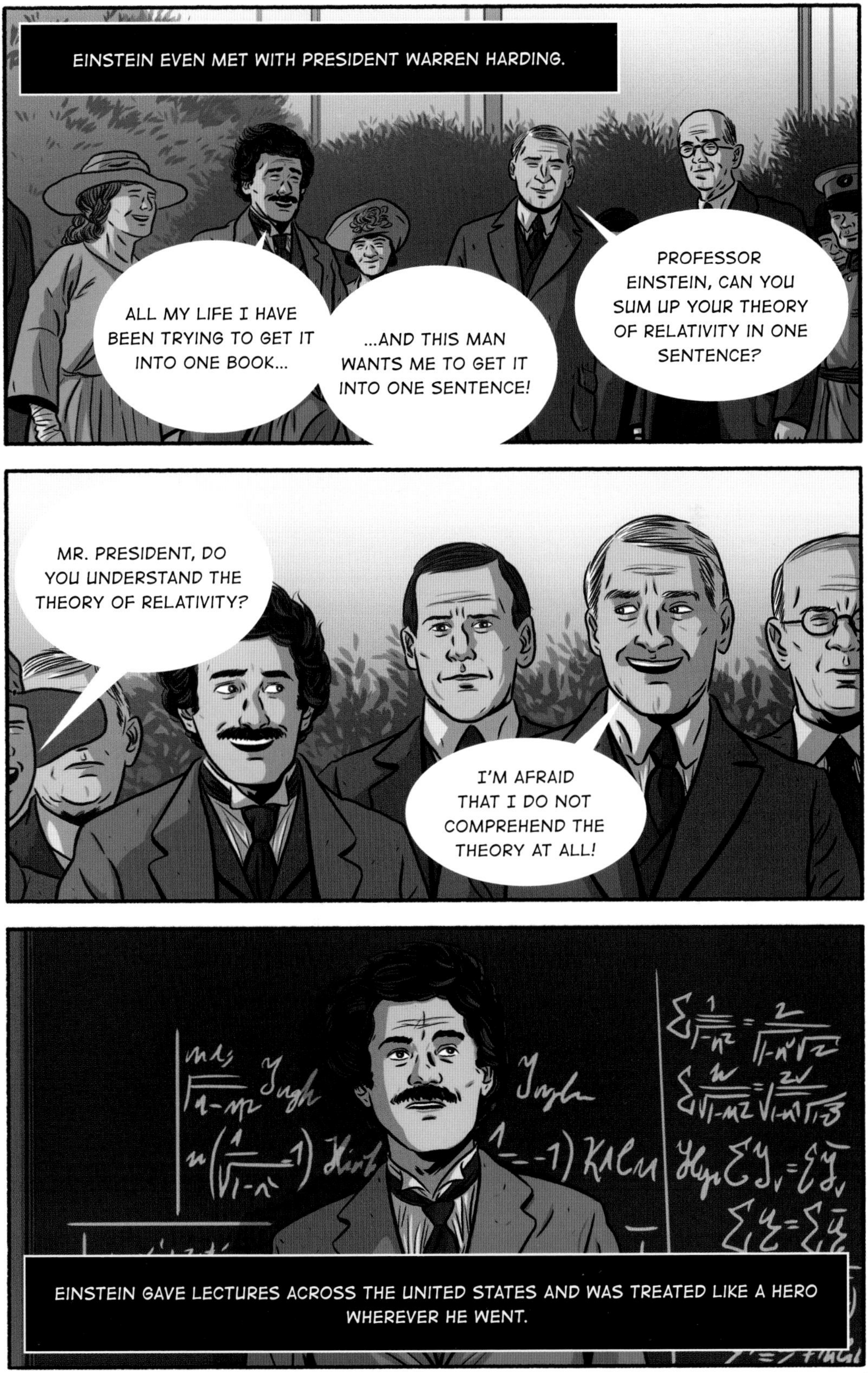
EINSTEIN EVEN MET WITH PRESIDENT WARREN HARDING.
PROFESSOR EINSTEIN, CAN YOU SUM UP YOUR THEORY OF RELATIVITY IN ONE SENTENCE?
ALL MY LIFE I HAVE BEEN TRYING TO GET IT INTO ONE BOOK...
...AND THIS MAN WANTS ME TO GET IT INTO ONE SENTENCE!
MR. PRESIDENT, DO YOU UNDERSTAND THE THEORY OF RELATIVITY?
I'M AFRAID THAT I DO NOT COMPREHEND THE THEORY AT ALL!
EINSTEIN GAVE LECTURES ACROSS THE UNITED STATES AND WAS TREATED LIKE A HERO WHEREVER HE WENT.

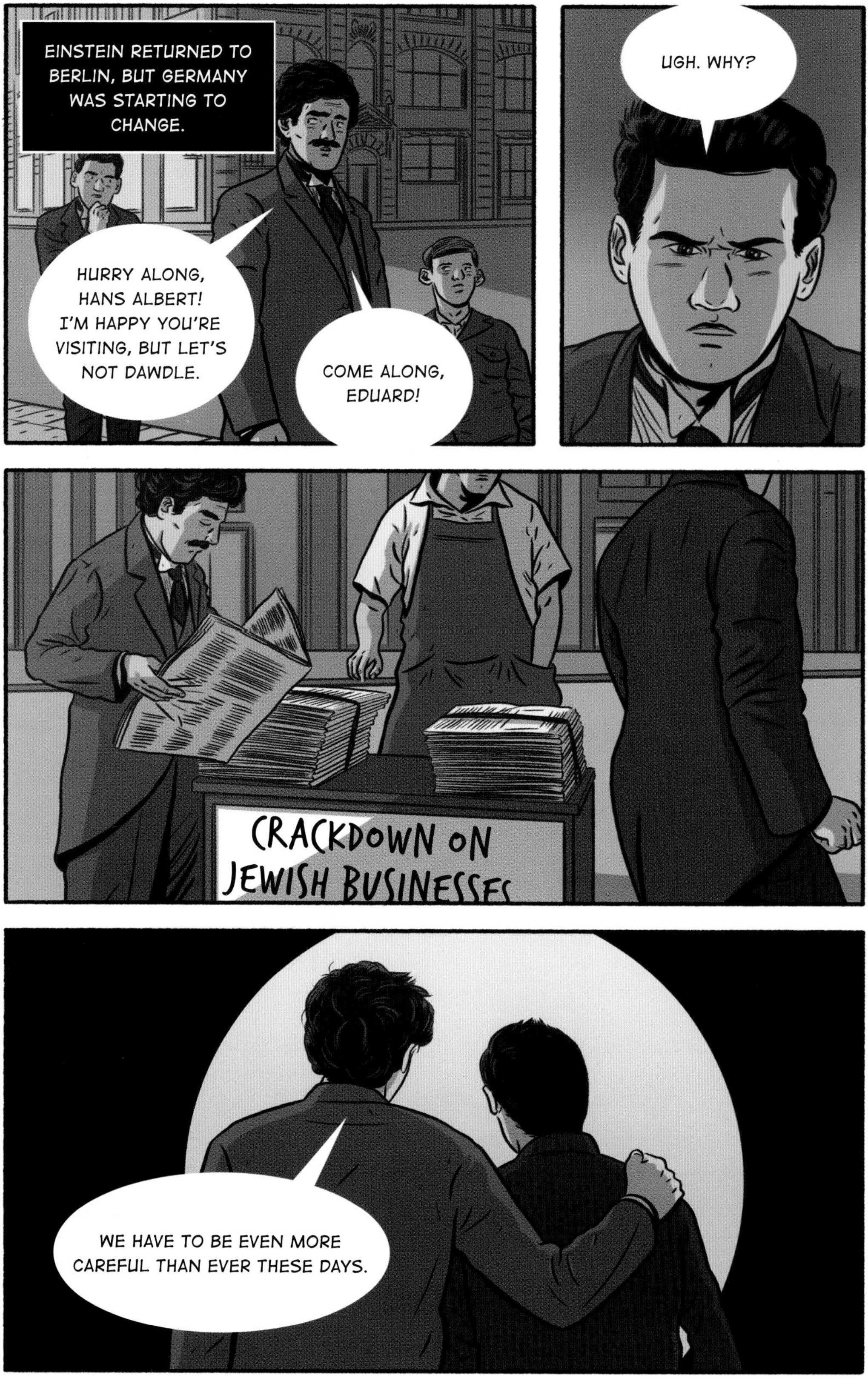
EINSTEIN RETURNED TO BERLIN, BUT GERMANY WAS STARTING TO CHANGE.
HURRY ALONG, HANS ALBERT! I'M HAPPY YOU'RE VISITING, BUT LET'S NOT DAWDLE.
COME ALONG, EDUARD!
UGH. WHY?
CRACKDOWN ON JEWISH BUSINESSES
WE HAVE TO BE EVEN MORE CAREFUL THAN EVER THESE DAYS.

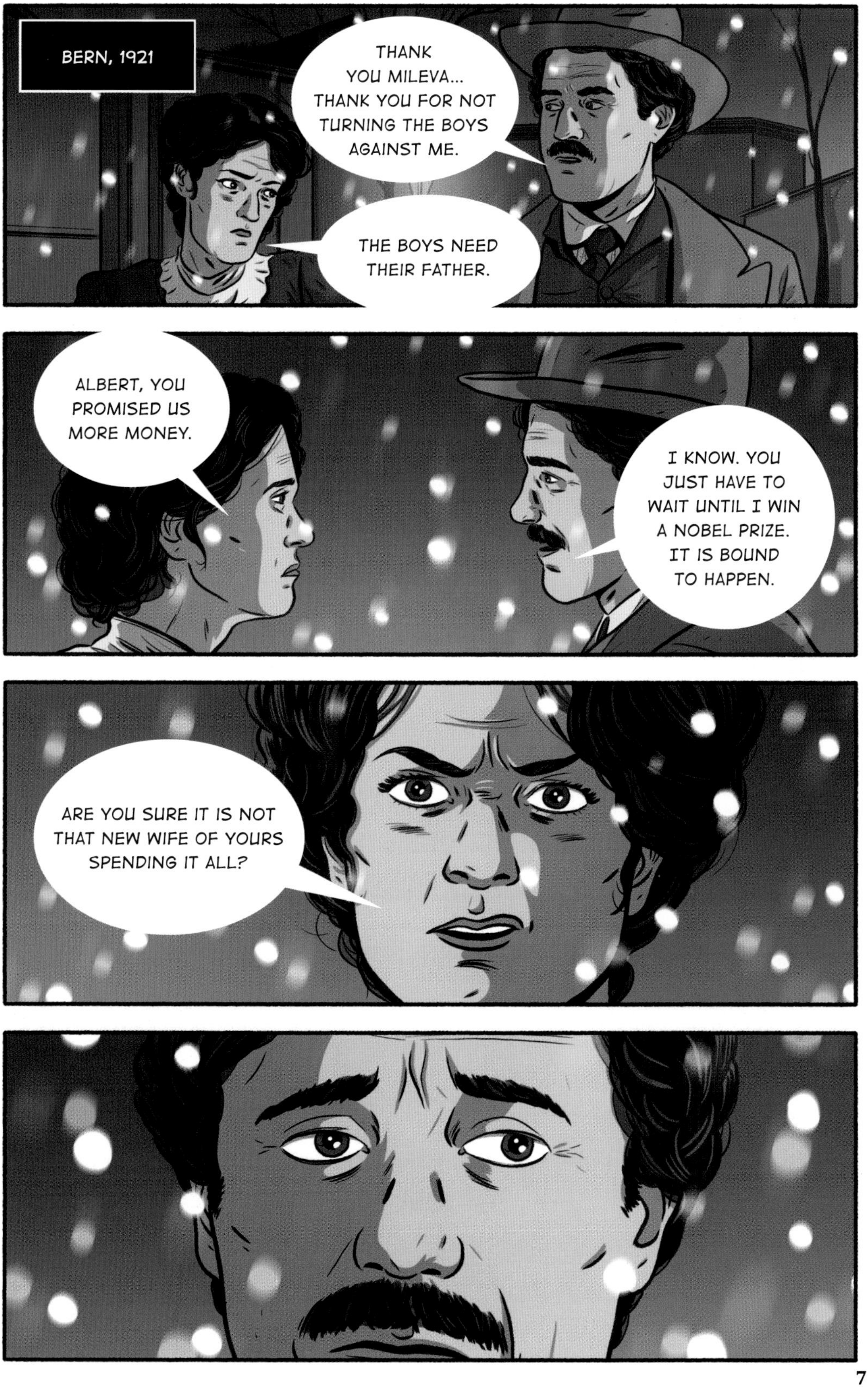
BERN, 1921
THANK YOU MILEVA... THANK YOU FOR NOT TURNING THE BOYS AGAINST ME.
THE BOYS NEED THEIR FATHER.
ALBERT, YOU PROMISED US MORE MONEY.
I KNOW. YOU JUST HAVE TO WAIT UNTIL I WIN A NOBEL PRIZE. IT IS BOUND TO HAPPEN.
ARE YOU SURE IT IS NOT THAT NEW WIFE OF YOURS SPENDING IT ALL?

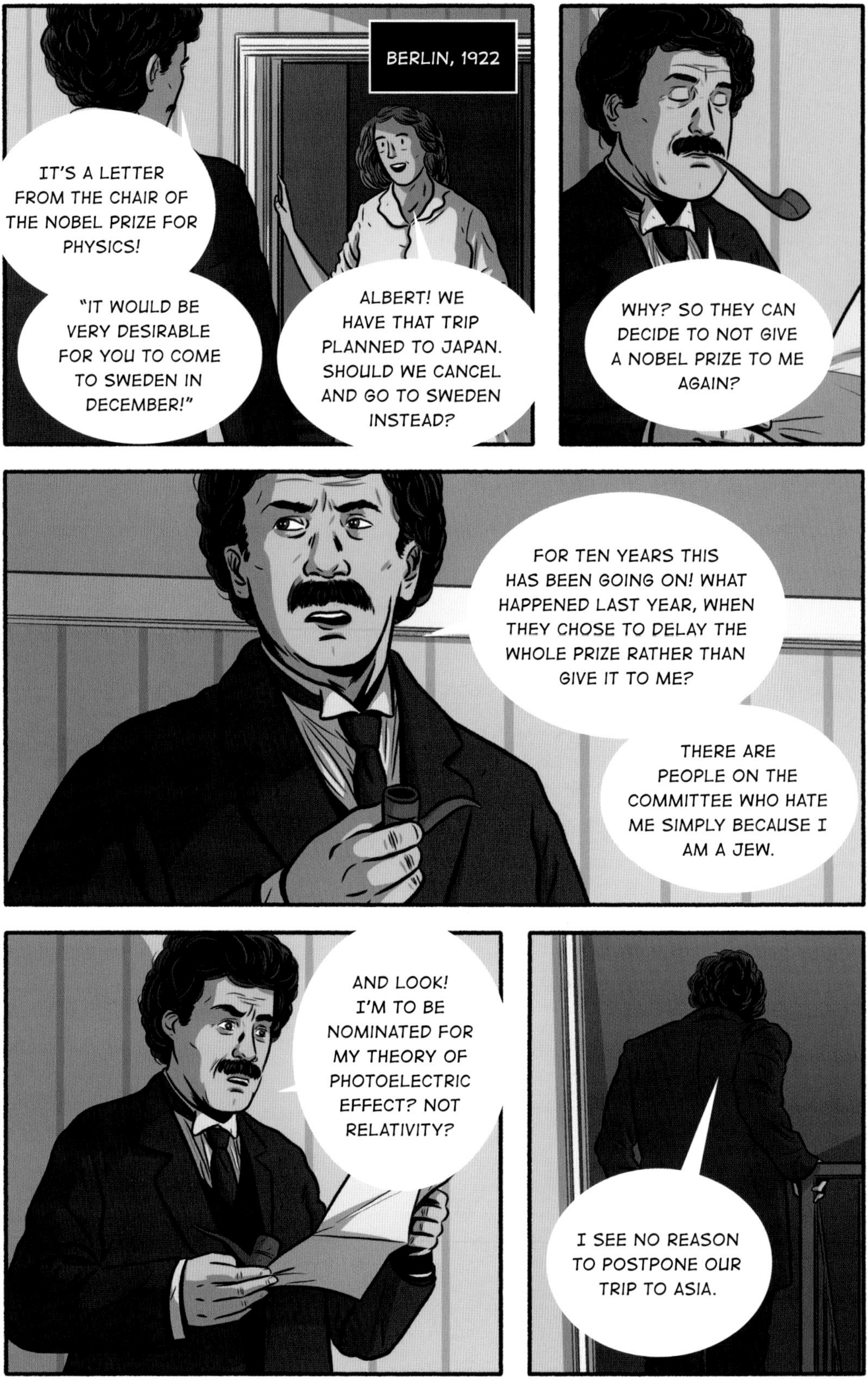
BERLIN, 1922
IT'S A LETTER FROM THE CHAIR OF THE NOBEL PRIZE FOR PHYSICS!
"IT WOULD BE VERY DESIRABLE FOR YOU TO COME TO SWEDEN IN DECEMBER!"
ALBERT! WE HAVE THAT TRIP PLANNED TO JAPAN. SHOULD WE CANCEL AND GO TO SWEDEN INSTEAD?
WHY? SO THEY CAN DECIDE TO NOT GIVE A NOBEL PRIZE TO ME AGAIN?
FOR TEN YEARS THIS HAS BEEN GOING ON! WHAT HAPPENED LAST YEAR, WHEN THEY CHOSE TO DELAY THE WHOLE PRIZE RATHER THAN GIVE IT TO ME?
THERE ARE PEOPLE ON THE COMMITTEE WHO HATE ME SIMPLY BECAUSE I AM A JEW.
AND LOOK! I'M TO BE NOMINATED FOR MY THEORY OF PHOTOELECTRIC EFFECT? NOT RELATIVITY?
I SEE NO REASON TO POSTPONE OUR TRIP TO ASIA.

JAPAN, DECEMBER 10, 1922

EINSTEIN WAS ON A LECTURE TOUR IN JAPAN WHEN THE NOBEL PRIZES WERE AWARDED, SO HE DID NOT ATTEND THE AWARDS CEREMONY IN SWEDEN.

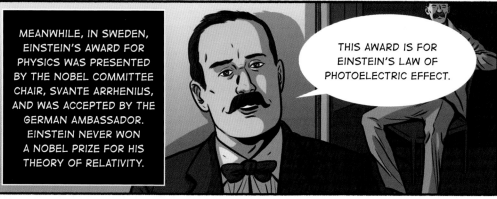

MEANWHILE, IN SWEDEN, EINSTEIN'S AWARD FOR PHYSICS WAS PRESENTED BY THE NOBEL COMMITTEE CHAIR, SVANTE ARRHENIUS, AND WAS ACCEPTED BY THE GERMAN AMBASSADOR. EINSTEIN NEVER WON A NOBEL PRIZE FOR HIS THEORY OF RELATIVITY.

THIS AWARD IS FOR EINSTEIN'S LAW OF PHOTOELECTRIC EFFECT.

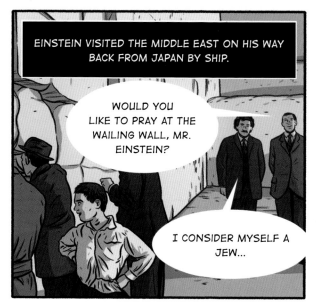

EINSTEIN VISITED THE MIDDLE EAST ON HIS WAY BACK FROM JAPAN BY SHIP.

WOULD YOU LIKE TO PRAY AT THE WAILING WALL, MR. EINSTEIN?

I CONSIDER MYSELF A JEW...

...BUT I WOULD CALL MYSELF A "RELIGIOUS NONBELIEVER."

I SEE THE BEAUTY AND HARMONY—THE MIND OF GOD—EXPRESSED IN THE CREATION OF THE UNIVERSE AND ITS LAWS.

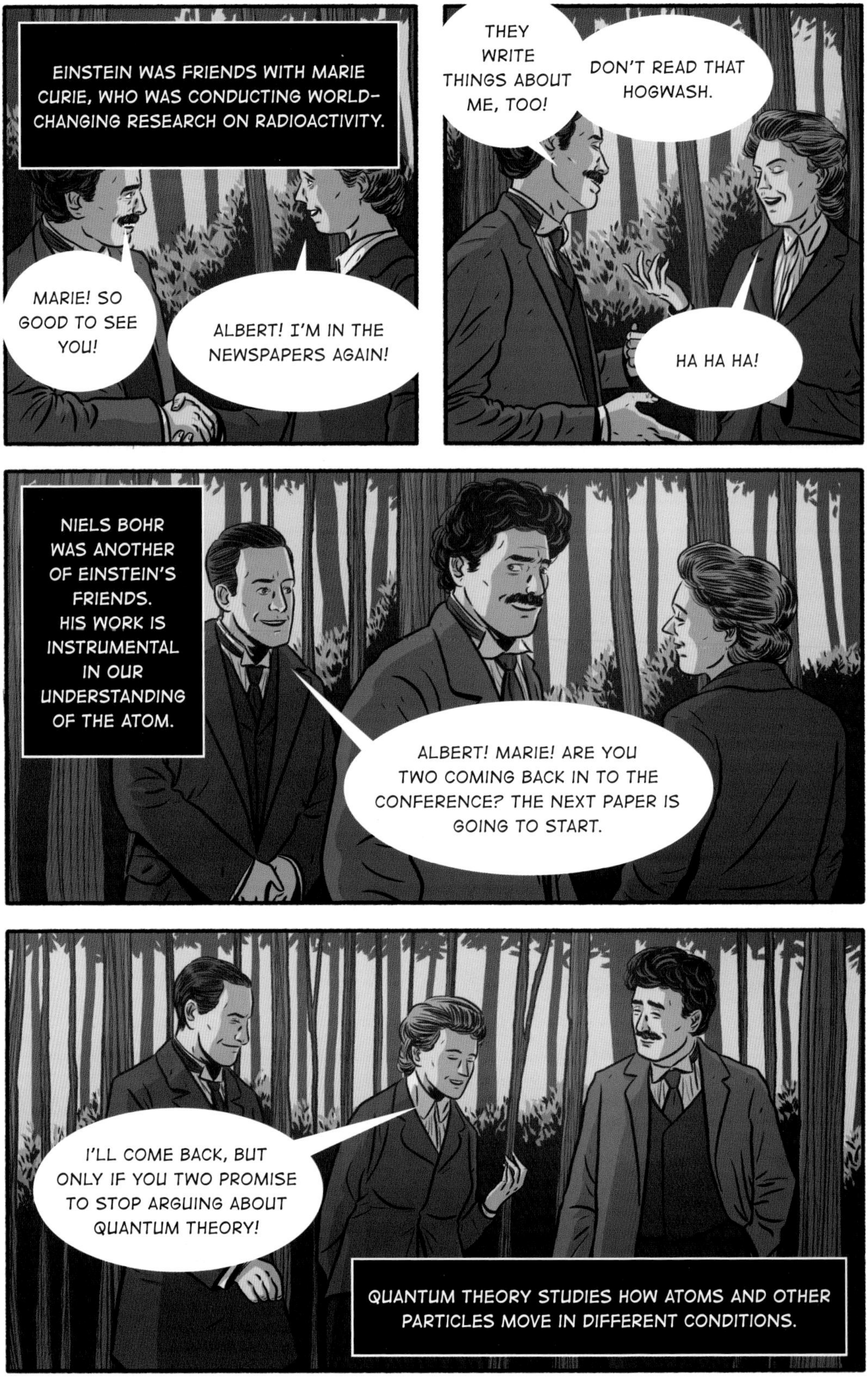
EINSTEIN WAS FRIENDS WITH MARIE CURIE, WHO WAS CONDUCTING WORLD-CHANGING RESEARCH ON RADIOACTIVITY.
MARIE! SO GOOD TO SEE YOU!
ALBERT! I'M IN THE NEWSPAPERS AGAIN!
THEY WRITE THINGS ABOUT ME, TOO!
DON'T READ THAT HOGWASH.
HA HA HA!
NIELS BOHR WAS ANOTHER OF EINSTEIN'S FRIENDS. HIS WORK IS INSTRUMENTAL IN OUR UNDERSTANDING OF THE ATOM.
ALBERT! MARIE! ARE YOU TWO COMING BACK IN TO THE CONFERENCE? THE NEXT PAPER IS GOING TO START.
I'LL COME BACK, BUT ONLY IF YOU TWO PROMISE TO STOP ARGUING ABOUT QUANTUM THEORY!
QUANTUM THEORY STUDIES HOW ATOMS AND OTHER PARTICLES MOVE IN DIFFERENT CONDITIONS.

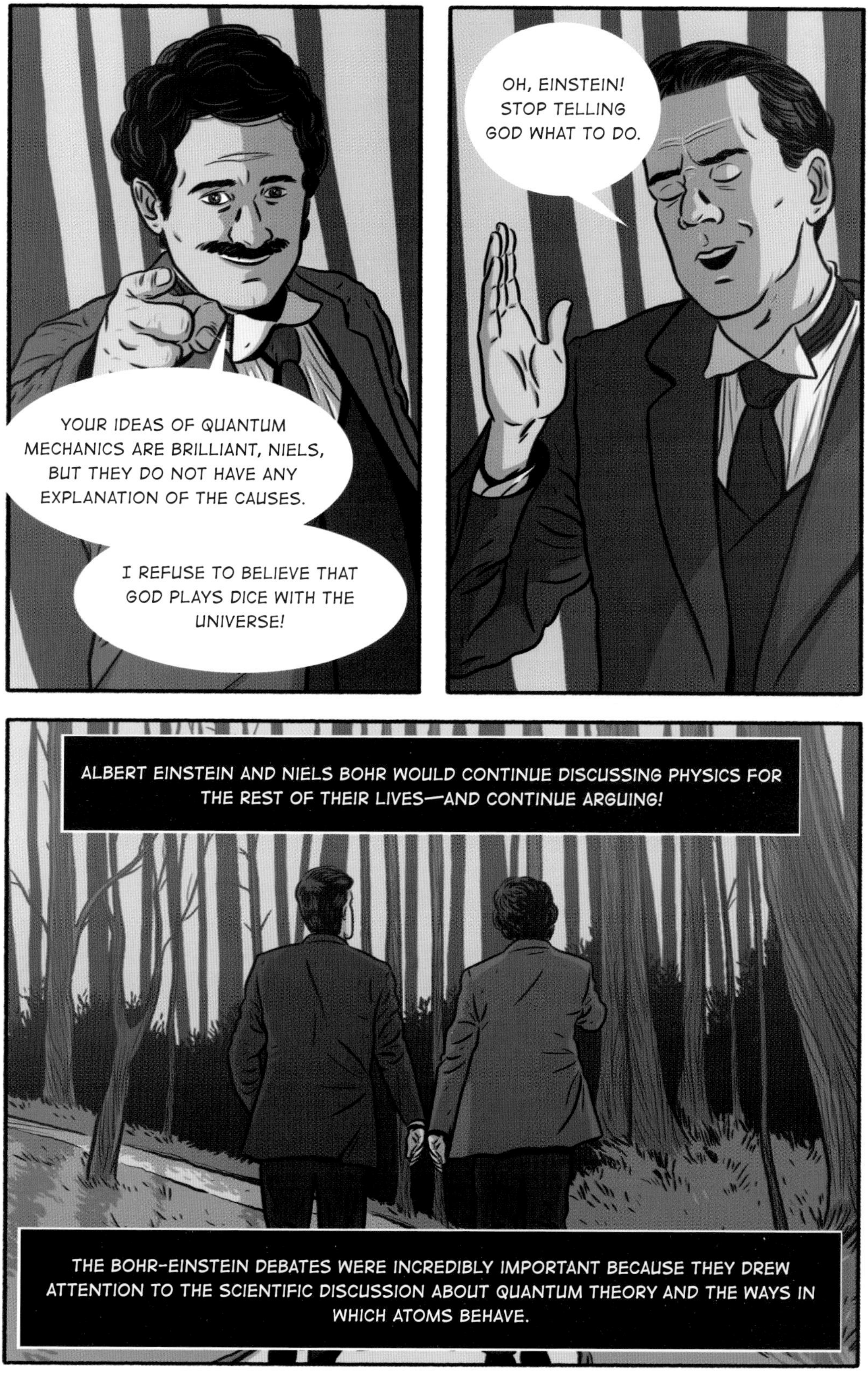
YOUR IDEAS OF QUANTUM MECHANICS ARE BRILLIANT, NIELS, BUT THEY DO NOT HAVE ANY EXPLANATION OF THE CAUSES.
I REFUSE TO BELIEVE THAT GOD PLAYS DICE WITH THE UNIVERSE!
OH, EINSTEIN! STOP TELLING GOD WHAT TO DO.
ALBERT EINSTEIN AND NIELS BOHR WOULD CONTINUE DISCUSSING PHYSICS FOR THE REST OF THEIR LIVES—AND CONTINUE ARGUING!
THE BOHR-EINSTEIN DEBATES WERE INCREDIBLY IMPORTANT BECAUSE THEY DREW ATTENTION TO THE SCIENTIFIC DISCUSSION ABOUT QUANTUM THEORY AND THE WAYS IN WHICH ATOMS BEHAVE.

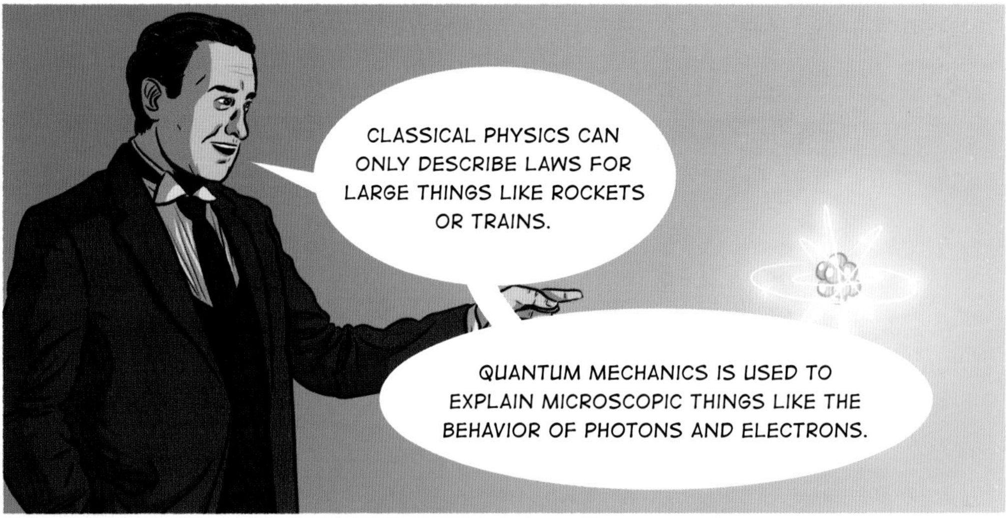
CLASSICAL PHYSICS CAN ONLY DESCRIBE LAWS FOR LARGE THINGS LIKE ROCKETS OR TRAINS.
QUANTUM MECHANICS IS USED TO EXPLAIN MICROSCOPIC THINGS LIKE THE BEHAVIOR OF PHOTONS AND ELECTRONS.

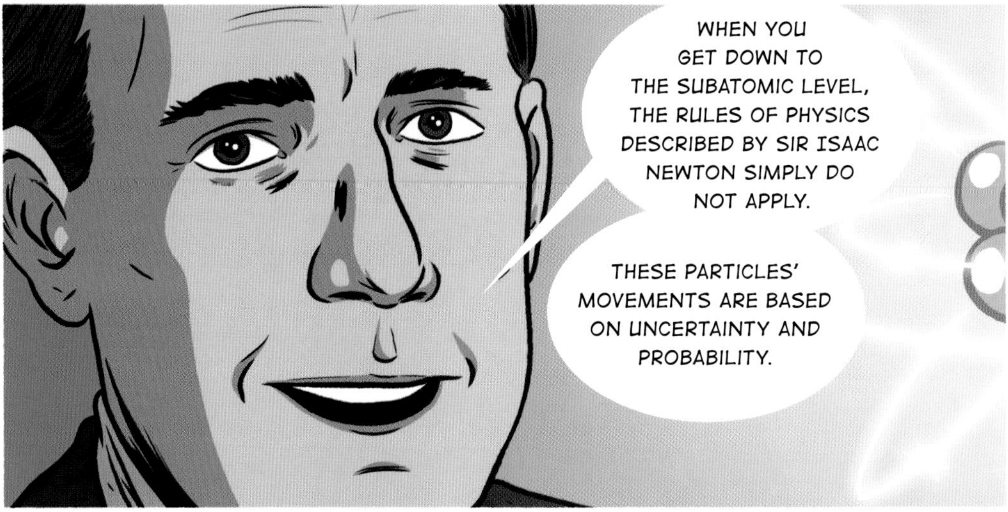
WHEN YOU GET DOWN TO THE SUBATOMIC LEVEL, THE RULES OF PHYSICS DESCRIBED BY SIR ISAAC NEWTON SIMPLY DO NOT APPLY.
THESE PARTICLES' MOVEMENTS ARE BASED ON UNCERTAINTY AND PROBABILITY.

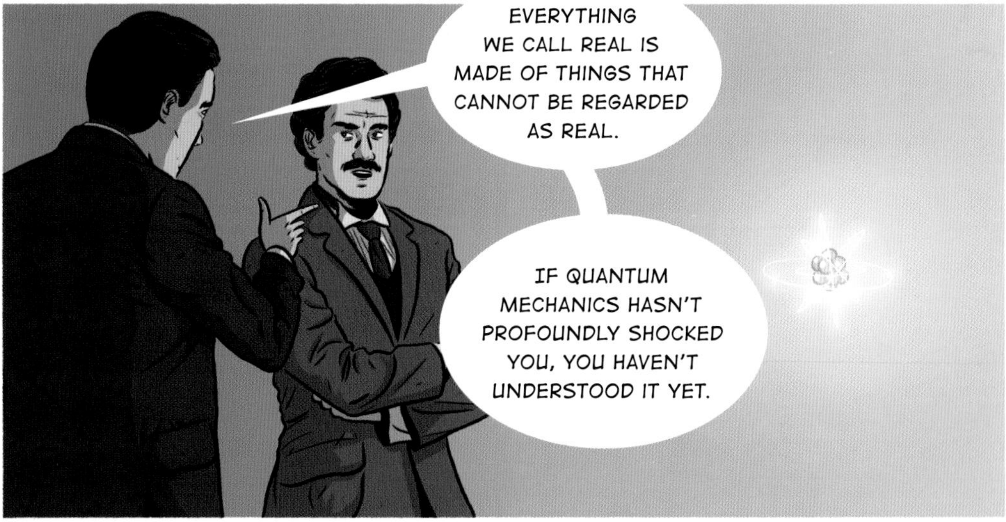
EVERYTHING WE CALL REAL IS MADE OF THINGS THAT CANNOT BE REGARDED AS REAL.
IF QUANTUM MECHANICS HASN'T PROFOUNDLY SHOCKED YOU, YOU HAVEN'T UNDERSTOOD IT YET.

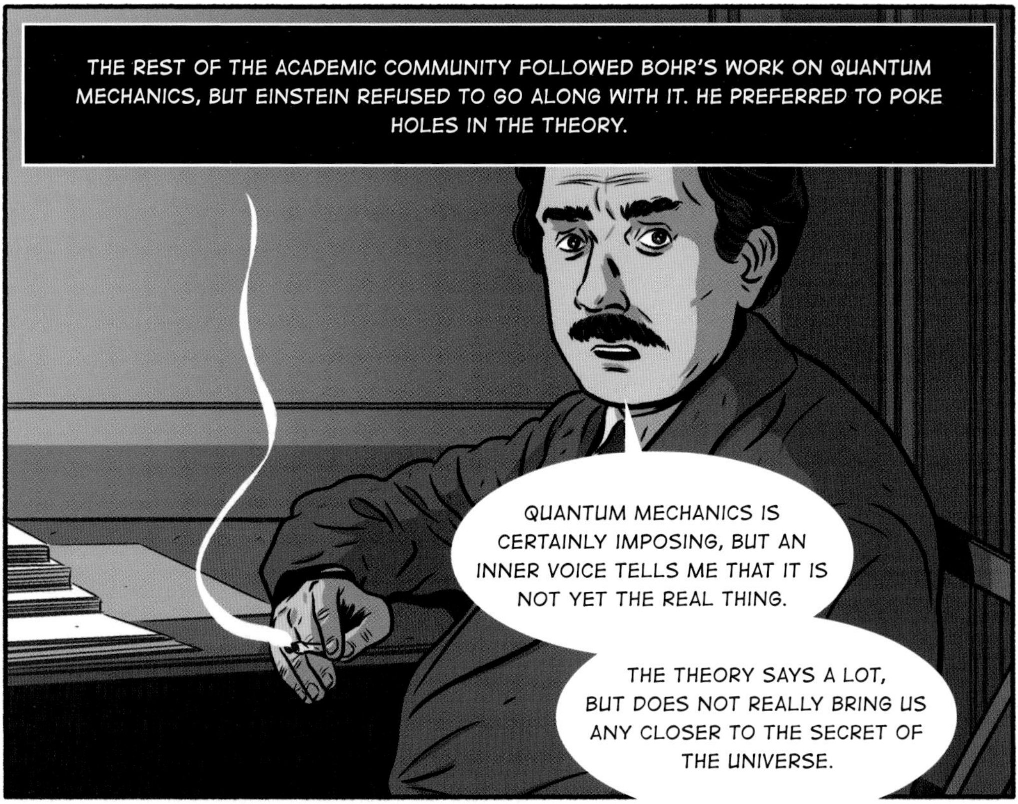
THE REST OF THE ACADEMIC COMMUNITY FOLLOWED BOHR'S WORK ON QUANTUM MECHANICS, BUT EINSTEIN REFUSED TO GO ALONG WITH IT. HE PREFERRED TO POKE HOLES IN THE THEORY.
QUANTUM MECHANICS IS CERTAINLY IMPOSING, BUT AN INNER VOICE TELLS ME THAT IT IS NOT YET THE REAL THING.
THE THEORY SAYS A LOT, BUT DOES NOT REALLY BRING US ANY CLOSER TO THE SECRET OF THE UNIVERSE.

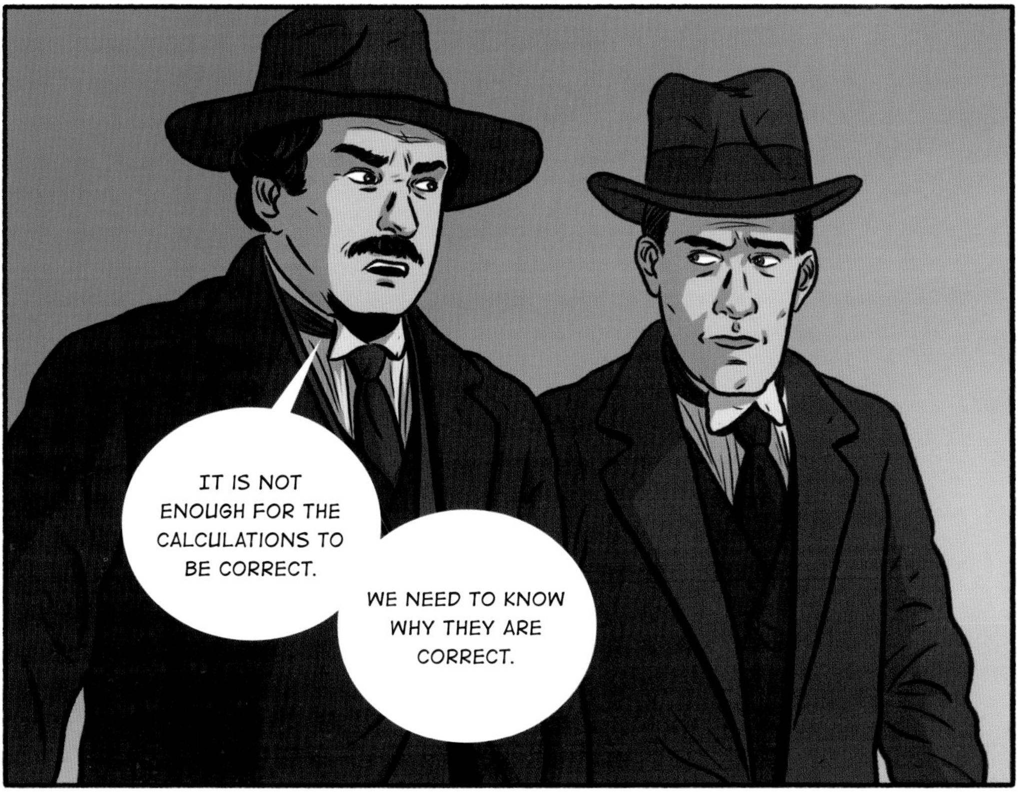
IT IS NOT ENOUGH FOR THE CALCULATIONS TO BE CORRECT.
WE NEED TO KNOW WHY THEY ARE CORRECT.

NEW YORK, 1931

NOT ALL OF EINSTEIN'S FRIENDS WERE SCIENTISTS. ON A TRIP TO THE UNITED STATES, HE BECAME FRIENDS WITH SILENT-MOVIE STAR CHARLIE CHAPLIN.

WHAT I ADMIRE MOST ABOUT YOUR ART IS ITS UNIVERSALITY.

YOU DON'T SAY A WORD, AND YET EVERYONE UNDERSTANDS YOU.

NOW PLAYING HERE
CHARLIE CHAPLIN IN CITY LIG
ALSO BIG STAGE PRESE

EINSTEIN AND CHAPLIN REMAINED FRIENDS FOR YEARS, BOTH FASCINATED BY EACH OTHER'S DIFFERENT CAREERS.

YES, BUT YOUR FAME IS EVEN GREATER.

THE WORLD ADMIRES YOU, YET NO ONE UNDERSTANDS YOU.

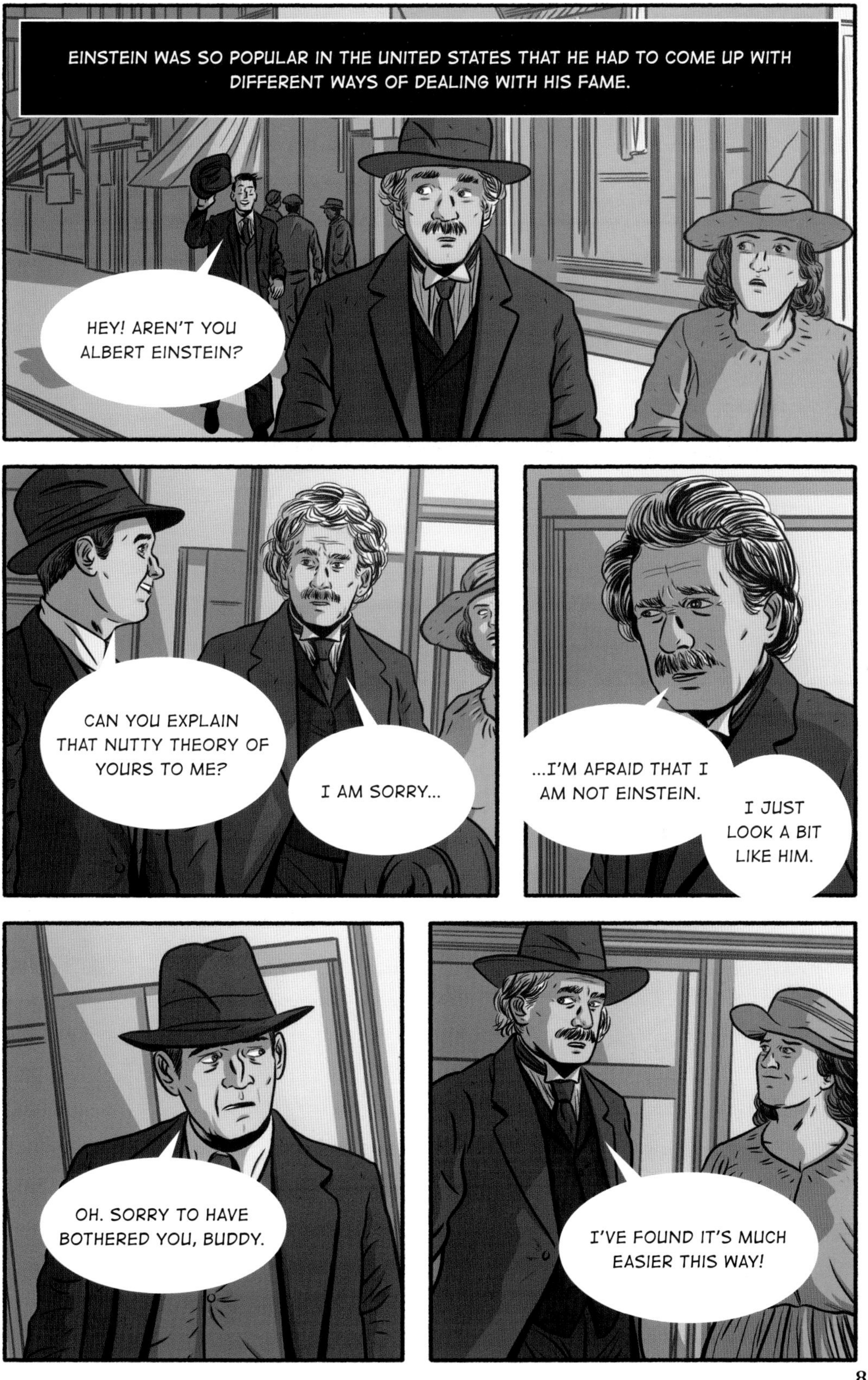
EINSTEIN WAS SO POPULAR IN THE UNITED STATES THAT HE HAD TO COME UP WITH DIFFERENT WAYS OF DEALING WITH HIS FAME.
HEY! AREN'T YOU ALBERT EINSTEIN?
CAN YOU EXPLAIN THAT NUTTY THEORY OF YOURS TO ME?
I AM SORRY...
...I'M AFRAID THAT I AM NOT EINSTEIN.
I JUST LOOK A BIT LIKE HIM.
OH. SORRY TO HAVE BOTHERED YOU, BUDDY.
I'VE FOUND IT'S MUCH EASIER THIS WAY!

CHAPTER 7

The Rise of the Nazis

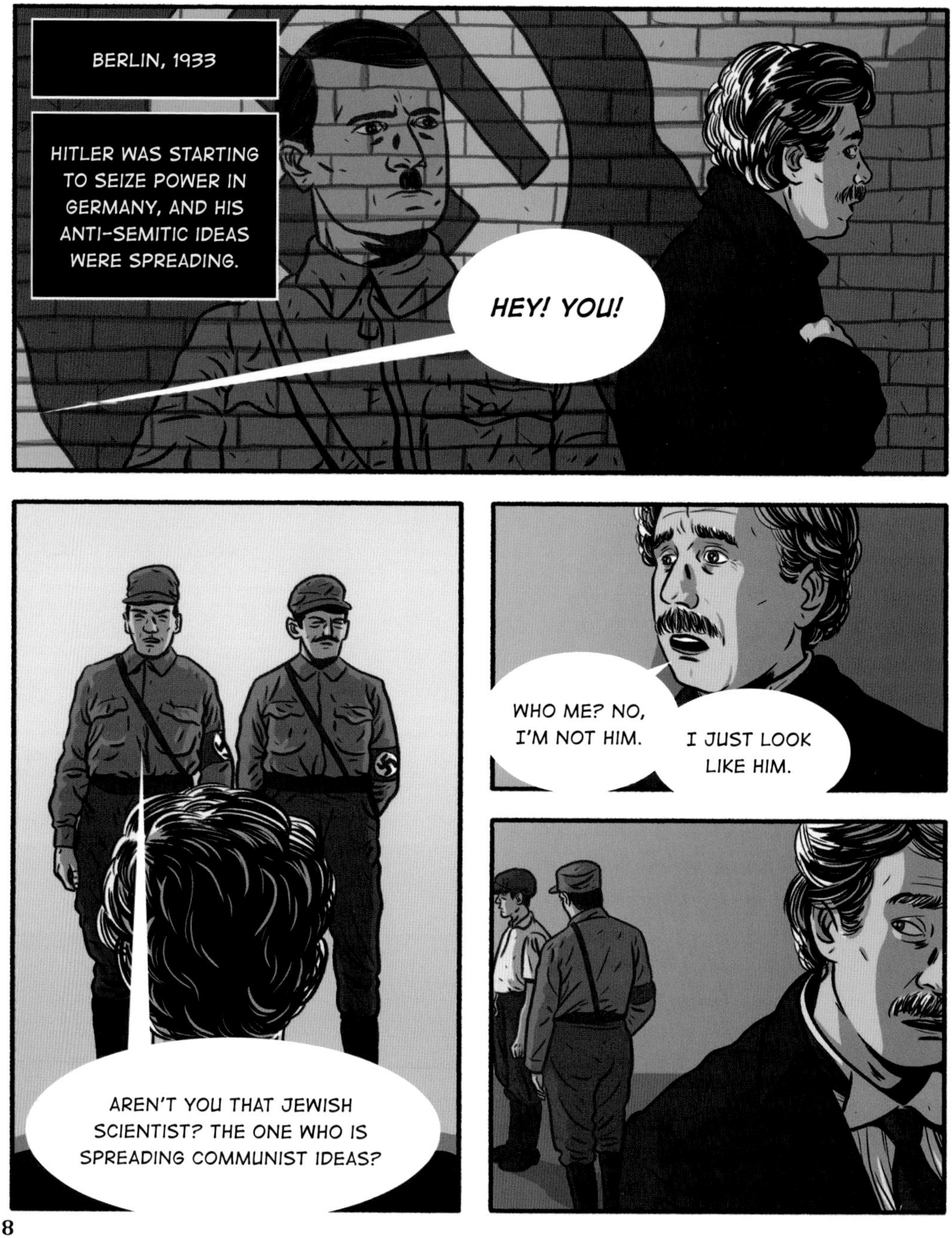
BERLIN, 1933
HITLER WAS STARTING TO SEIZE POWER IN GERMANY, AND HIS ANTI-SEMITIC IDEAS WERE SPREADING.
HEY! YOU!
AREN'T YOU THAT JEWISH SCIENTIST? THE ONE WHO IS SPREADING COMMUNIST IDEAS?
WHO ME? NO, I'M NOT HIM.
I JUST LOOK LIKE HIM.

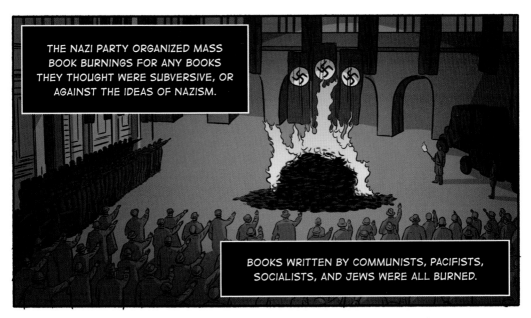

THE NAZI PARTY ORGANIZED MASS BOOK BURNINGS FOR ANY BOOKS THEY THOUGHT WERE SUBVERSIVE, OR AGAINST THE IDEAS OF NAZISM.

BOOKS WRITTEN BY COMMUNISTS, PACIFISTS, SOCIALISTS, AND JEWS WERE ALL BURNED.

EINSTEIN'S BOOKS WERE BURNED BECAUSE HE WAS JEWISH.

ALBERT EINSTEIN - THE MEANING OF RELATIVITY

JEWISH INTELLECTUALISM IS DEAD!

WE NEED TO CLEANSE GERMANY FROM THIS UN-GERMAN SPIRIT!

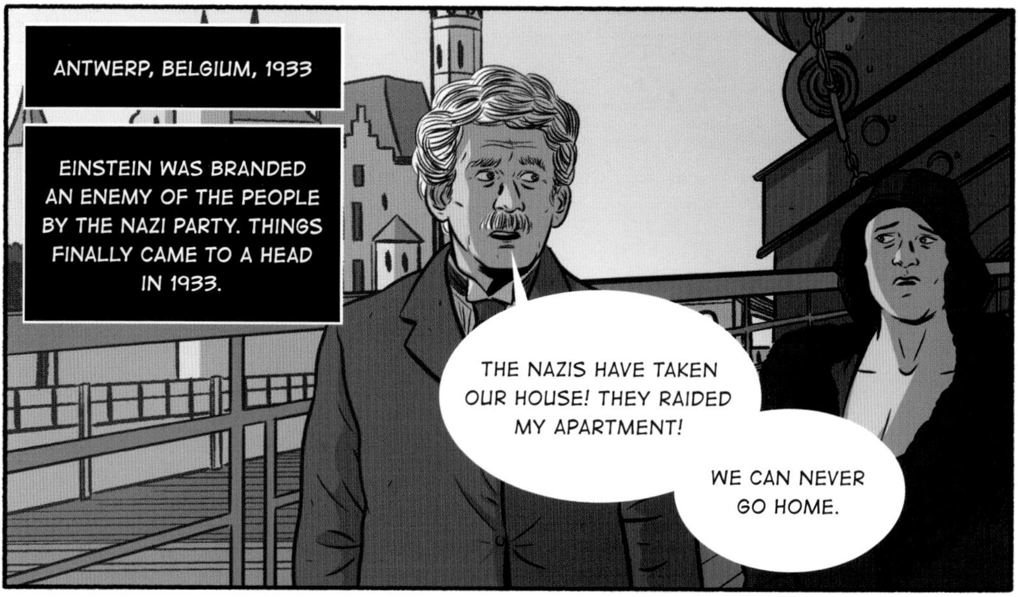
ANTWERP, BELGIUM, 1933
EINSTEIN WAS BRANDED AN ENEMY OF THE PEOPLE BY THE NAZI PARTY. THINGS FINALLY CAME TO A HEAD IN 1933.
THE NAZIS HAVE TAKEN OUR HOUSE! THEY RAIDED MY APARTMENT!
WE CAN NEVER GO HOME.

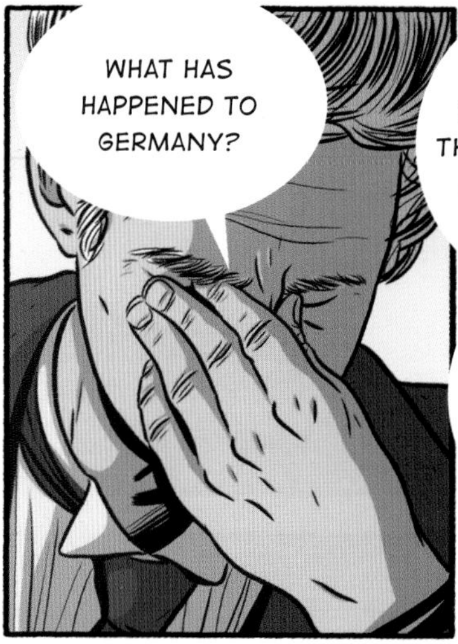
WHAT HAS HAPPENED TO GERMANY?

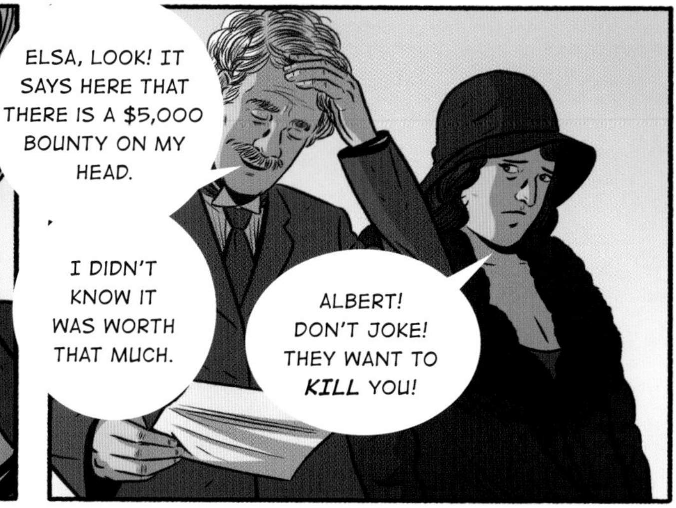
ELSA, LOOK! IT SAYS HERE THAT THERE IS A $5,000 BOUNTY ON MY HEAD.
I DIDN'T KNOW IT WAS WORTH THAT MUCH.
ALBERT! DON'T JOKE! THEY WANT TO ***KILL*** YOU!

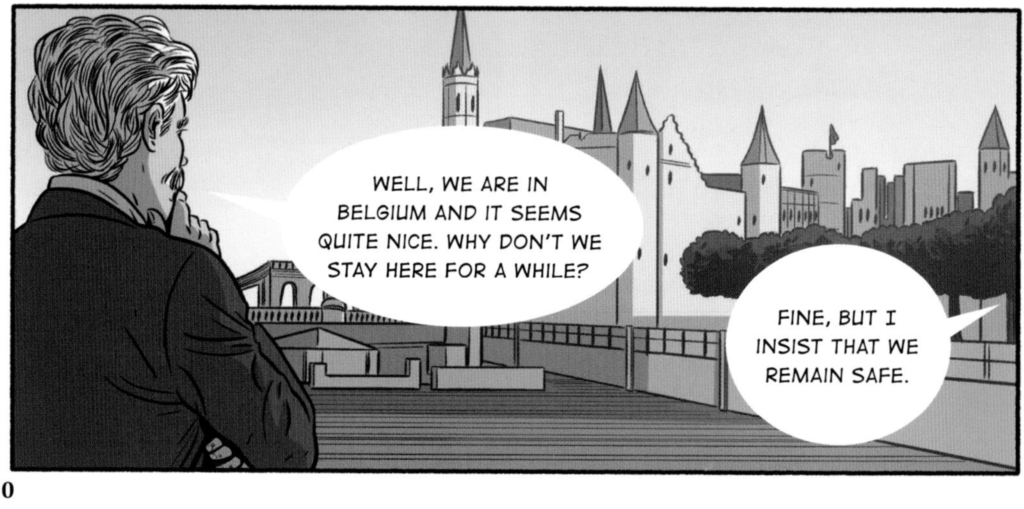
WELL, WE ARE IN BELGIUM AND IT SEEMS QUITE NICE. WHY DON'T WE STAY HERE FOR A WHILE?
FINE, BUT I INSIST THAT WE REMAIN SAFE.

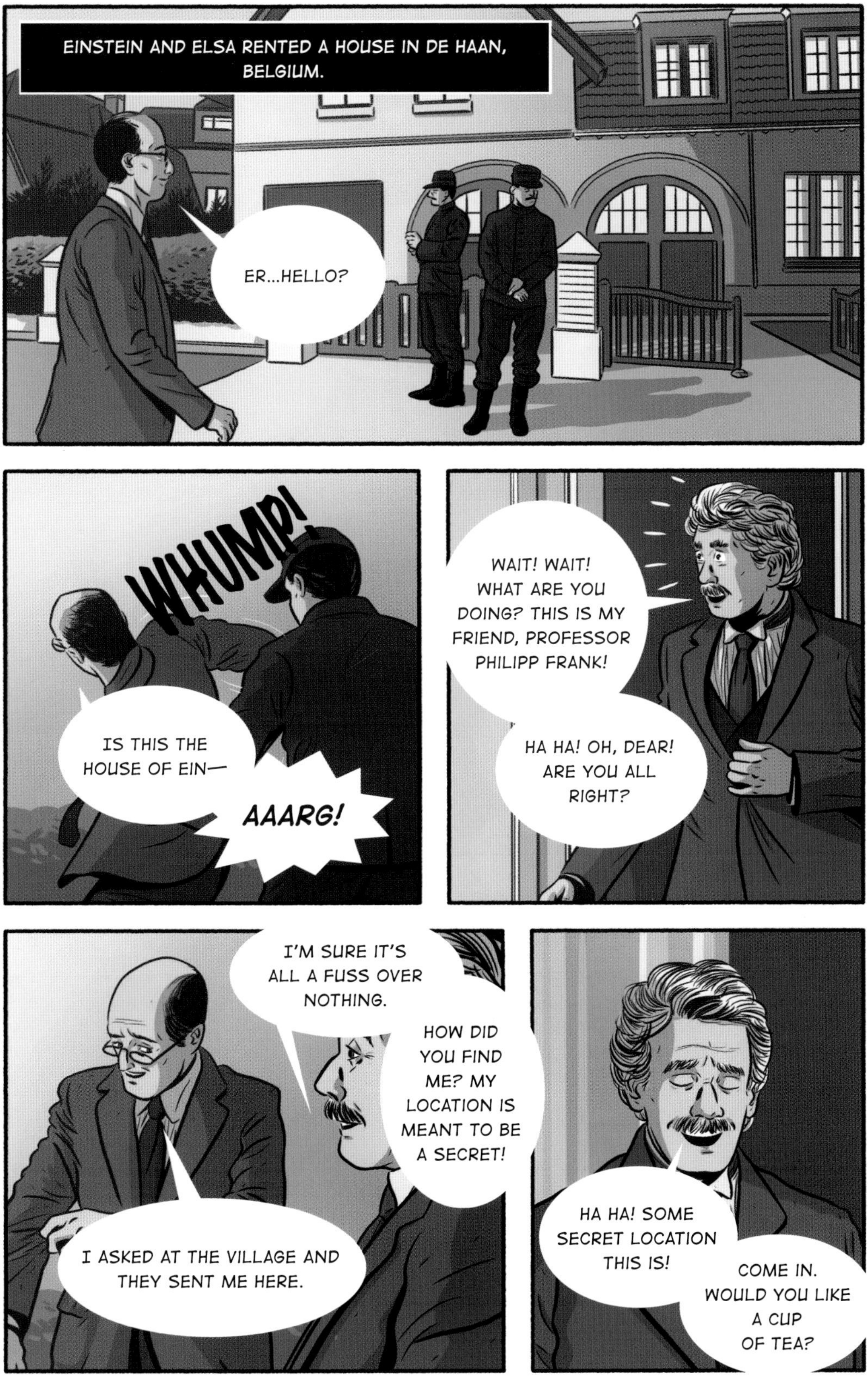
EINSTEIN AND ELSA RENTED A HOUSE IN DE HAAN, BELGIUM.
ER...HELLO?
WHUMP!
IS THIS THE HOUSE OF EIN—
AAARG!
WAIT! WAIT! WHAT ARE YOU DOING? THIS IS MY FRIEND, PROFESSOR PHILIPP FRANK!
HA HA! OH, DEAR! ARE YOU ALL RIGHT?
I'M SURE IT'S ALL A FUSS OVER NOTHING.
HOW DID YOU FIND ME? MY LOCATION IS MEANT TO BE A SECRET!
I ASKED AT THE VILLAGE AND THEY SENT ME HERE.
HA HA! SOME SECRET LOCATION THIS IS!
COME IN. WOULD YOU LIKE A CUP OF TEA?

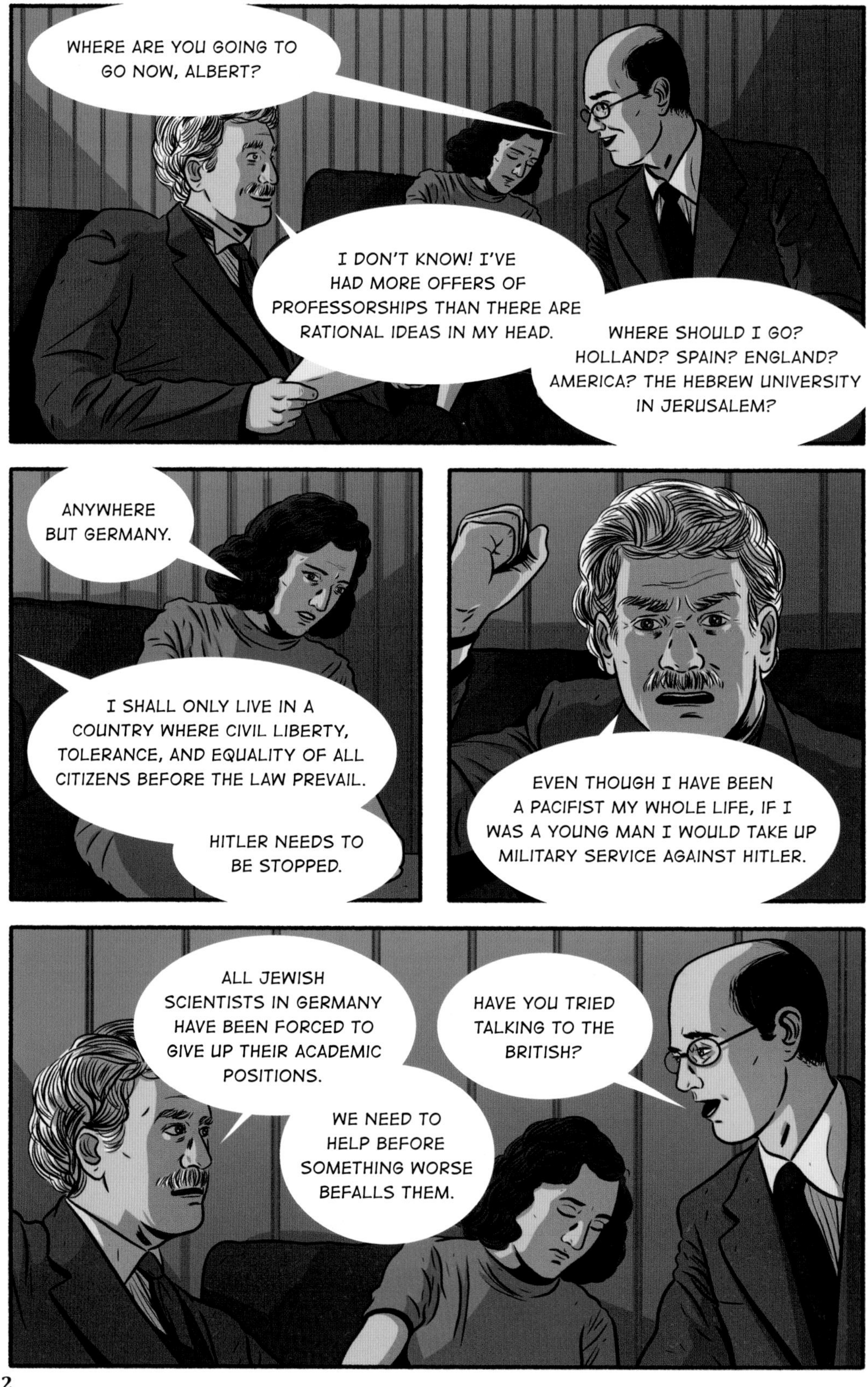
WHERE ARE YOU GOING TO GO NOW, ALBERT?
I DON'T KNOW! I'VE HAD MORE OFFERS OF PROFESSORSHIPS THAN THERE ARE RATIONAL IDEAS IN MY HEAD.
WHERE SHOULD I GO? HOLLAND? SPAIN? ENGLAND? AMERICA? THE HEBREW UNIVERSITY IN JERUSALEM?
ANYWHERE BUT GERMANY.
I SHALL ONLY LIVE IN A COUNTRY WHERE CIVIL LIBERTY, TOLERANCE, AND EQUALITY OF ALL CITIZENS BEFORE THE LAW PREVAIL.
HITLER NEEDS TO BE STOPPED.
EVEN THOUGH I HAVE BEEN A PACIFIST MY WHOLE LIFE, IF I WAS A YOUNG MAN I WOULD TAKE UP MILITARY SERVICE AGAINST HITLER.
ALL JEWISH SCIENTISTS IN GERMANY HAVE BEEN FORCED TO GIVE UP THEIR ACADEMIC POSITIONS.
WE NEED TO HELP BEFORE SOMETHING WORSE BEFALLS THEM.
HAVE YOU TRIED TALKING TO THE BRITISH?

ENGLAND, 1933

EINSTEIN CONTACTED COMMANDER OLIVER LOCKER-LAMPSON, A POLITICIAN AND NAVAL OFFICER WHOM HE HAD MET PREVIOUSLY.

COMMANDER LOCKER-LAMPSON...

OLIVER, I MUST CONFESS, I'M NOT ENTIRELY SURE WHAT IS GOING ON HERE.

YOU NEED HELP. I'M TAKING YOU TO SEE SOMEONE WHO CAN HELP, OLD BEAN.

THOUGHT I'D BRING SOME SHOTGUNS FOR PROTECTION!

ENGLAND IS A MOST EXTRAORDINARY PLACE.

LOCKER-LAMPSON PUT EINSTEIN IN TOUCH WITH SOME VERY IMPORTANT PEOPLE.

ALBERT EINSTEIN, THIS IS WINSTON CHURCHILL.

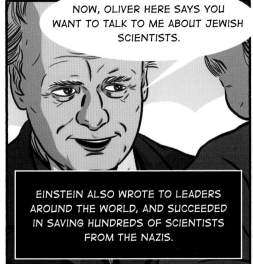

NOW, OLIVER HERE SAYS YOU WANT TO TALK TO ME ABOUT JEWISH SCIENTISTS.

EINSTEIN ALSO WROTE TO LEADERS AROUND THE WORLD, AND SUCCEEDED IN SAVING HUNDREDS OF SCIENTISTS FROM THE NAZIS.

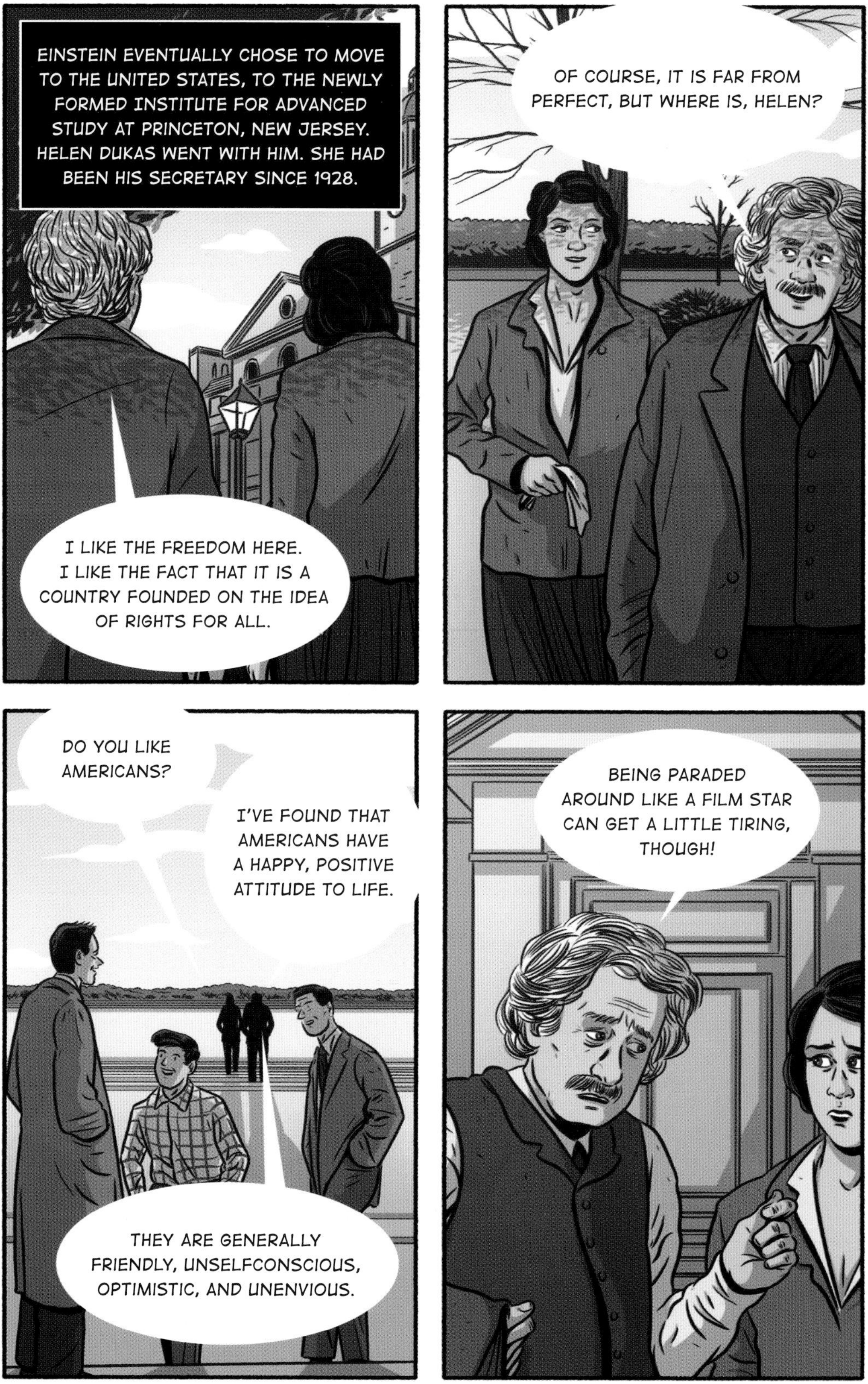
EINSTEIN EVENTUALLY CHOSE TO MOVE TO THE UNITED STATES, TO THE NEWLY FORMED INSTITUTE FOR ADVANCED STUDY AT PRINCETON, NEW JERSEY. HELEN DUKAS WENT WITH HIM. SHE HAD BEEN HIS SECRETARY SINCE 1928.
I LIKE THE FREEDOM HERE. I LIKE THE FACT THAT IT IS A COUNTRY FOUNDED ON THE IDEA OF RIGHTS FOR ALL.
OF COURSE, IT IS FAR FROM PERFECT, BUT WHERE IS, HELEN?
DO YOU LIKE AMERICANS?
I'VE FOUND THAT AMERICANS HAVE A HAPPY, POSITIVE ATTITUDE TO LIFE.
THEY ARE GENERALLY FRIENDLY, UNSELFCONSCIOUS, OPTIMISTIC, AND UNENVIOUS.
BEING PARADED AROUND LIKE A FILM STAR CAN GET A LITTLE TIRING, THOUGH!

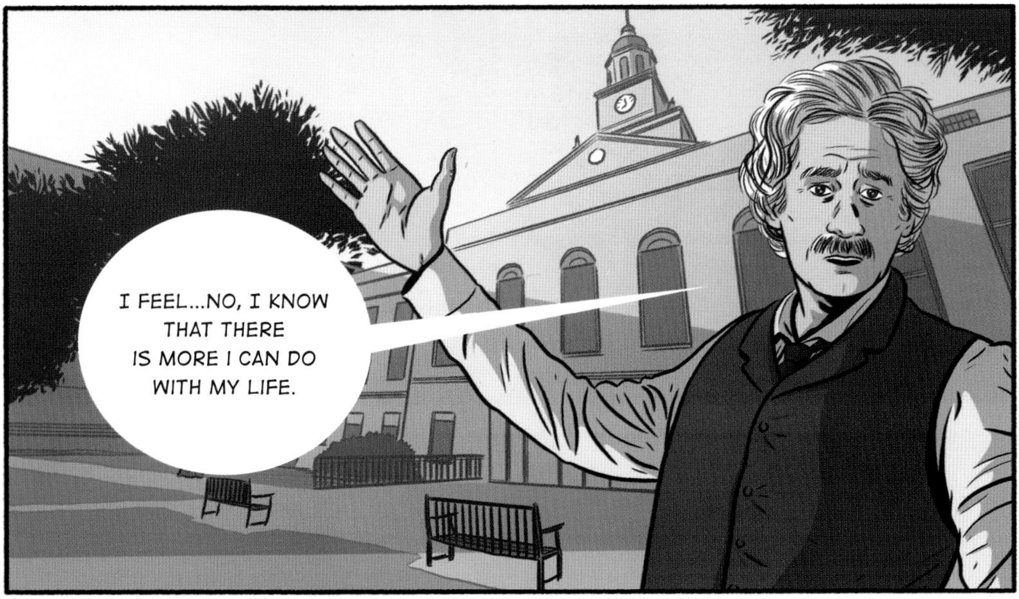
I FEEL...NO, I KNOW THAT THERE IS MORE I CAN DO WITH MY LIFE.

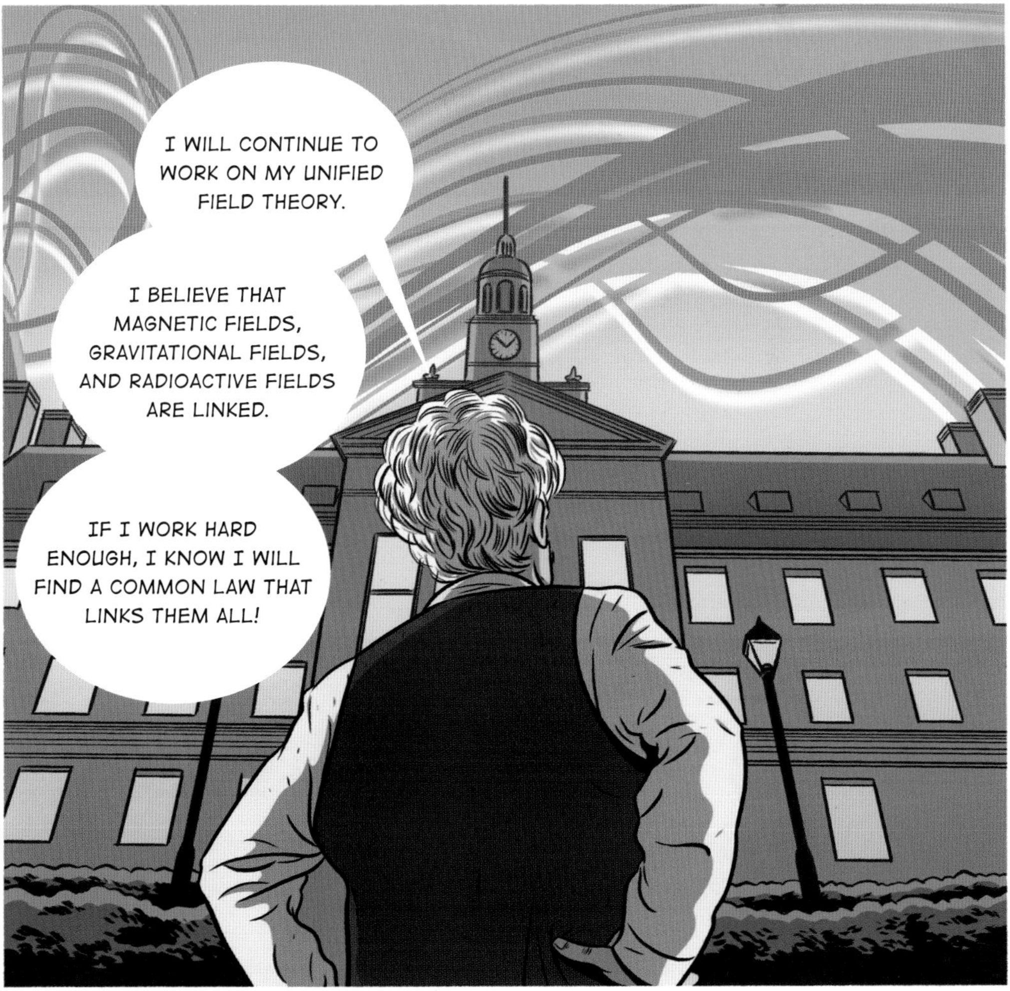
I WILL CONTINUE TO WORK ON MY UNIFIED FIELD THEORY.
I BELIEVE THAT MAGNETIC FIELDS, GRAVITATIONAL FIELDS, AND RADIOACTIVE FIELDS ARE LINKED.
IF I WORK HARD ENOUGH, I KNOW I WILL FIND A COMMON LAW THAT LINKS THEM ALL!

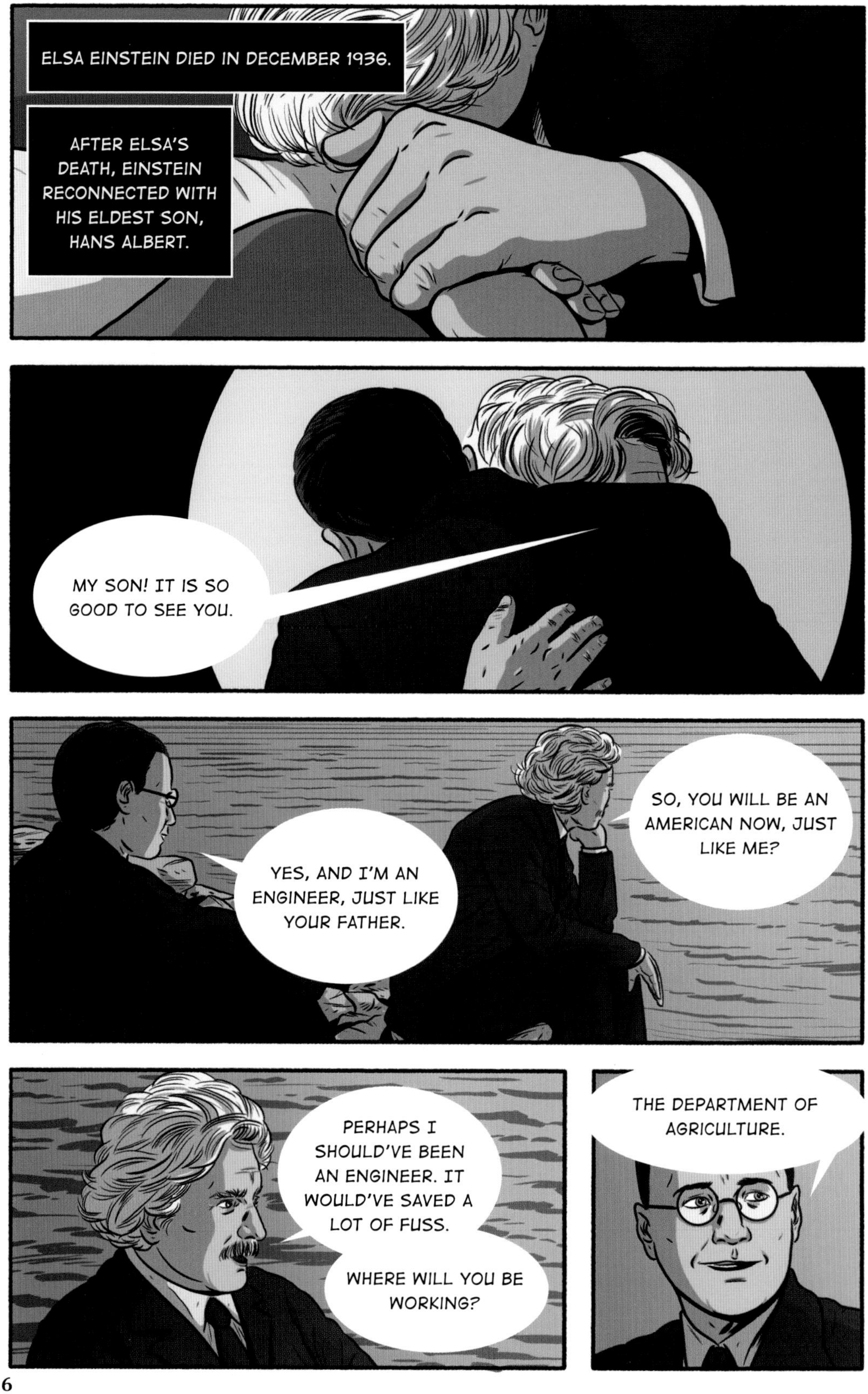
ELSA EINSTEIN DIED IN DECEMBER 1936.
AFTER ELSA'S DEATH, EINSTEIN RECONNECTED WITH HIS ELDEST SON, HANS ALBERT.
MY SON! IT IS SO GOOD TO SEE YOU.
SO, YOU WILL BE AN AMERICAN NOW, JUST LIKE ME?
YES, AND I'M AN ENGINEER, JUST LIKE YOUR FATHER.
PERHAPS I SHOULD'VE BEEN AN ENGINEER. IT WOULD'VE SAVED A LOT OF FUSS.
WHERE WILL YOU BE WORKING?
THE DEPARTMENT OF AGRICULTURE.

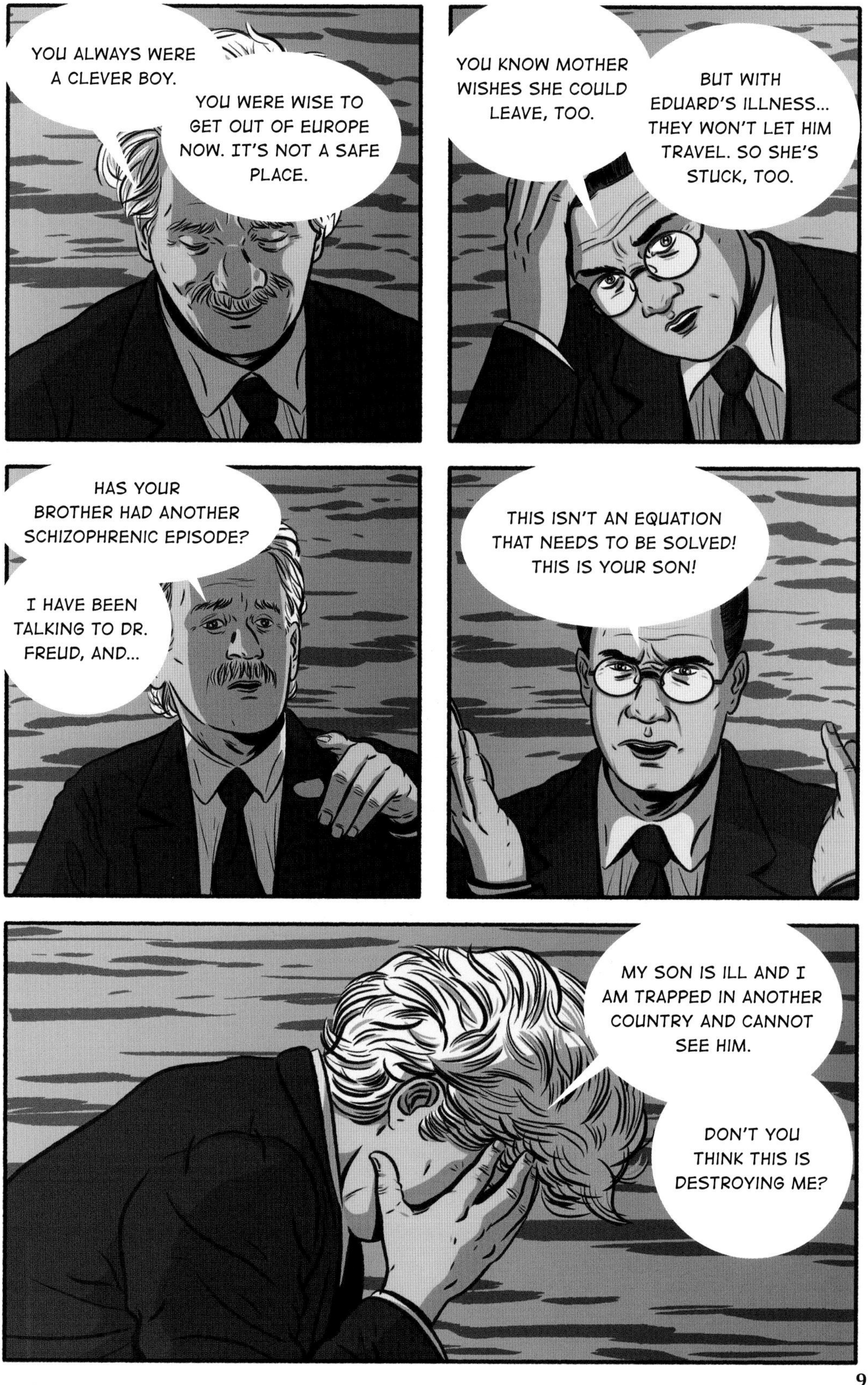
YOU ALWAYS WERE A CLEVER BOY.
YOU WERE WISE TO GET OUT OF EUROPE NOW. IT'S NOT A SAFE PLACE.
YOU KNOW MOTHER WISHES SHE COULD LEAVE, TOO.
BUT WITH EDUARD'S ILLNESS... THEY WON'T LET HIM TRAVEL. SO SHE'S STUCK, TOO.
HAS YOUR BROTHER HAD ANOTHER SCHIZOPHRENIC EPISODE?
I HAVE BEEN TALKING TO DR. FREUD, AND...
THIS ISN'T AN EQUATION THAT NEEDS TO BE SOLVED! THIS IS YOUR SON!
MY SON IS ILL AND I AM TRAPPED IN ANOTHER COUNTRY AND CANNOT SEE HIM.
DON'T YOU THINK THIS IS DESTROYING ME?

CHAPTER 8

The Manhattan Project

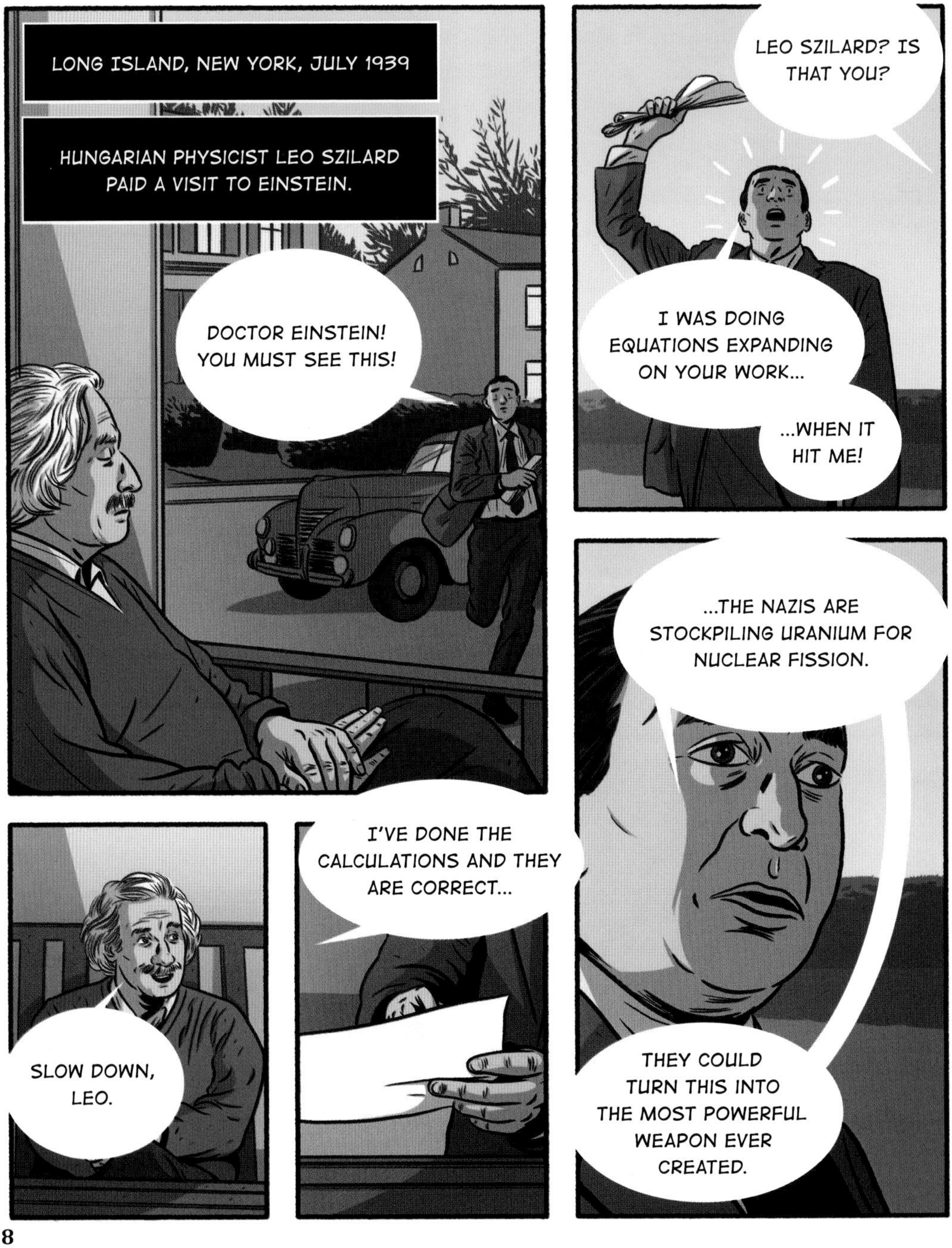
LONG ISLAND, NEW YORK, JULY 1939
HUNGARIAN PHYSICIST LEO SZILARD PAID A VISIT TO EINSTEIN.
DOCTOR EINSTEIN! YOU MUST SEE THIS!
LEO SZILARD? IS THAT YOU?
I WAS DOING EQUATIONS EXPANDING ON YOUR WORK...
...WHEN IT HIT ME!
SLOW DOWN, LEO.
I'VE DONE THE CALCULATIONS AND THEY ARE CORRECT...
...THE NAZIS ARE STOCKPILING URANIUM FOR NUCLEAR FISSION.
THEY COULD TURN THIS INTO THE MOST POWERFUL WEAPON EVER CREATED.

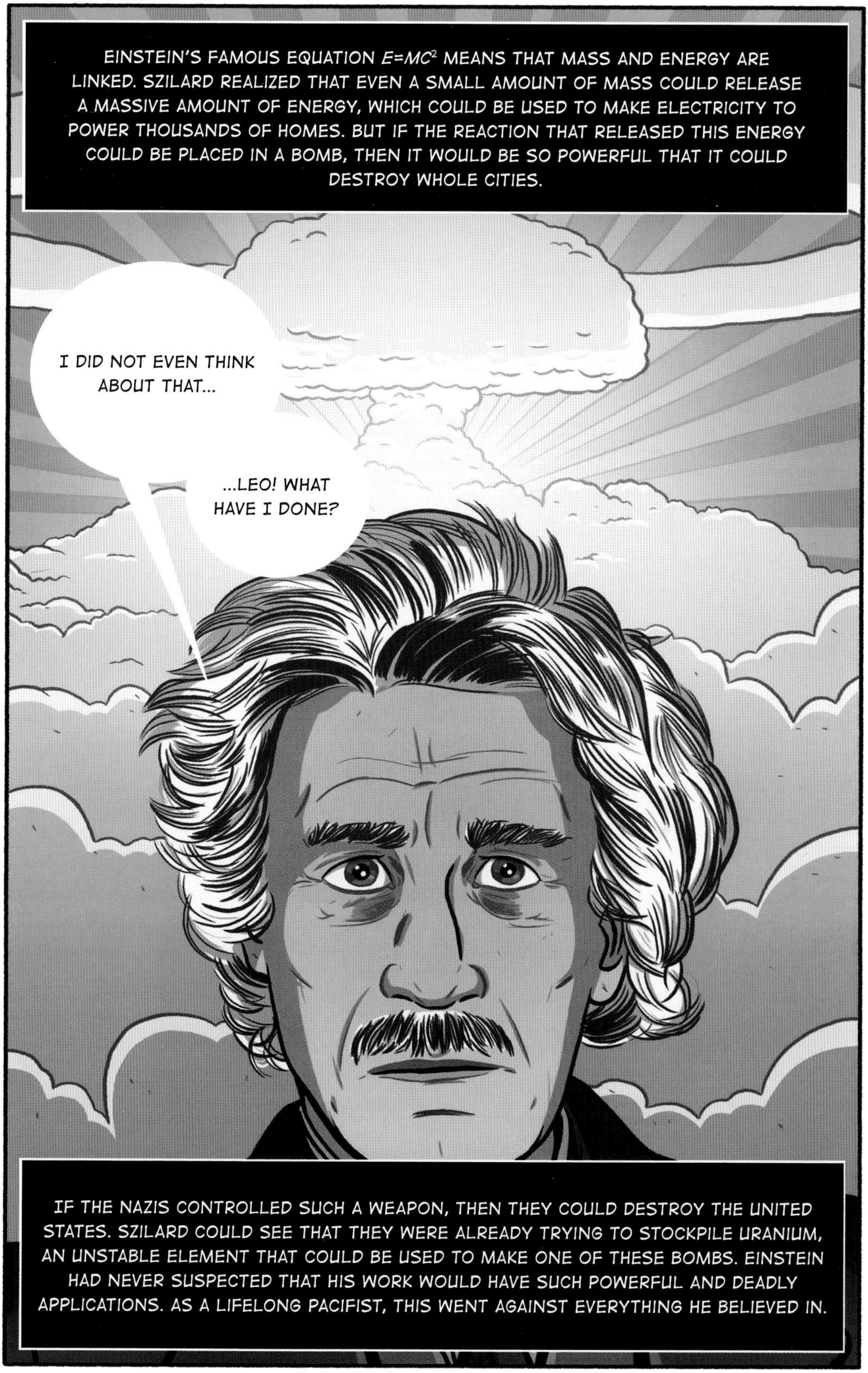
EINSTEIN'S FAMOUS EQUATION E=MC² MEANS THAT MASS AND ENERGY ARE LINKED. SZILARD REALIZED THAT EVEN A SMALL AMOUNT OF MASS COULD RELEASE A MASSIVE AMOUNT OF ENERGY, WHICH COULD BE USED TO MAKE ELECTRICITY TO POWER THOUSANDS OF HOMES. BUT IF THE REACTION THAT RELEASED THIS ENERGY COULD BE PLACED IN A BOMB, THEN IT WOULD BE SO POWERFUL THAT IT COULD DESTROY WHOLE CITIES.
I DID NOT EVEN THINK ABOUT THAT...
...LEO! WHAT HAVE I DONE?
IF THE NAZIS CONTROLLED SUCH A WEAPON, THEN THEY COULD DESTROY THE UNITED STATES. SZILARD COULD SEE THAT THEY WERE ALREADY TRYING TO STOCKPILE URANIUM, AN UNSTABLE ELEMENT THAT COULD BE USED TO MAKE ONE OF THESE BOMBS. EINSTEIN HAD NEVER SUSPECTED THAT HIS WORK WOULD HAVE SUCH POWERFUL AND DEADLY APPLICATIONS. AS A LIFELONG PACIFIST, THIS WENT AGAINST EVERYTHING HE BELIEVED IN.

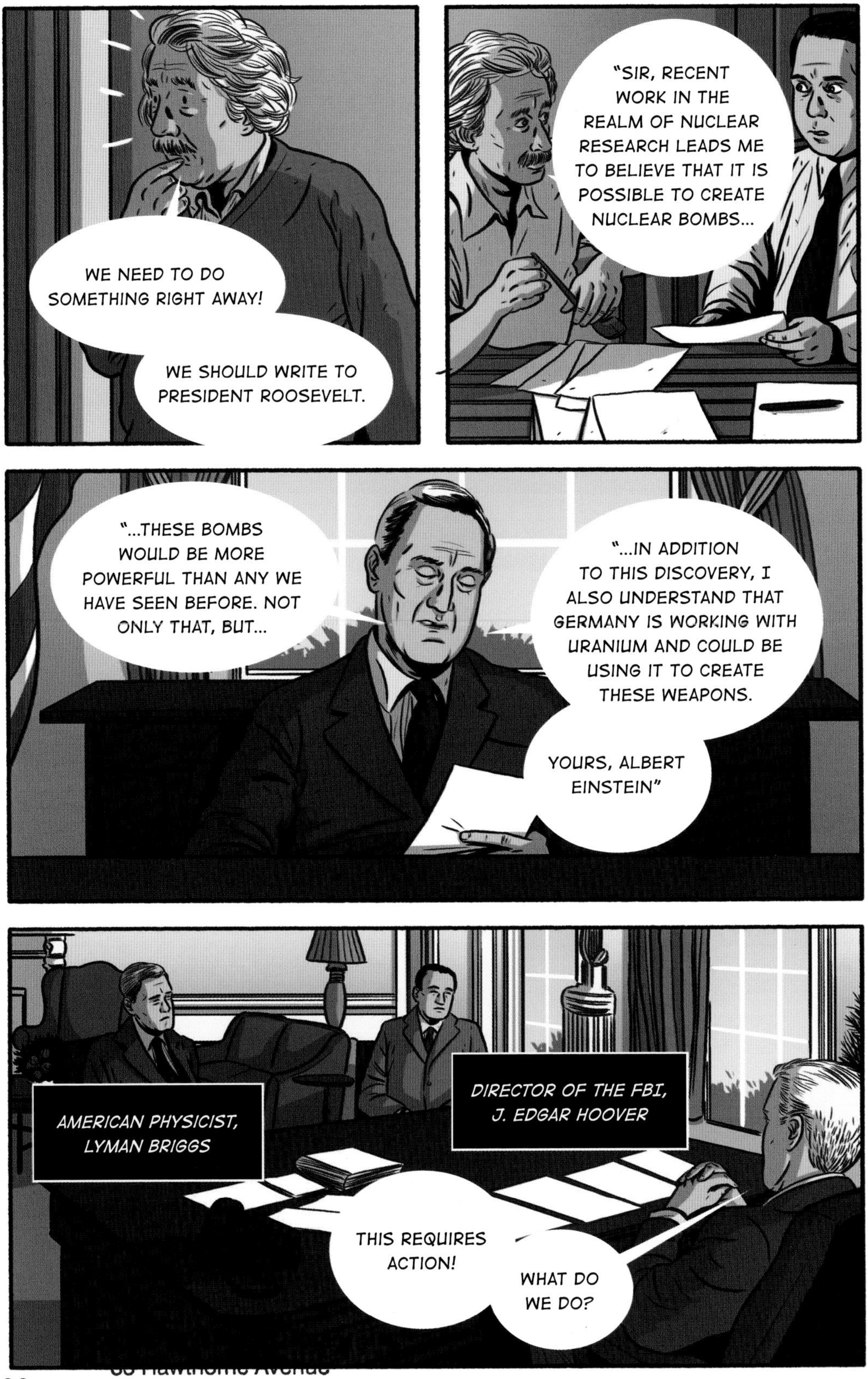
WE NEED TO DO SOMETHING RIGHT AWAY!
WE SHOULD WRITE TO PRESIDENT ROOSEVELT.
"SIR, RECENT WORK IN THE REALM OF NUCLEAR RESEARCH LEADS ME TO BELIEVE THAT IT IS POSSIBLE TO CREATE NUCLEAR BOMBS...
"...THESE BOMBS WOULD BE MORE POWERFUL THAN ANY WE HAVE SEEN BEFORE. NOT ONLY THAT, BUT...
"...IN ADDITION TO THIS DISCOVERY, I ALSO UNDERSTAND THAT GERMANY IS WORKING WITH URANIUM AND COULD BE USING IT TO CREATE THESE WEAPONS.
YOURS, ALBERT EINSTEIN"
AMERICAN PHYSICIST, LYMAN BRIGGS
DIRECTOR OF THE FBI, J. EDGAR HOOVER
THIS REQUIRES ACTION!
WHAT DO WE DO?

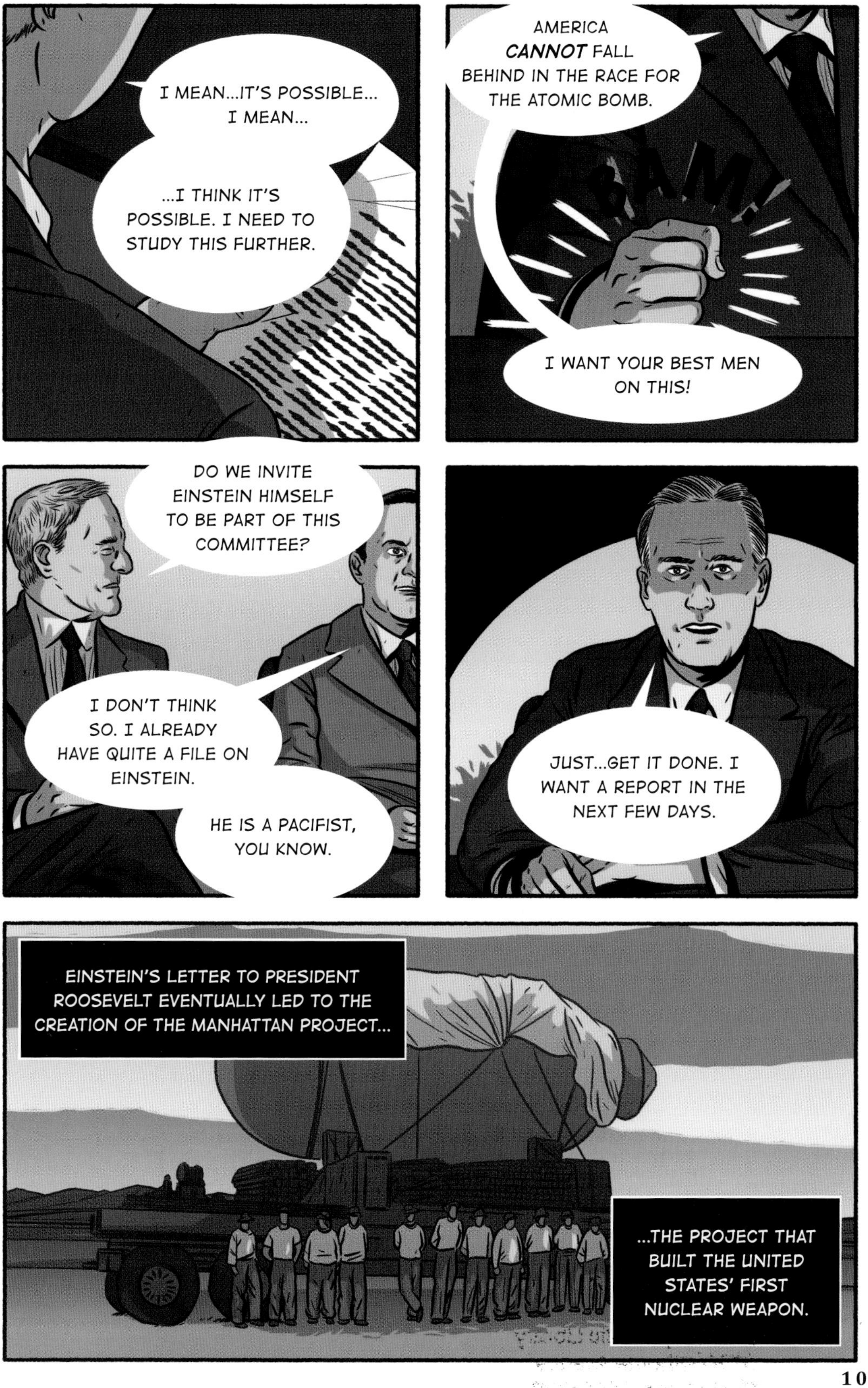
I MEAN...IT'S POSSIBLE... I MEAN...
...I THINK IT'S POSSIBLE. I NEED TO STUDY THIS FURTHER.
AMERICA *CANNOT* FALL BEHIND IN THE RACE FOR THE ATOMIC BOMB.
BAM!
I WANT YOUR BEST MEN ON THIS!
DO WE INVITE EINSTEIN HIMSELF TO BE PART OF THIS COMMITTEE?
I DON'T THINK SO. I ALREADY HAVE QUITE A FILE ON EINSTEIN.
HE IS A PACIFIST, YOU KNOW.
JUST...GET IT DONE. I WANT A REPORT IN THE NEXT FEW DAYS.
EINSTEIN'S LETTER TO PRESIDENT ROOSEVELT EVENTUALLY LED TO THE CREATION OF THE MANHATTAN PROJECT...
...THE PROJECT THAT BUILT THE UNITED STATES' FIRST NUCLEAR WEAPON.

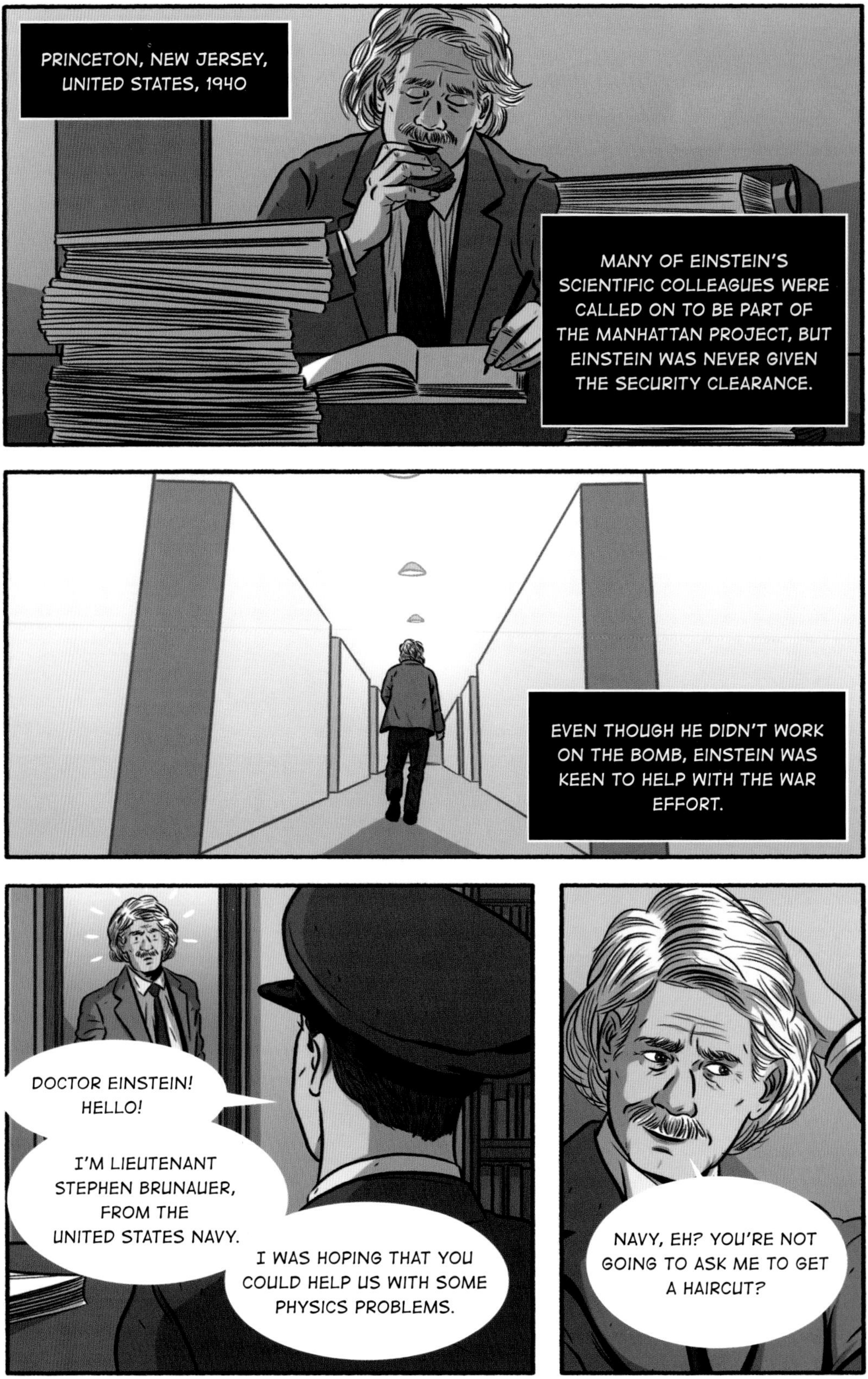
PRINCETON, NEW JERSEY, UNITED STATES, 1940
MANY OF EINSTEIN'S SCIENTIFIC COLLEAGUES WERE CALLED ON TO BE PART OF THE MANHATTAN PROJECT, BUT EINSTEIN WAS NEVER GIVEN THE SECURITY CLEARANCE.
EVEN THOUGH HE DIDN'T WORK ON THE BOMB, EINSTEIN WAS KEEN TO HELP WITH THE WAR EFFORT.
DOCTOR EINSTEIN! HELLO!
I'M LIEUTENANT STEPHEN BRUNAUER, FROM THE UNITED STATES NAVY.
I WAS HOPING THAT YOU COULD HELP US WITH SOME PHYSICS PROBLEMS.
NAVY, EH? YOU'RE NOT GOING TO ASK ME TO GET A HAIRCUT?

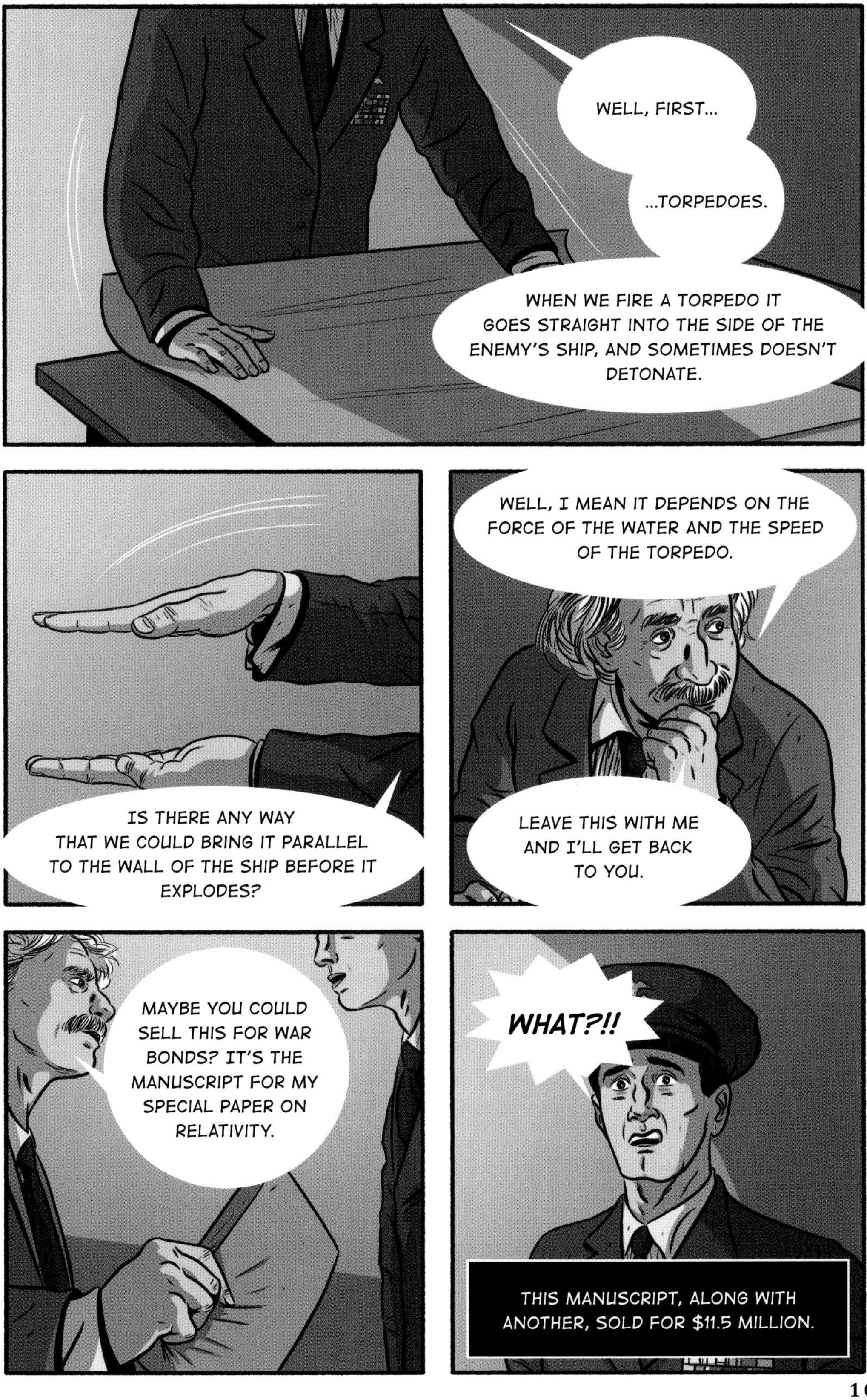
WELL, FIRST...
...TORPEDOES.
WHEN WE FIRE A TORPEDO IT GOES STRAIGHT INTO THE SIDE OF THE ENEMY'S SHIP, AND SOMETIMES DOESN'T DETONATE.
IS THERE ANY WAY THAT WE COULD BRING IT PARALLEL TO THE WALL OF THE SHIP BEFORE IT EXPLODES?
WELL, I MEAN IT DEPENDS ON THE FORCE OF THE WATER AND THE SPEED OF THE TORPEDO.
LEAVE THIS WITH ME AND I'LL GET BACK TO YOU.
MAYBE YOU COULD SELL THIS FOR WAR BONDS? IT'S THE MANUSCRIPT FOR MY SPECIAL PAPER ON RELATIVITY.
WHAT?!!
THIS MANUSCRIPT, ALONG WITH ANOTHER, SOLD FOR $11.5 MILLION.

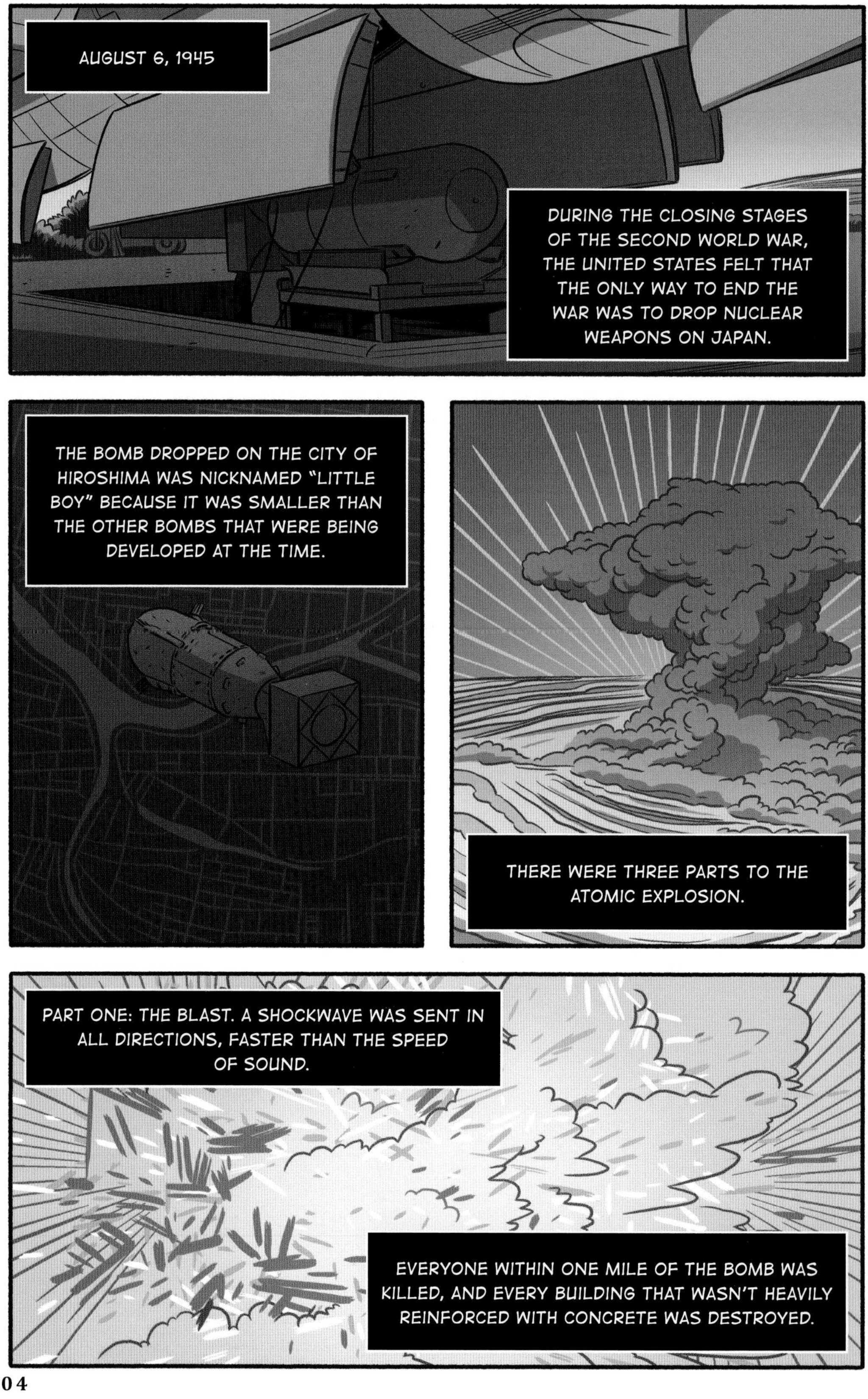
AUGUST 6, 1945
DURING THE CLOSING STAGES OF THE SECOND WORLD WAR, THE UNITED STATES FELT THAT THE ONLY WAY TO END THE WAR WAS TO DROP NUCLEAR WEAPONS ON JAPAN.
THE BOMB DROPPED ON THE CITY OF HIROSHIMA WAS NICKNAMED "LITTLE BOY" BECAUSE IT WAS SMALLER THAN THE OTHER BOMBS THAT WERE BEING DEVELOPED AT THE TIME.
THERE WERE THREE PARTS TO THE ATOMIC EXPLOSION.
PART ONE: THE BLAST. A SHOCKWAVE WAS SENT IN ALL DIRECTIONS, FASTER THAN THE SPEED OF SOUND.
EVERYONE WITHIN ONE MILE OF THE BOMB WAS KILLED, AND EVERY BUILDING THAT WASN'T HEAVILY REINFORCED WITH CONCRETE WAS DESTROYED.

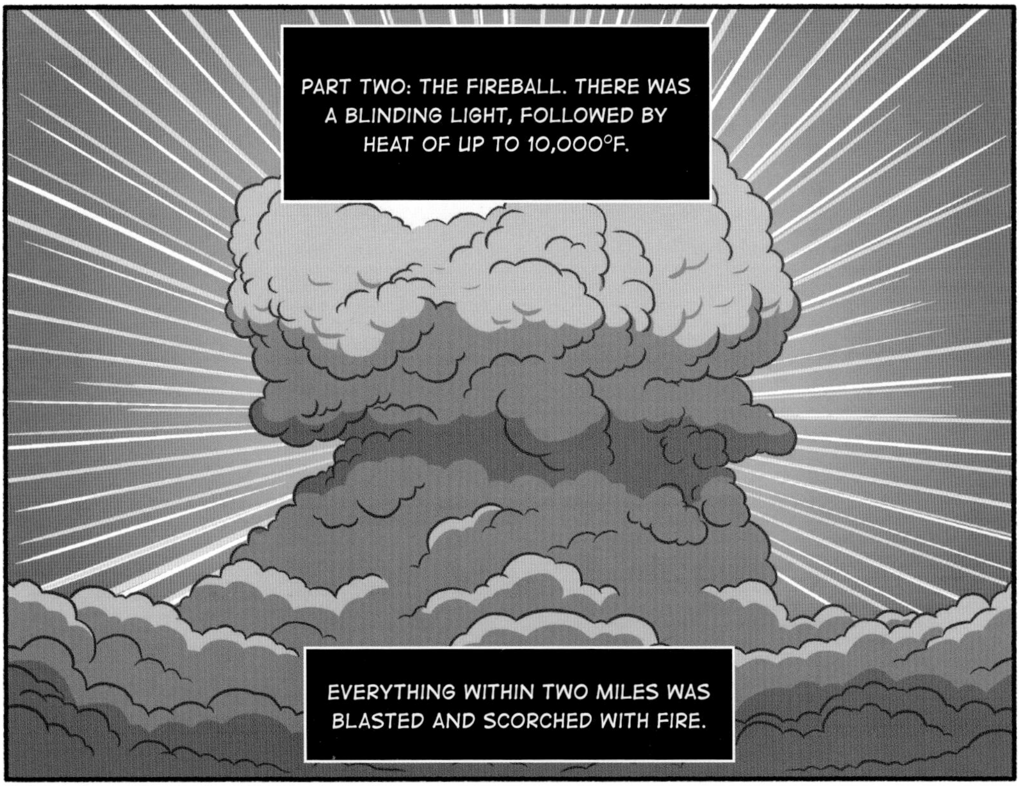
PART TWO: THE FIREBALL. THERE WAS A BLINDING LIGHT, FOLLOWED BY HEAT OF UP TO 10,000°F.
EVERYTHING WITHIN TWO MILES WAS BLASTED AND SCORCHED WITH FIRE.

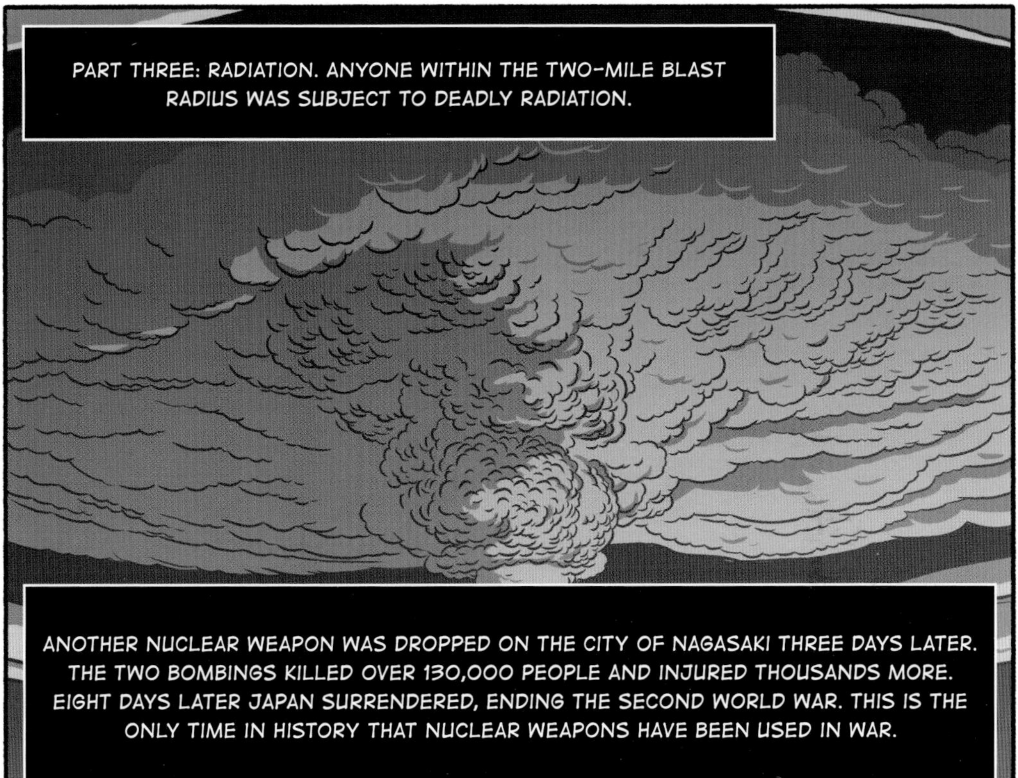
PART THREE: RADIATION. ANYONE WITHIN THE TWO-MILE BLAST RADIUS WAS SUBJECT TO DEADLY RADIATION.
ANOTHER NUCLEAR WEAPON WAS DROPPED ON THE CITY OF NAGASAKI THREE DAYS LATER. THE TWO BOMBINGS KILLED OVER 130,000 PEOPLE AND INJURED THOUSANDS MORE. EIGHT DAYS LATER JAPAN SURRENDERED, ENDING THE SECOND WORLD WAR. THIS IS THE ONLY TIME IN HISTORY THAT NUCLEAR WEAPONS HAVE BEEN USED IN WAR.

EINSTEIN WAS ON VACATION IN SARANAC LAKE IN THE ADIRONDACK MOUNTAINS IN NORTHEASTERN NEW YORK STATE WHEN HE HEARD THE NEWS ABOUT HIROSHIMA.

OH, MY GOD.

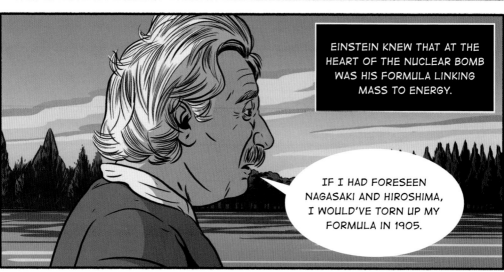

EINSTEIN KNEW THAT AT THE HEART OF THE NUCLEAR BOMB WAS HIS FORMULA LINKING MASS TO ENERGY.

IF I HAD FORESEEN NAGASAKI AND HIROSHIMA, I WOULD'VE TORN UP MY FORMULA IN 1905.

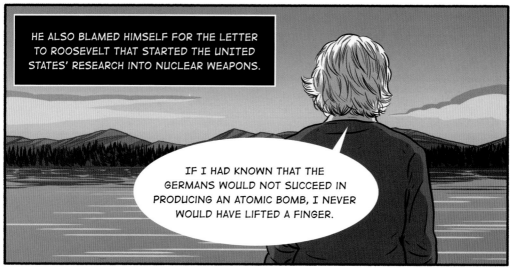

HE ALSO BLAMED HIMSELF FOR THE LETTER TO ROOSEVELT THAT STARTED THE UNITED STATES' RESEARCH INTO NUCLEAR WEAPONS.

IF I HAD KNOWN THAT THE GERMANS WOULD NOT SUCCEED IN PRODUCING AN ATOMIC BOMB, I NEVER WOULD HAVE LIFTED A FINGER.

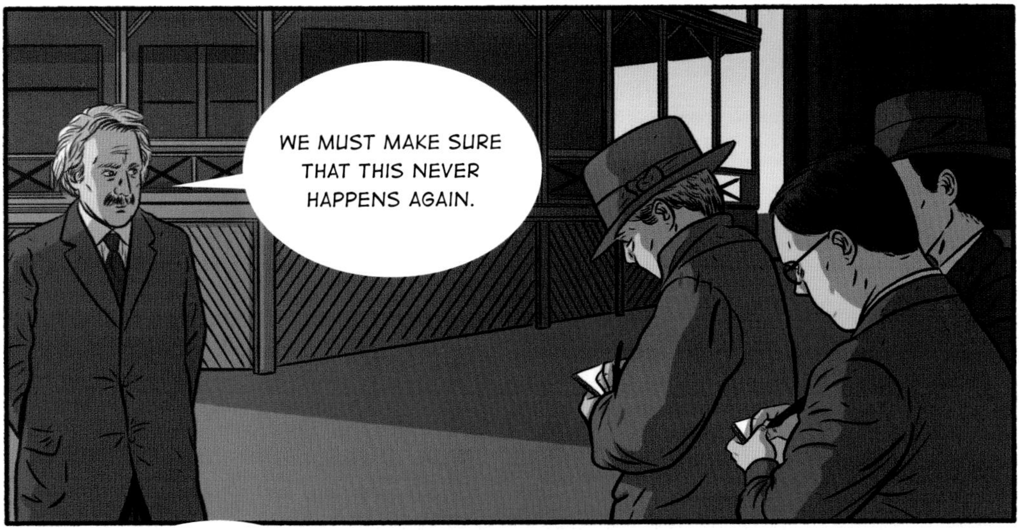
WE MUST MAKE SURE THAT THIS NEVER HAPPENS AGAIN.

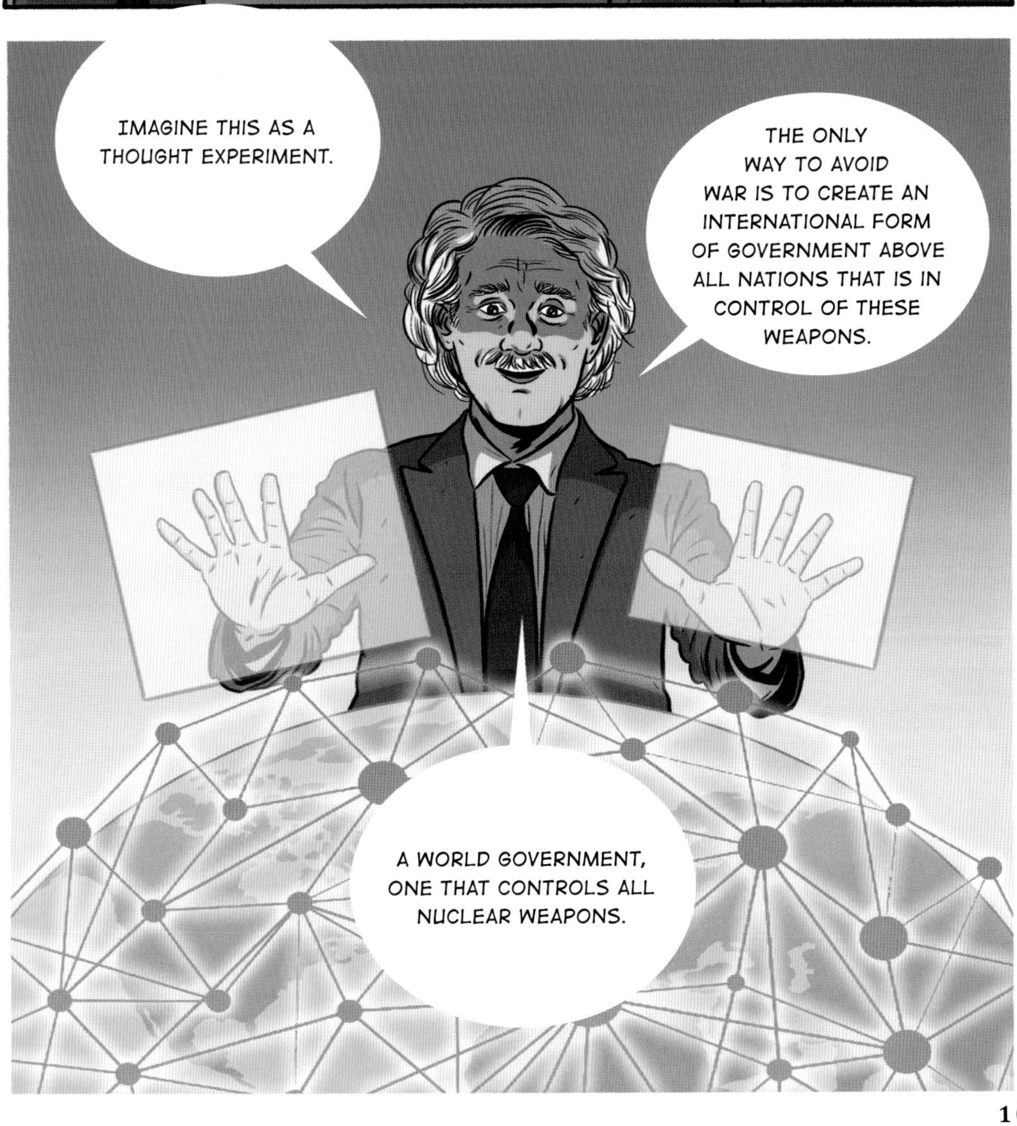
IMAGINE THIS AS A THOUGHT EXPERIMENT.
THE ONLY WAY TO AVOID WAR IS TO CREATE AN INTERNATIONAL FORM OF GOVERNMENT ABOVE ALL NATIONS THAT IS IN CONTROL OF THESE WEAPONS.
A WORLD GOVERNMENT, ONE THAT CONTROLS ALL NUCLEAR WEAPONS.

CHAPTER 9

Life After the Bomb

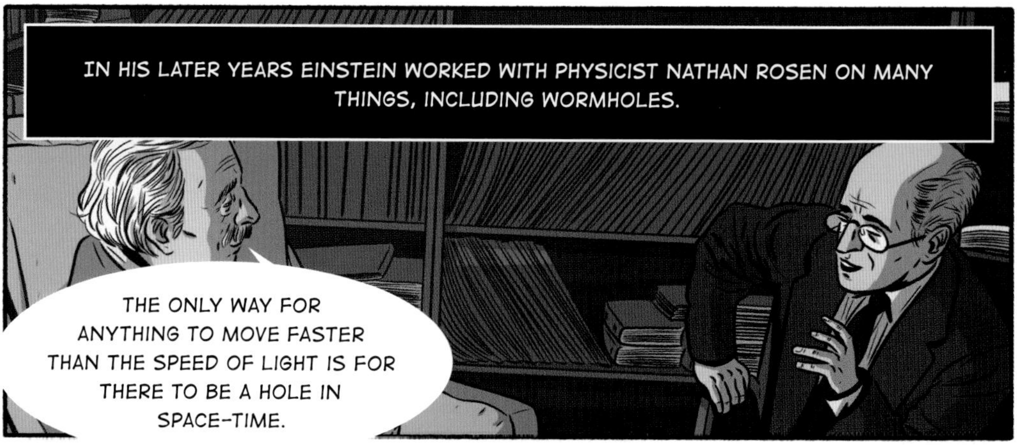
IN HIS LATER YEARS EINSTEIN WORKED WITH PHYSICIST NATHAN ROSEN ON MANY THINGS, INCLUDING WORMHOLES.
THE ONLY WAY FOR ANYTHING TO MOVE FASTER THAN THE SPEED OF LIGHT IS FOR THERE TO BE A HOLE IN SPACE-TIME.

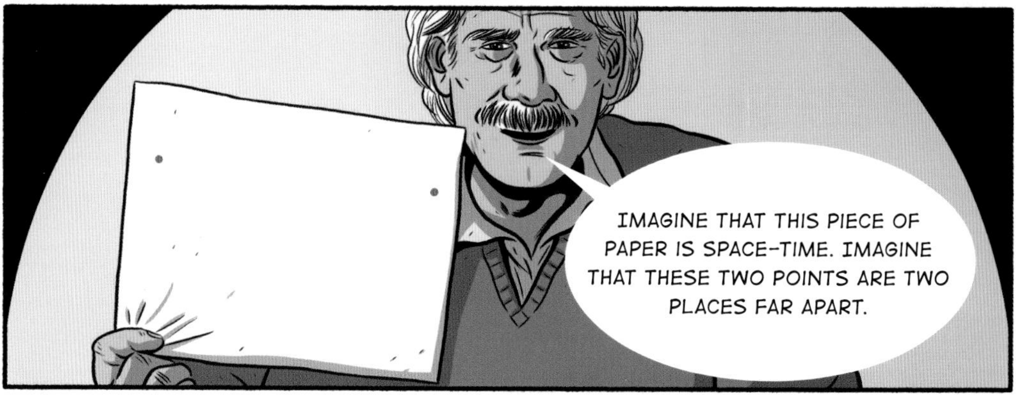
IMAGINE THAT THIS PIECE OF PAPER IS SPACE-TIME. IMAGINE THAT THESE TWO POINTS ARE TWO PLACES FAR APART.

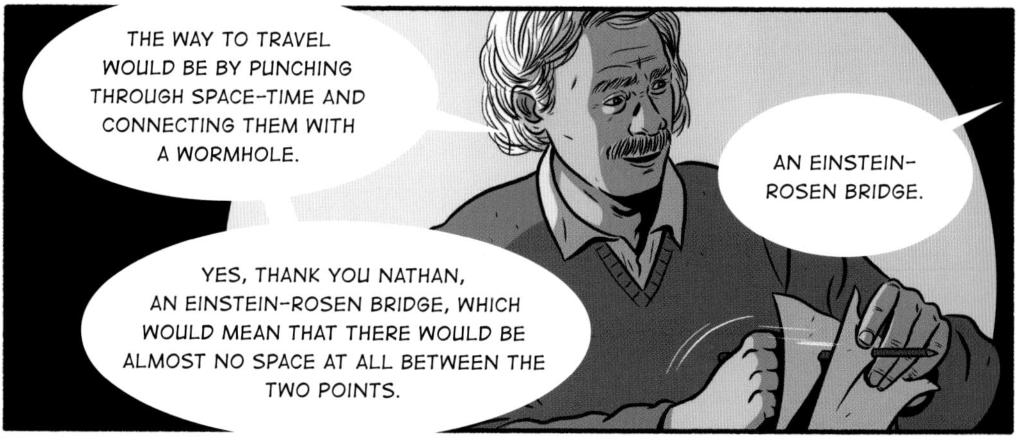
THE WAY TO TRAVEL WOULD BE BY PUNCHING THROUGH SPACE-TIME AND CONNECTING THEM WITH A WORMHOLE.
AN EINSTEIN-ROSEN BRIDGE.
YES, THANK YOU NATHAN, AN EINSTEIN-ROSEN BRIDGE, WHICH WOULD MEAN THAT THERE WOULD BE ALMOST NO SPACE AT ALL BETWEEN THE TWO POINTS.

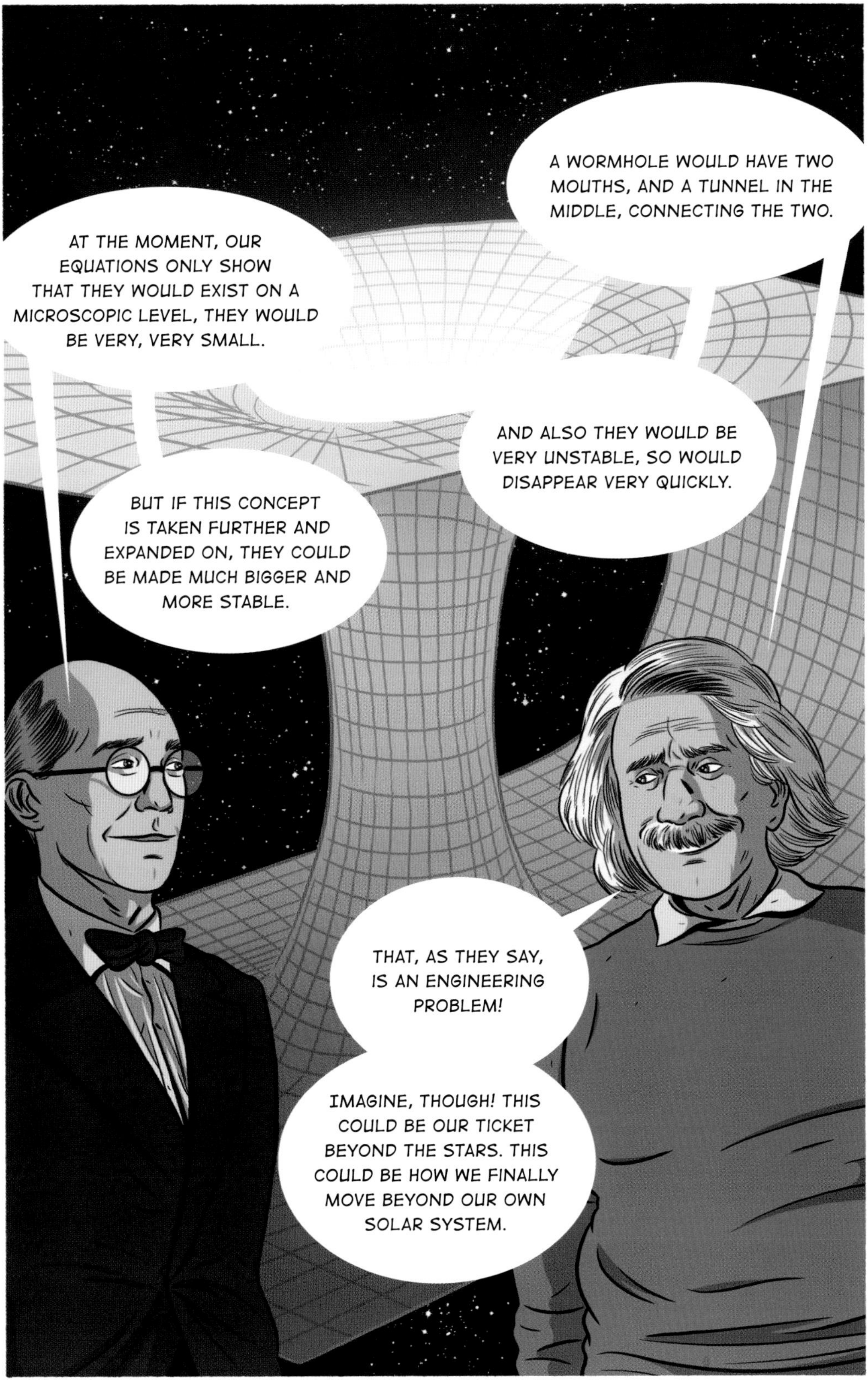
A WORMHOLE WOULD HAVE TWO MOUTHS, AND A TUNNEL IN THE MIDDLE, CONNECTING THE TWO.
AT THE MOMENT, OUR EQUATIONS ONLY SHOW THAT THEY WOULD EXIST ON A MICROSCOPIC LEVEL, THEY WOULD BE VERY, VERY SMALL.
AND ALSO THEY WOULD BE VERY UNSTABLE, SO WOULD DISAPPEAR VERY QUICKLY.
BUT IF THIS CONCEPT IS TAKEN FURTHER AND EXPANDED ON, THEY COULD BE MADE MUCH BIGGER AND MORE STABLE.
THAT, AS THEY SAY, IS AN ENGINEERING PROBLEM!
IMAGINE, THOUGH! THIS COULD BE OUR TICKET BEYOND THE STARS. THIS COULD BE HOW WE FINALLY MOVE BEYOND OUR OWN SOLAR SYSTEM.

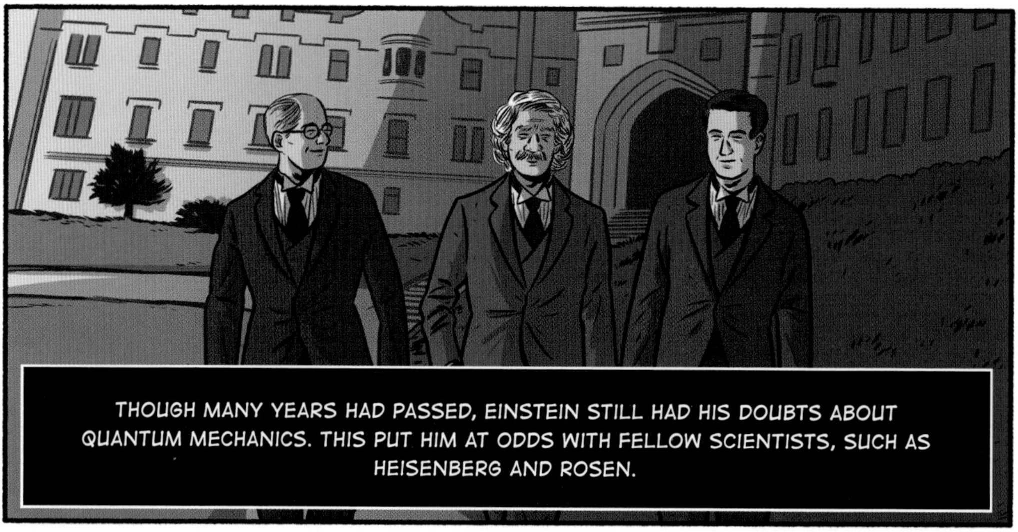
THOUGH MANY YEARS HAD PASSED, EINSTEIN STILL HAD HIS DOUBTS ABOUT QUANTUM MECHANICS. THIS PUT HIM AT ODDS WITH FELLOW SCIENTISTS, SUCH AS HEISENBERG AND ROSEN.

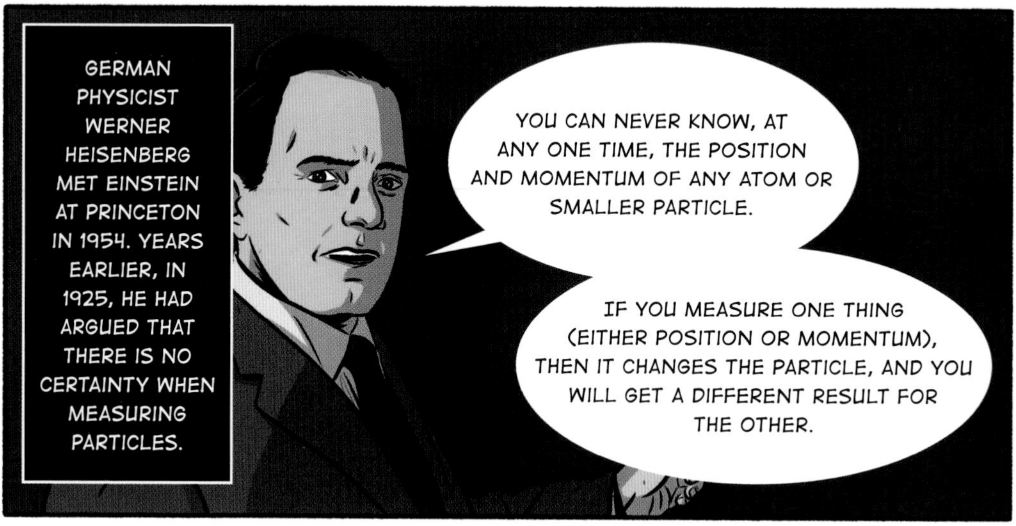
GERMAN PHYSICIST WERNER HEISENBERG MET EINSTEIN AT PRINCETON IN 1954. YEARS EARLIER, IN 1925, HE HAD ARGUED THAT THERE IS NO CERTAINTY WHEN MEASURING PARTICLES.
YOU CAN NEVER KNOW, AT ANY ONE TIME, THE POSITION AND MOMENTUM OF ANY ATOM OR SMALLER PARTICLE.
IF YOU MEASURE ONE THING (EITHER POSITION OR MOMENTUM), THEN IT CHANGES THE PARTICLE, AND YOU WILL GET A DIFFERENT RESULT FOR THE OTHER.

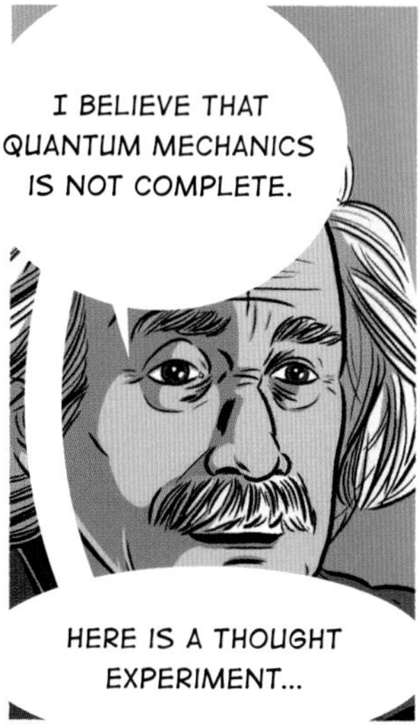
I BELIEVE THAT QUANTUM MECHANICS IS NOT COMPLETE.
HERE IS A THOUGHT EXPERIMENT...

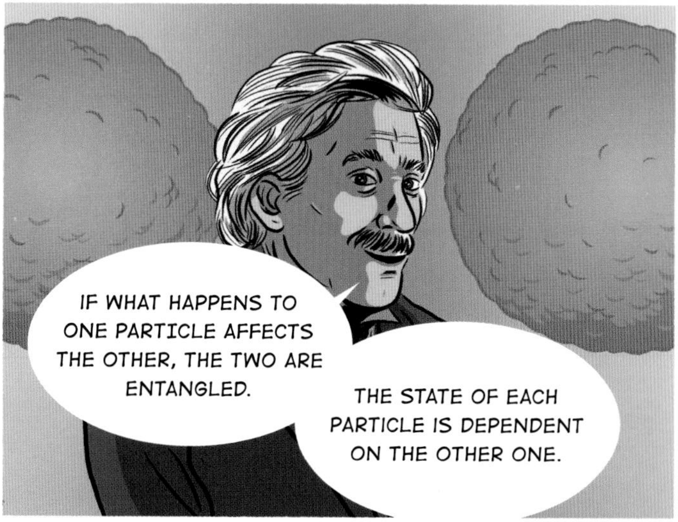
IF WHAT HAPPENS TO ONE PARTICLE AFFECTS THE OTHER, THE TWO ARE ENTANGLED.
THE STATE OF EACH PARTICLE IS DEPENDENT ON THE OTHER ONE.

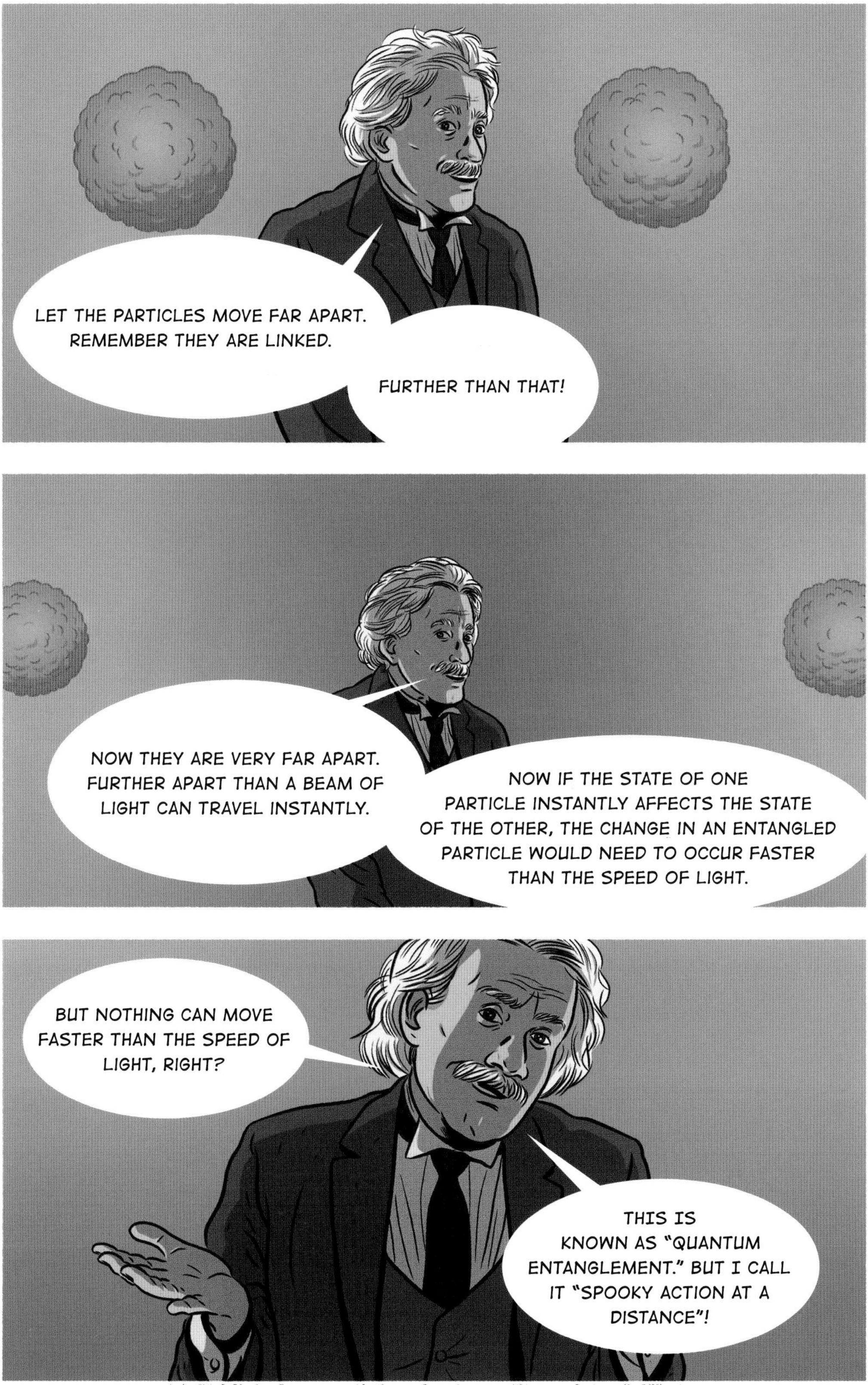
LET THE PARTICLES MOVE FAR APART. REMEMBER THEY ARE LINKED.
FURTHER THAN THAT!
NOW THEY ARE VERY FAR APART. FURTHER APART THAN A BEAM OF LIGHT CAN TRAVEL INSTANTLY.
NOW IF THE STATE OF ONE PARTICLE INSTANTLY AFFECTS THE STATE OF THE OTHER, THE CHANGE IN AN ENTANGLED PARTICLE WOULD NEED TO OCCUR FASTER THAN THE SPEED OF LIGHT.
BUT NOTHING CAN MOVE FASTER THAN THE SPEED OF LIGHT, RIGHT?
THIS IS KNOWN AS "QUANTUM ENTANGLEMENT." BUT I CALL IT "SPOOKY ACTION AT A DISTANCE"!

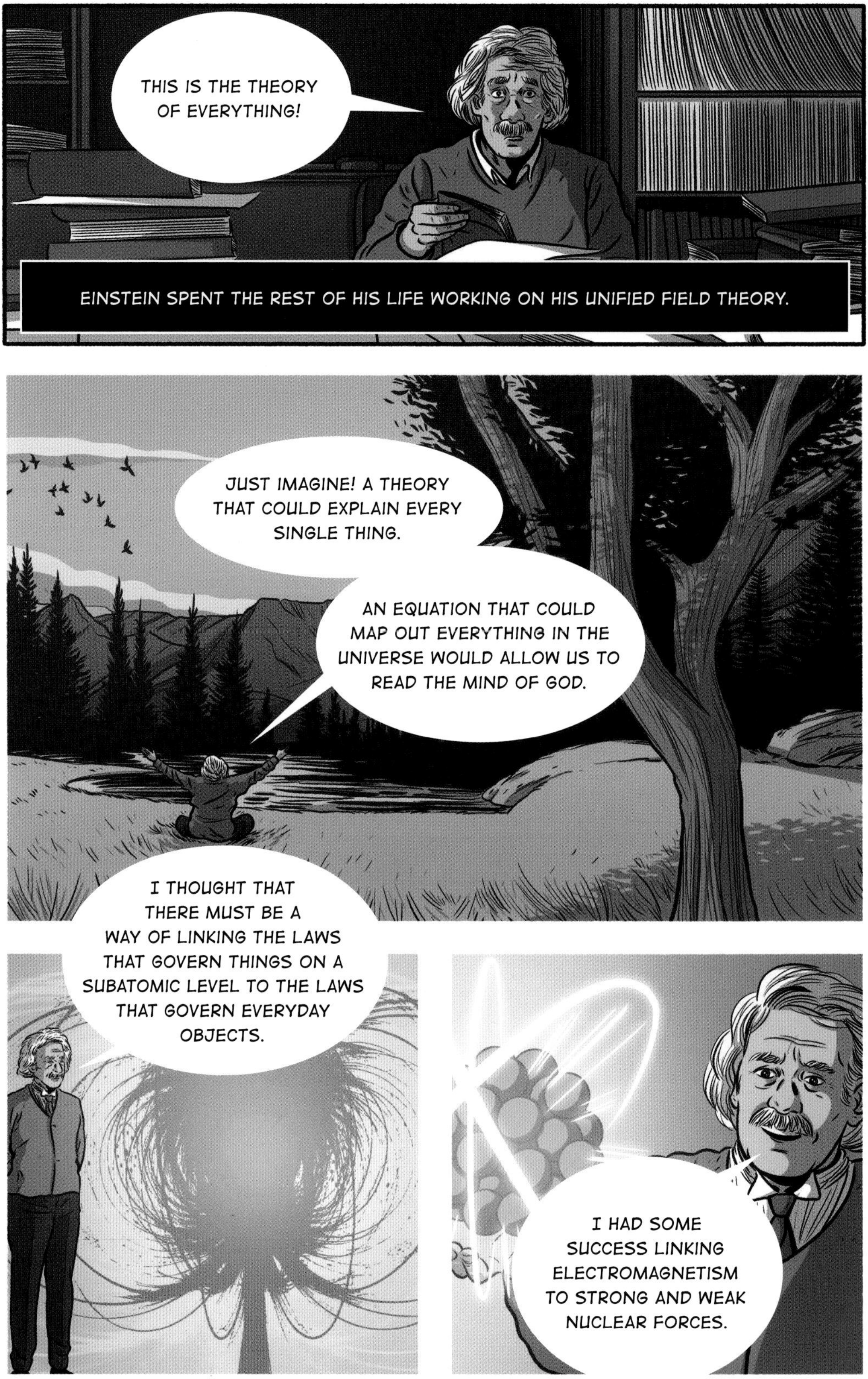
THIS IS THE THEORY OF EVERYTHING!
EINSTEIN SPENT THE REST OF HIS LIFE WORKING ON HIS UNIFIED FIELD THEORY.
JUST IMAGINE! A THEORY THAT COULD EXPLAIN EVERY SINGLE THING.
AN EQUATION THAT COULD MAP OUT EVERYTHING IN THE UNIVERSE WOULD ALLOW US TO READ THE MIND OF GOD.
I THOUGHT THAT THERE MUST BE A WAY OF LINKING THE LAWS THAT GOVERN THINGS ON A SUBATOMIC LEVEL TO THE LAWS THAT GOVERN EVERYDAY OBJECTS.
I HAD SOME SUCCESS LINKING ELECTROMAGNETISM TO STRONG AND WEAK NUCLEAR FORCES.

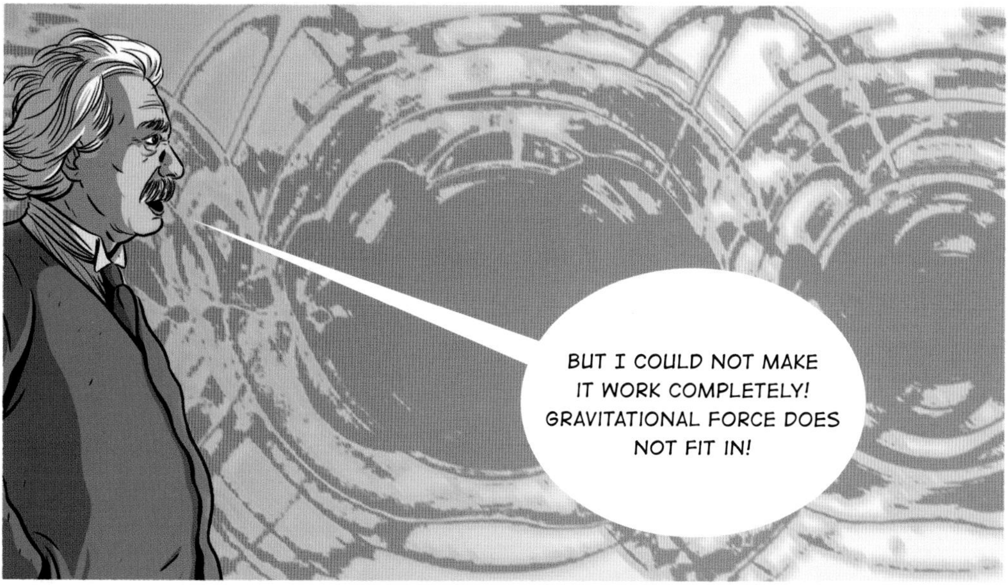
BUT I COULD NOT MAKE IT WORK COMPLETELY! GRAVITATIONAL FORCE DOES NOT FIT IN!

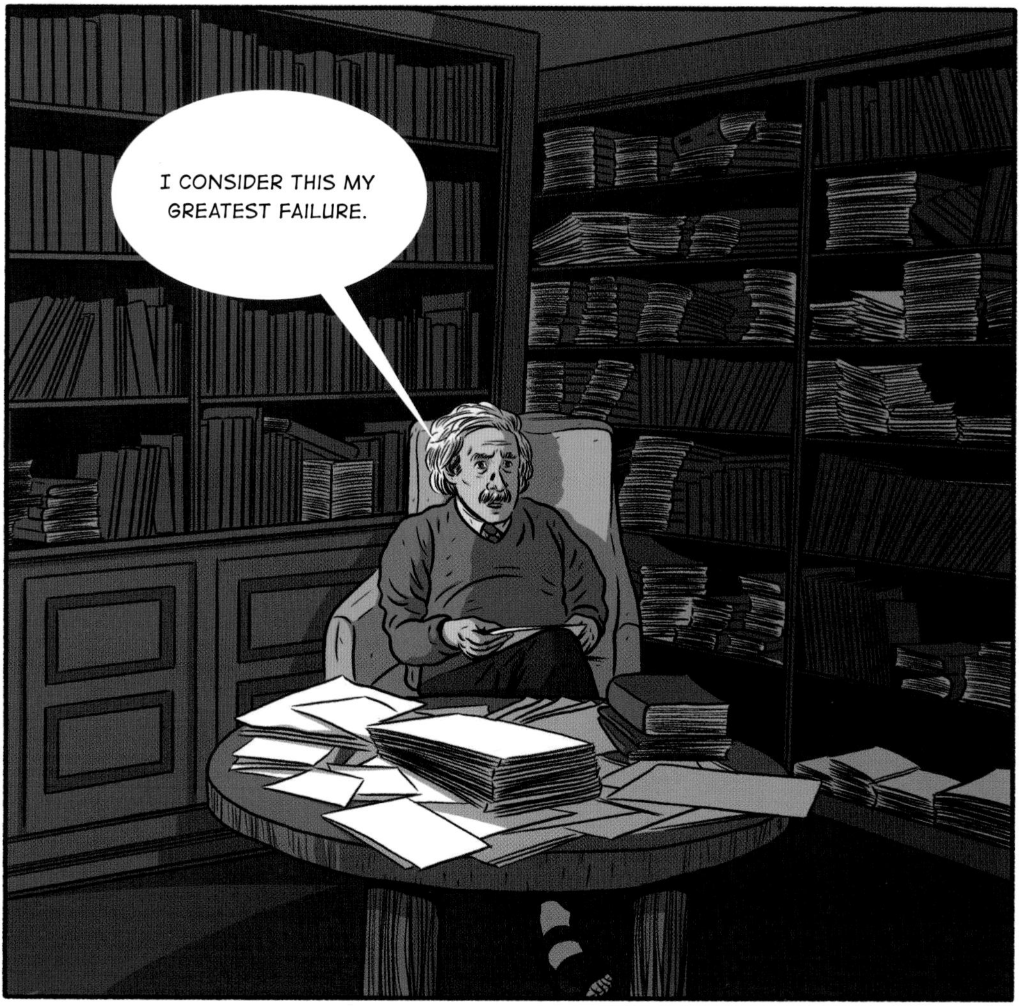
I CONSIDER THIS MY GREATEST FAILURE.

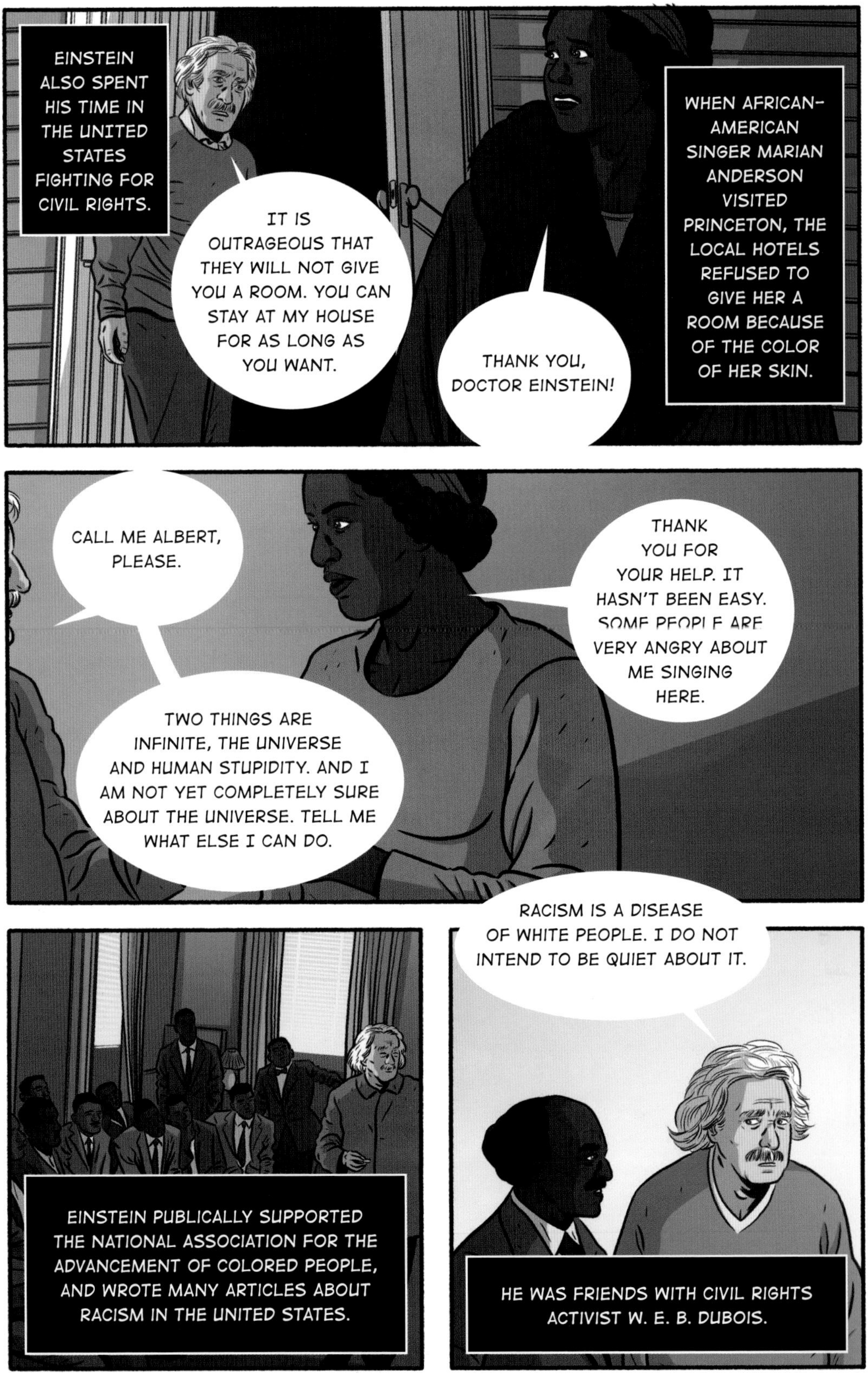
EINSTEIN ALSO SPENT HIS TIME IN THE UNITED STATES FIGHTING FOR CIVIL RIGHTS.
WHEN AFRICAN-AMERICAN SINGER MARIAN ANDERSON VISITED PRINCETON, THE LOCAL HOTELS REFUSED TO GIVE HER A ROOM BECAUSE OF THE COLOR OF HER SKIN.
IT IS OUTRAGEOUS THAT THEY WILL NOT GIVE YOU A ROOM. YOU CAN STAY AT MY HOUSE FOR AS LONG AS YOU WANT.
THANK YOU, DOCTOR EINSTEIN!
CALL ME ALBERT, PLEASE.
THANK YOU FOR YOUR HELP. IT HASN'T BEEN EASY. SOME PEOPLE ARE VERY ANGRY ABOUT ME SINGING HERE.
TWO THINGS ARE INFINITE, THE UNIVERSE AND HUMAN STUPIDITY. AND I AM NOT YET COMPLETELY SURE ABOUT THE UNIVERSE. TELL ME WHAT ELSE I CAN DO.
EINSTEIN PUBLICALLY SUPPORTED THE NATIONAL ASSOCIATION FOR THE ADVANCEMENT OF COLORED PEOPLE, AND WROTE MANY ARTICLES ABOUT RACISM IN THE UNITED STATES.
RACISM IS A DISEASE OF WHITE PEOPLE. I DO NOT INTEND TO BE QUIET ABOUT IT.
HE WAS FRIENDS WITH CIVIL RIGHTS ACTIVIST W. E. B. DUBOIS.

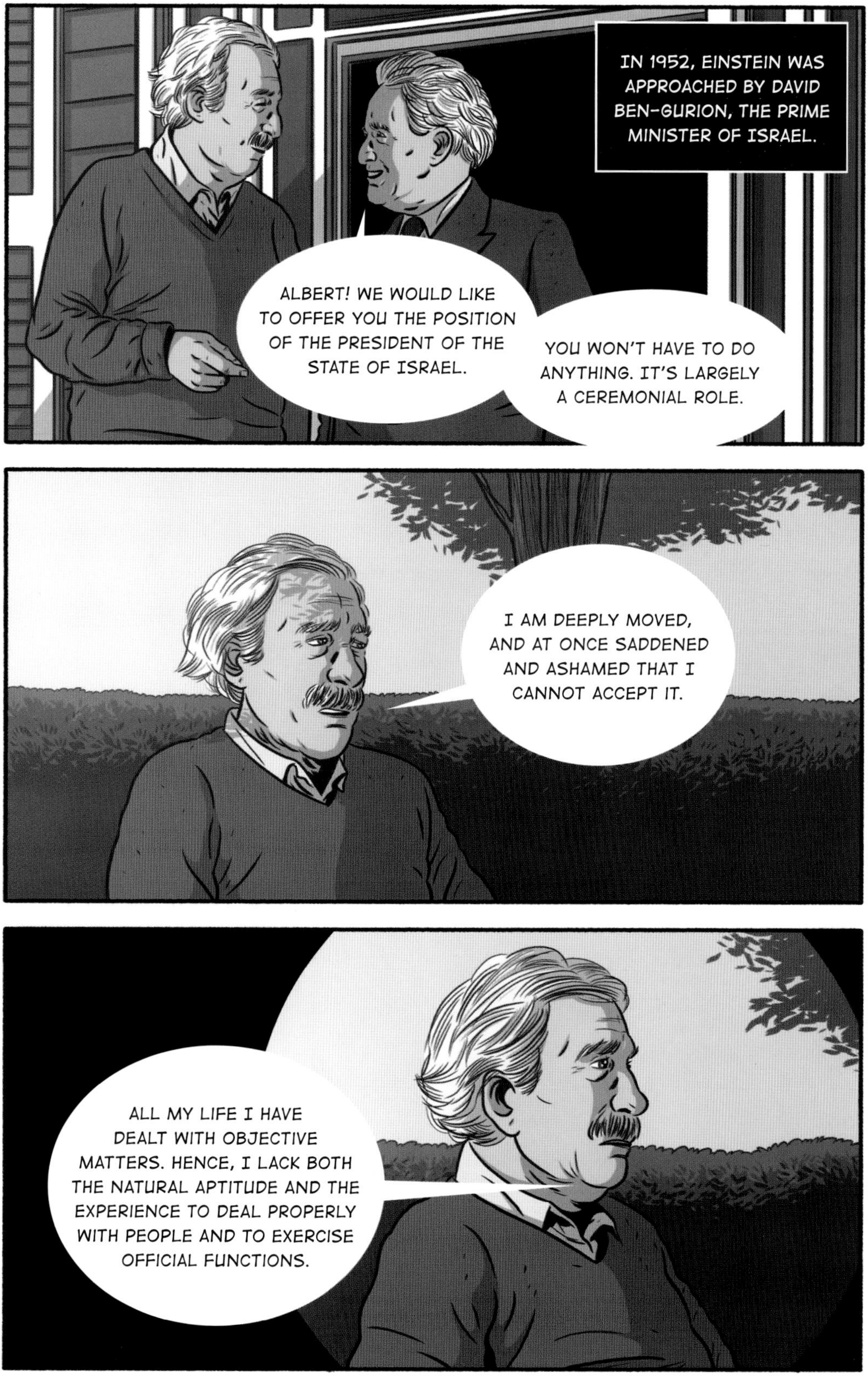
IN 1952, EINSTEIN WAS APPROACHED BY DAVID BEN-GURION, THE PRIME MINISTER OF ISRAEL.
ALBERT! WE WOULD LIKE TO OFFER YOU THE POSITION OF THE PRESIDENT OF THE STATE OF ISRAEL.
YOU WON'T HAVE TO DO ANYTHING. IT'S LARGELY A CEREMONIAL ROLE.
I AM DEEPLY MOVED, AND AT ONCE SADDENED AND ASHAMED THAT I CANNOT ACCEPT IT.
ALL MY LIFE I HAVE DEALT WITH OBJECTIVE MATTERS. HENCE, I LACK BOTH THE NATURAL APTITUDE AND THE EXPERIENCE TO DEAL PROPERLY WITH PEOPLE AND TO EXERCISE OFFICIAL FUNCTIONS.

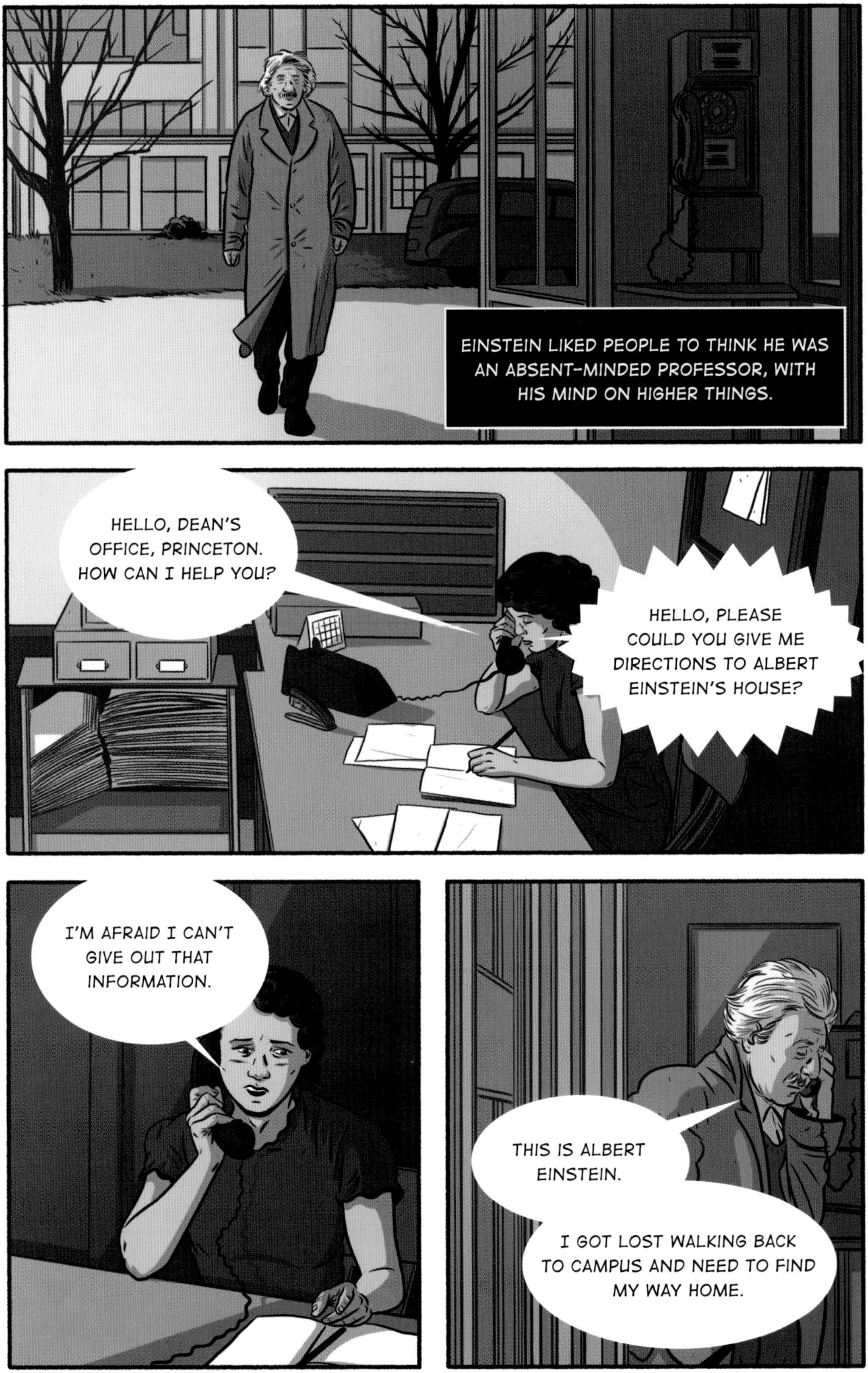
EINSTEIN LIKED PEOPLE TO THINK HE WAS AN ABSENT-MINDED PROFESSOR, WITH HIS MIND ON HIGHER THINGS.
HELLO, DEAN'S OFFICE, PRINCETON. HOW CAN I HELP YOU?
HELLO, PLEASE COULD YOU GIVE ME DIRECTIONS TO ALBERT EINSTEIN'S HOUSE?
I'M AFRAID I CAN'T GIVE OUT THAT INFORMATION.
THIS IS ALBERT EINSTEIN.
I GOT LOST WALKING BACK TO CAMPUS AND NEED TO FIND MY WAY HOME.

APRIL 17, 1955.

ALBERT EINSTEIN WAS ADMITTED TO PRINCETON HOSPITAL WITH BLEEDING FROM A BURST BLOOD VESSEL.

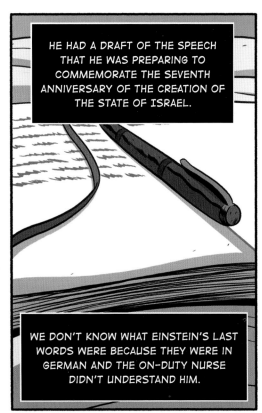

HE HAD A DRAFT OF THE SPEECH THAT HE WAS PREPARING TO COMMEMORATE THE SEVENTH ANNIVERSARY OF THE CREATION OF THE STATE OF ISRAEL.

WE DON'T KNOW WHAT EINSTEIN'S LAST WORDS WERE BECAUSE THEY WERE IN GERMAN AND THE ON-DUTY NURSE DIDN'T UNDERSTAND HIM.

...

ALBERT EINSTEIN DIED AT 1:15 A.M. ON APRIL 18, 1955, IN PRINCETON.

HE WAS 76 YEARS OLD.

CHAPTER 10

EINSTEIN'S LEGACY

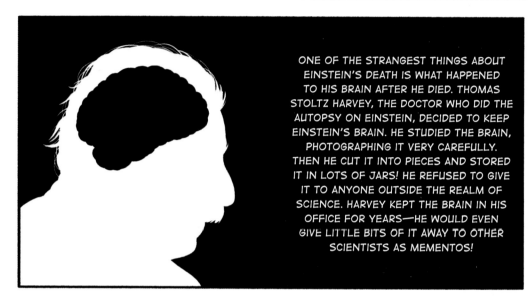

ONE OF THE STRANGEST THINGS ABOUT EINSTEIN'S DEATH IS WHAT HAPPENED TO HIS BRAIN AFTER HE DIED. THOMAS STOLTZ HARVEY, THE DOCTOR WHO DID THE AUTOPSY ON EINSTEIN, DECIDED TO KEEP EINSTEIN'S BRAIN. HE STUDIED THE BRAIN, PHOTOGRAPHING IT VERY CAREFULLY. THEN HE CUT IT INTO PIECES AND STORED IT IN LOTS OF JARS! HE REFUSED TO GIVE IT TO ANYONE OUTSIDE THE REALM OF SCIENCE. HARVEY KEPT THE BRAIN IN HIS OFFICE FOR YEARS—HE WOULD EVEN GIVE LITTLE BITS OF IT AWAY TO OTHER SCIENTISTS AS MEMENTOS!

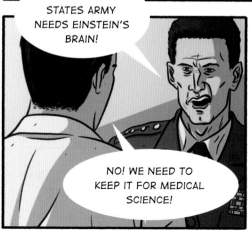

THE UNITED STATES ARMY NEEDS EINSTEIN'S BRAIN!

NO! WE NEED TO KEEP IT FOR MEDICAL SCIENCE!

EINSTEIN'S BRAIN IS NOW SAFELY STORED IN PRINCETON HOSPITAL.

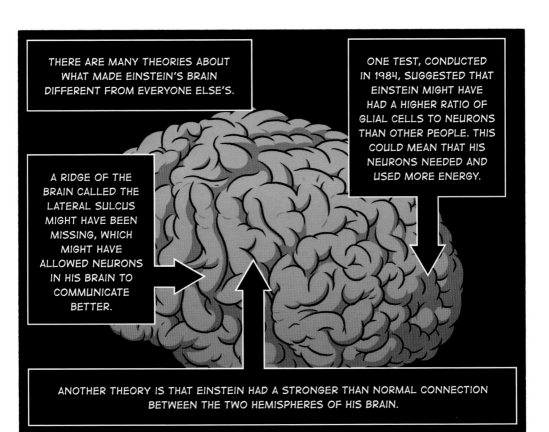

THERE ARE MANY THEORIES ABOUT WHAT MADE EINSTEIN'S BRAIN DIFFERENT FROM EVERYONE ELSE'S.

ONE TEST, CONDUCTED IN 1984, SUGGESTED THAT EINSTEIN MIGHT HAVE HAD A HIGHER RATIO OF GLIAL CELLS TO NEURONS THAN OTHER PEOPLE. THIS COULD MEAN THAT HIS NEURONS NEEDED AND USED MORE ENERGY.

A RIDGE OF THE BRAIN CALLED THE LATERAL SULCUS MIGHT HAVE BEEN MISSING, WHICH MIGHT HAVE ALLOWED NEURONS IN HIS BRAIN TO COMMUNICATE BETTER.

ANOTHER THEORY IS THAT EINSTEIN HAD A STRONGER THAN NORMAL CONNECTION BETWEEN THE TWO HEMISPHERES OF HIS BRAIN.

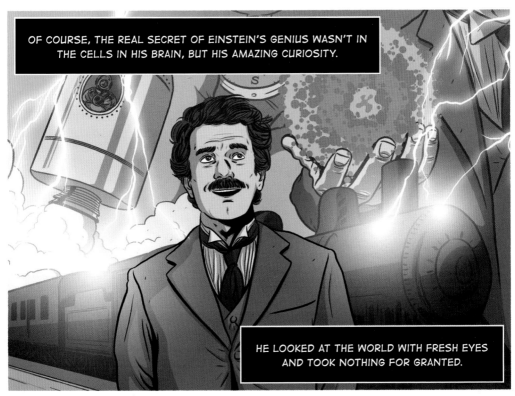

OF COURSE, THE REAL SECRET OF EINSTEIN'S GENIUS WASN'T IN THE CELLS IN HIS BRAIN, BUT HIS AMAZING CURIOSITY.

HE LOOKED AT THE WORLD WITH FRESH EYES AND TOOK NOTHING FOR GRANTED.

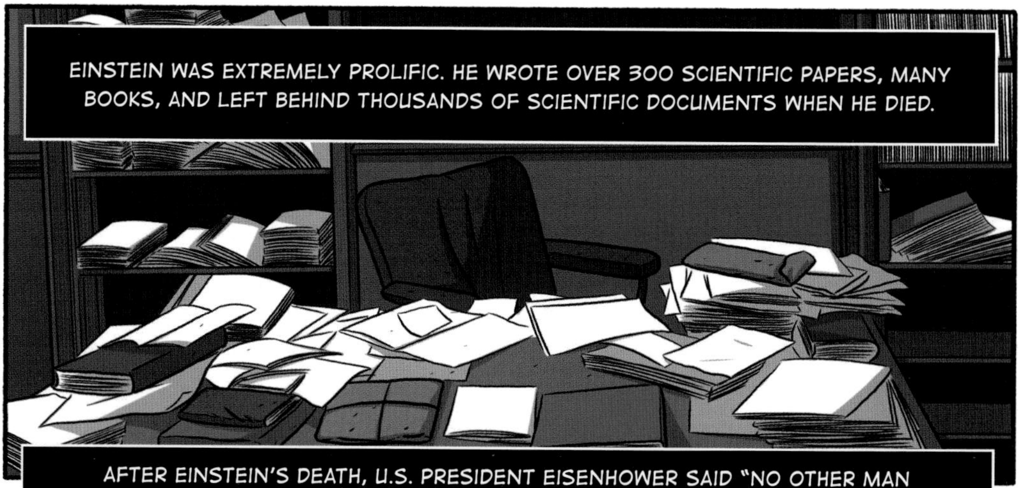
EINSTEIN WAS EXTREMELY PROLIFIC. HE WROTE OVER 300 SCIENTIFIC PAPERS, MANY BOOKS, AND LEFT BEHIND THOUSANDS OF SCIENTIFIC DOCUMENTS WHEN HE DIED.

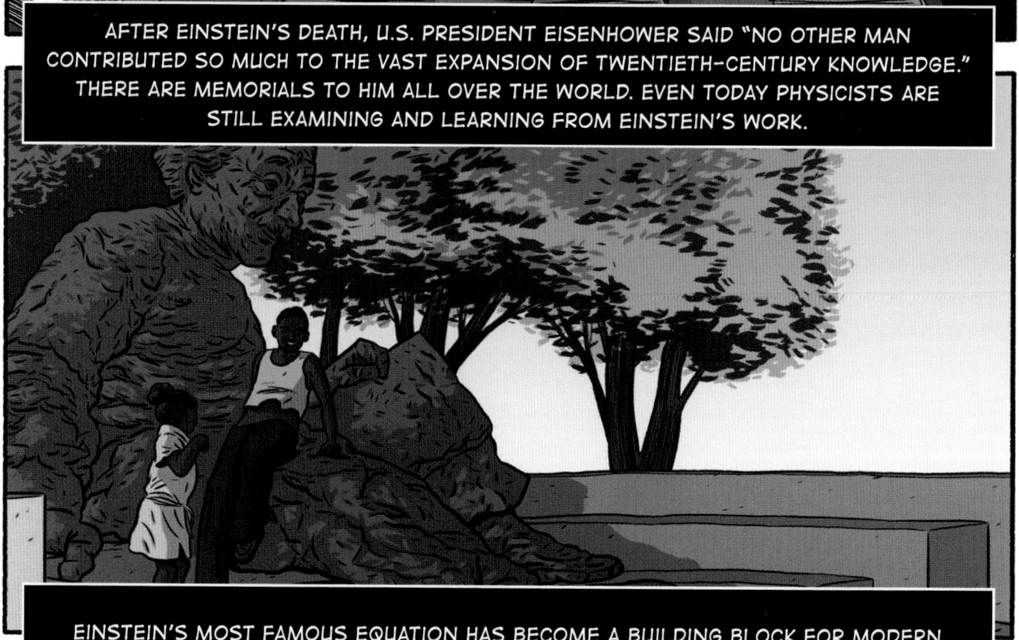
AFTER EINSTEIN'S DEATH, U.S. PRESIDENT EISENHOWER SAID "NO OTHER MAN CONTRIBUTED SO MUCH TO THE VAST EXPANSION OF TWENTIETH-CENTURY KNOWLEDGE." THERE ARE MEMORIALS TO HIM ALL OVER THE WORLD. EVEN TODAY PHYSICISTS ARE STILL EXAMINING AND LEARNING FROM EINSTEIN'S WORK.

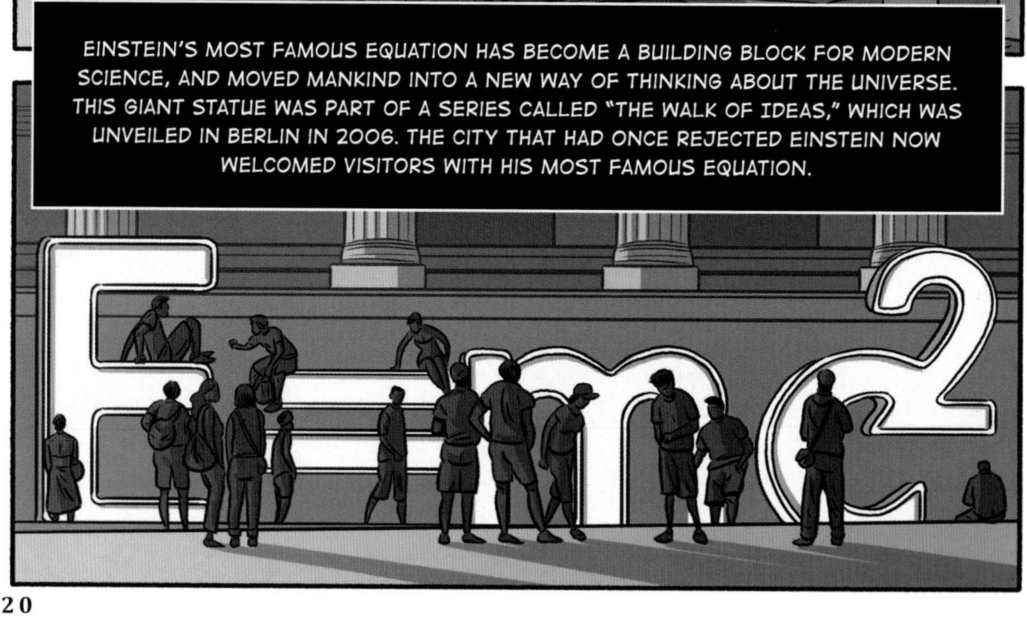
EINSTEIN'S MOST FAMOUS EQUATION HAS BECOME A BUILDING BLOCK FOR MODERN SCIENCE, AND MOVED MANKIND INTO A NEW WAY OF THINKING ABOUT THE UNIVERSE. THIS GIANT STATUE WAS PART OF A SERIES CALLED "THE WALK OF IDEAS," WHICH WAS UNVEILED IN BERLIN IN 2006. THE CITY THAT HAD ONCE REJECTED EINSTEIN NOW WELCOMED VISITORS WITH HIS MOST FAMOUS EQUATION.

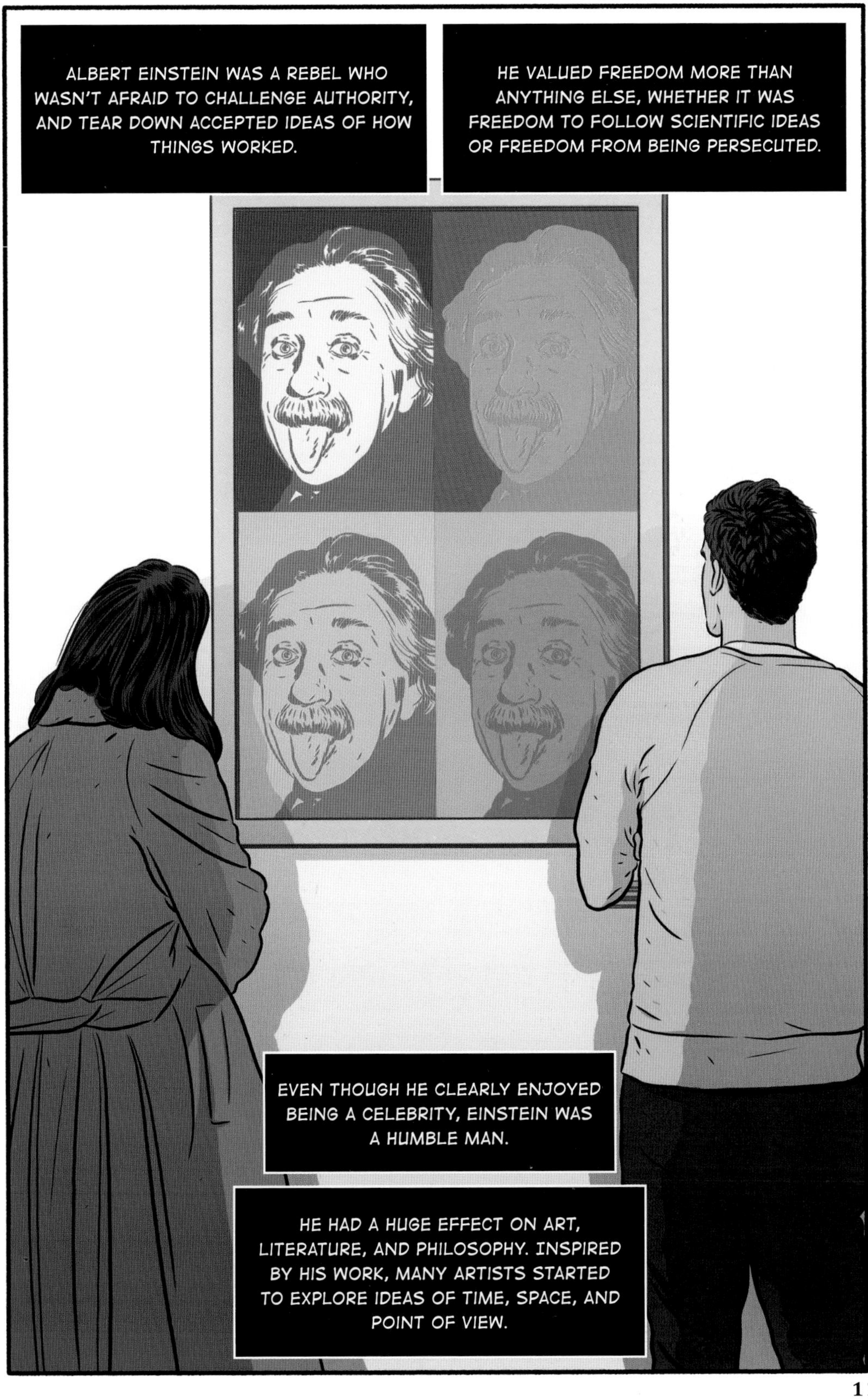
ALBERT EINSTEIN WAS A REBEL WHO WASN'T AFRAID TO CHALLENGE AUTHORITY, AND TEAR DOWN ACCEPTED IDEAS OF HOW THINGS WORKED.
HE VALUED FREEDOM MORE THAN ANYTHING ELSE, WHETHER IT WAS FREEDOM TO FOLLOW SCIENTIFIC IDEAS OR FREEDOM FROM BEING PERSECUTED.
EVEN THOUGH HE CLEARLY ENJOYED BEING A CELEBRITY, EINSTEIN WAS A HUMBLE MAN.
HE HAD A HUGE EFFECT ON ART, LITERATURE, AND PHILOSOPHY. INSPIRED BY HIS WORK, MANY ARTISTS STARTED TO EXPLORE IDEAS OF TIME, SPACE, AND POINT OF VIEW.

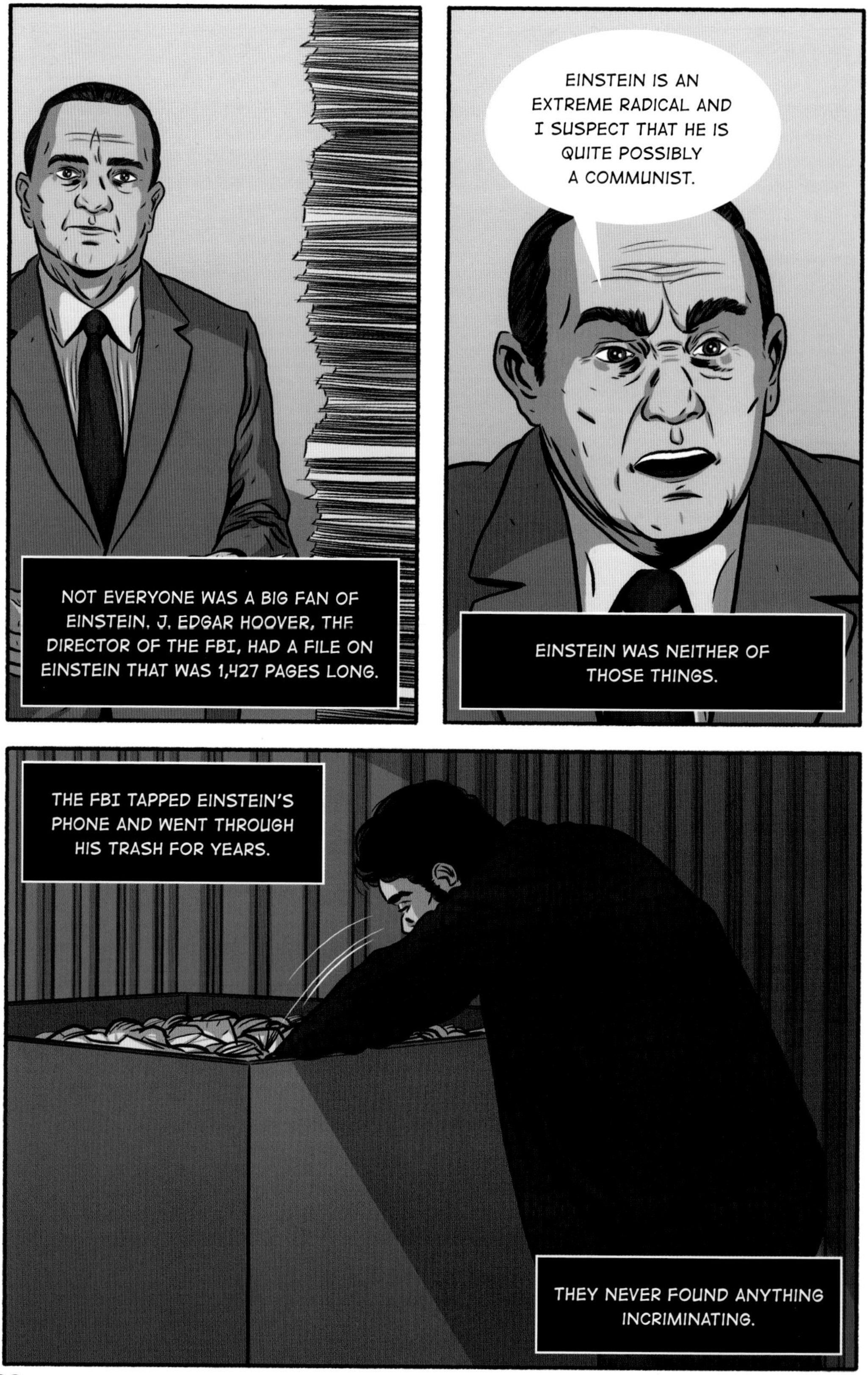
NOT EVERYONE WAS A BIG FAN OF EINSTEIN. J. EDGAR HOOVER, THE DIRECTOR OF THE FBI, HAD A FILE ON EINSTEIN THAT WAS 1,427 PAGES LONG.
EINSTEIN IS AN EXTREME RADICAL AND I SUSPECT THAT HE IS QUITE POSSIBLY A COMMUNIST.
EINSTEIN WAS NEITHER OF THOSE THINGS.
THE FBI TAPPED EINSTEIN'S PHONE AND WENT THROUGH HIS TRASH FOR YEARS.
THEY NEVER FOUND ANYTHING INCRIMINATING.

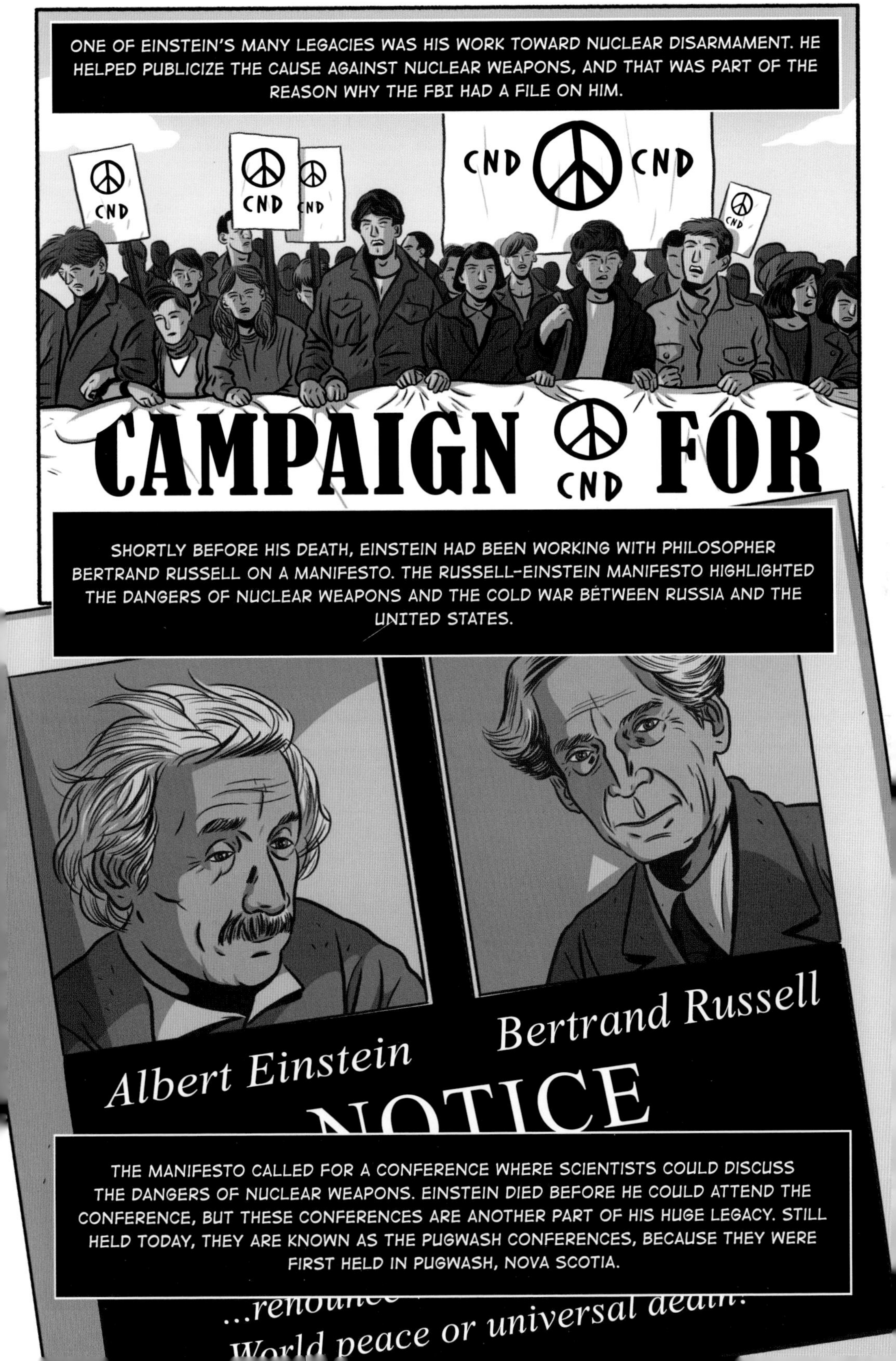
ONE OF EINSTEIN'S MANY LEGACIES WAS HIS WORK TOWARD NUCLEAR DISARMAMENT. HE HELPED PUBLICIZE THE CAUSE AGAINST NUCLEAR WEAPONS, AND THAT WAS PART OF THE REASON WHY THE FBI HAD A FILE ON HIM.
CND
CND
CND
CND CND
CND
CAMPAIGN CND FOR
SHORTLY BEFORE HIS DEATH, EINSTEIN HAD BEEN WORKING WITH PHILOSOPHER BERTRAND RUSSELL ON A MANIFESTO. THE RUSSELL-EINSTEIN MANIFESTO HIGHLIGHTED THE DANGERS OF NUCLEAR WEAPONS AND THE COLD WAR BETWEEN RUSSIA AND THE UNITED STATES.
Albert Einstein
Bertrand Russell
NOTICE
THE MANIFESTO CALLED FOR A CONFERENCE WHERE SCIENTISTS COULD DISCUSS THE DANGERS OF NUCLEAR WEAPONS. EINSTEIN DIED BEFORE HE COULD ATTEND THE CONFERENCE, BUT THESE CONFERENCES ARE ANOTHER PART OF HIS HUGE LEGACY. STILL HELD TODAY, THEY ARE KNOWN AS THE PUGWASH CONFERENCES, BECAUSE THEY WERE FIRST HELD IN PUGWASH, NOVA SCOTIA.

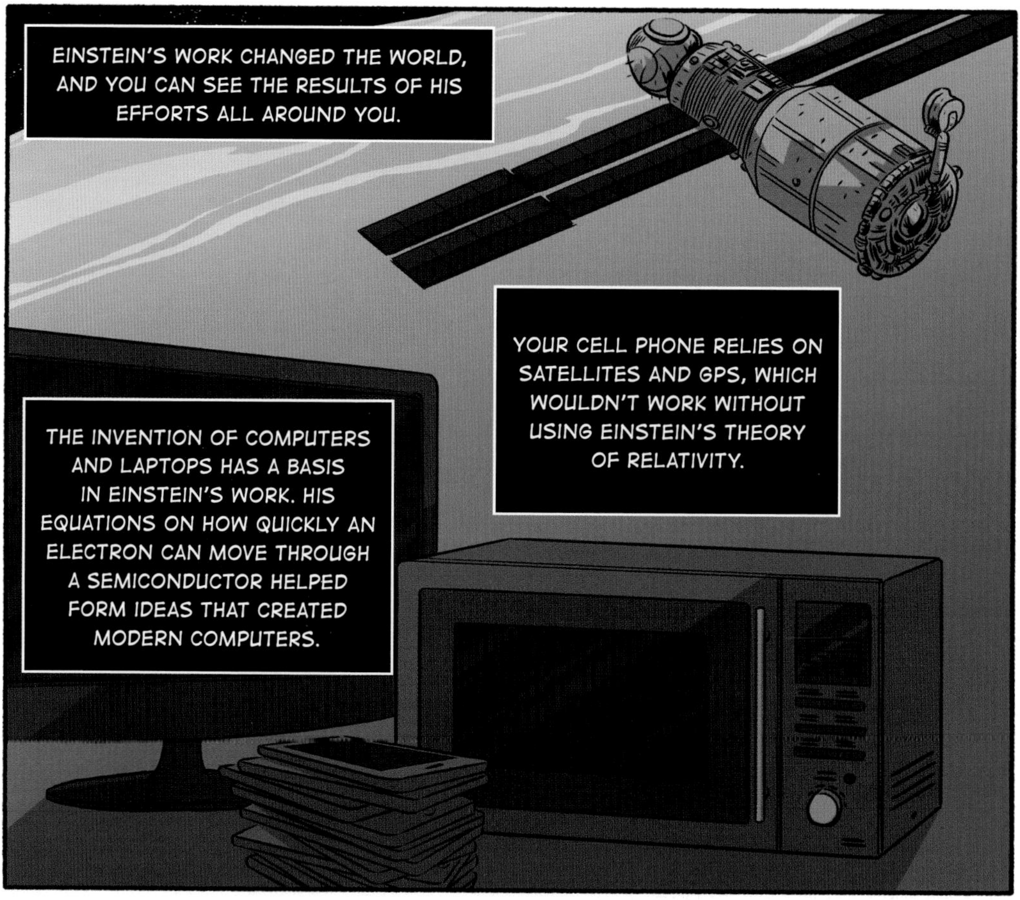
EINSTEIN'S WORK CHANGED THE WORLD, AND YOU CAN SEE THE RESULTS OF HIS EFFORTS ALL AROUND YOU.
YOUR CELL PHONE RELIES ON SATELLITES AND GPS, WHICH WOULDN'T WORK WITHOUT USING EINSTEIN'S THEORY OF RELATIVITY.
THE INVENTION OF COMPUTERS AND LAPTOPS HAS A BASIS IN EINSTEIN'S WORK. HIS EQUATIONS ON HOW QUICKLY AN ELECTRON CAN MOVE THROUGH A SEMICONDUCTOR HELPED FORM IDEAS THAT CREATED MODERN COMPUTERS.

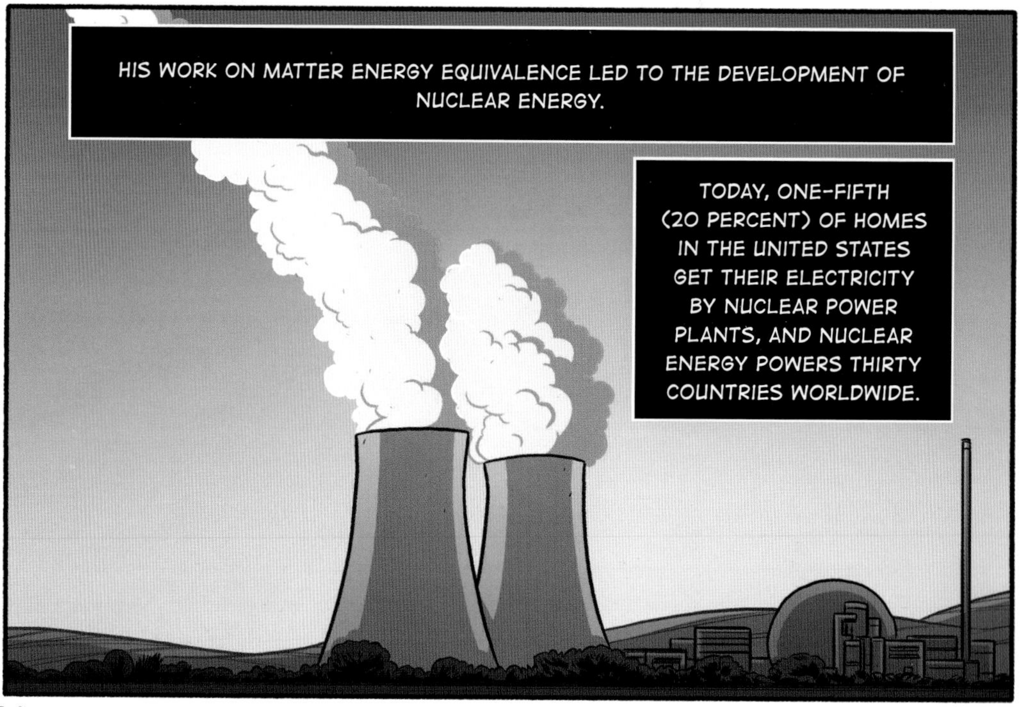
HIS WORK ON MATTER ENERGY EQUIVALENCE LED TO THE DEVELOPMENT OF NUCLEAR ENERGY.
TODAY, ONE-FIFTH (20 PERCENT) OF HOMES IN THE UNITED STATES GET THEIR ELECTRICITY BY NUCLEAR POWER PLANTS, AND NUCLEAR ENERGY POWERS THIRTY COUNTRIES WORLDWIDE.

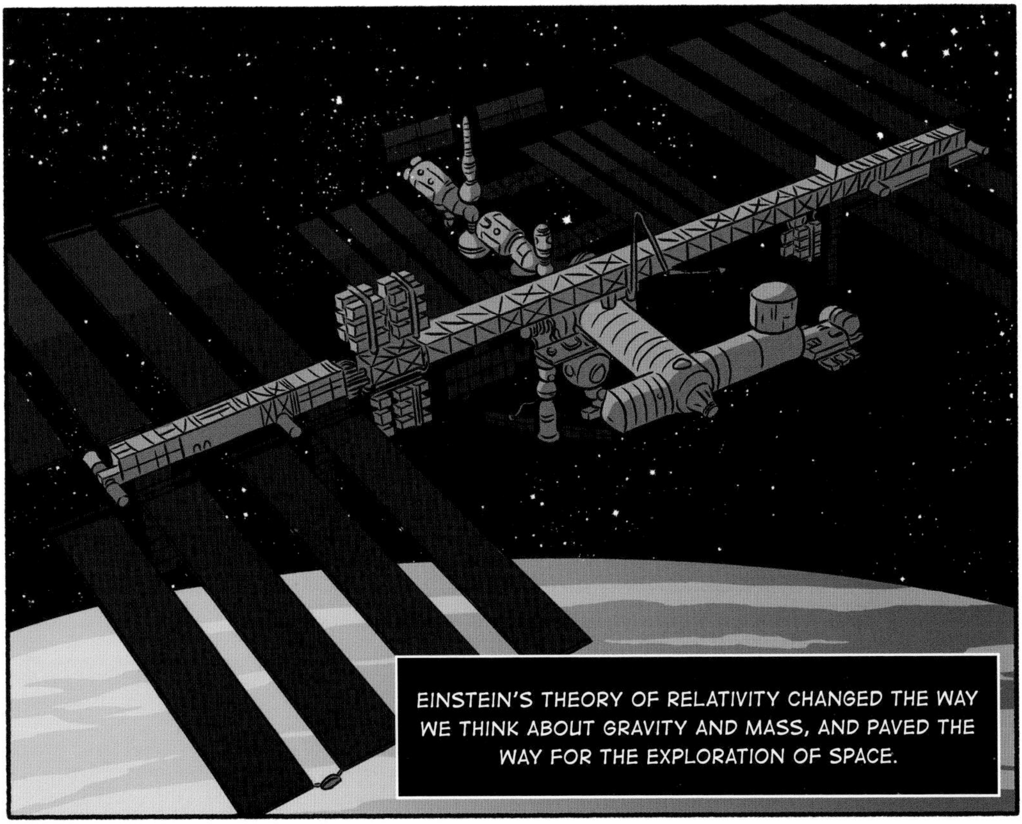
EINSTEIN'S THEORY OF RELATIVITY CHANGED THE WAY WE THINK ABOUT GRAVITY AND MASS, AND PAVED THE WAY FOR THE EXPLORATION OF SPACE.

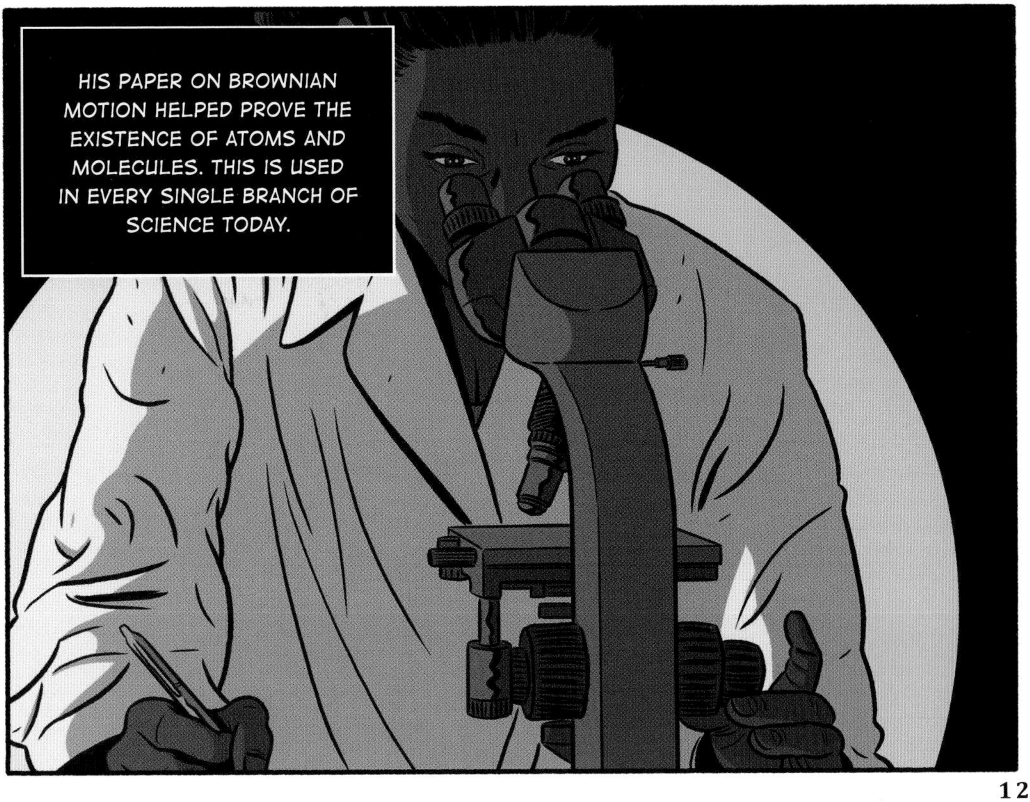
HIS PAPER ON BROWNIAN MOTION HELPED PROVE THE EXISTENCE OF ATOMS AND MOLECULES. THIS IS USED IN EVERY SINGLE BRANCH OF SCIENCE TODAY.

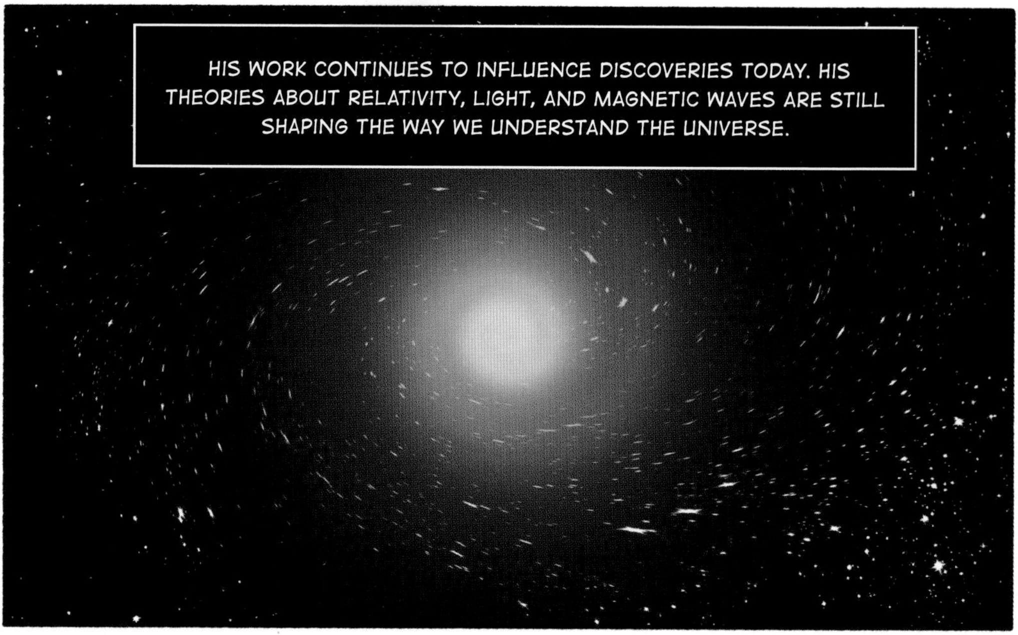
HIS WORK CONTINUES TO INFLUENCE DISCOVERIES TODAY. HIS THEORIES ABOUT RELATIVITY, LIGHT, AND MAGNETIC WAVES ARE STILL SHAPING THE WAY WE UNDERSTAND THE UNIVERSE.

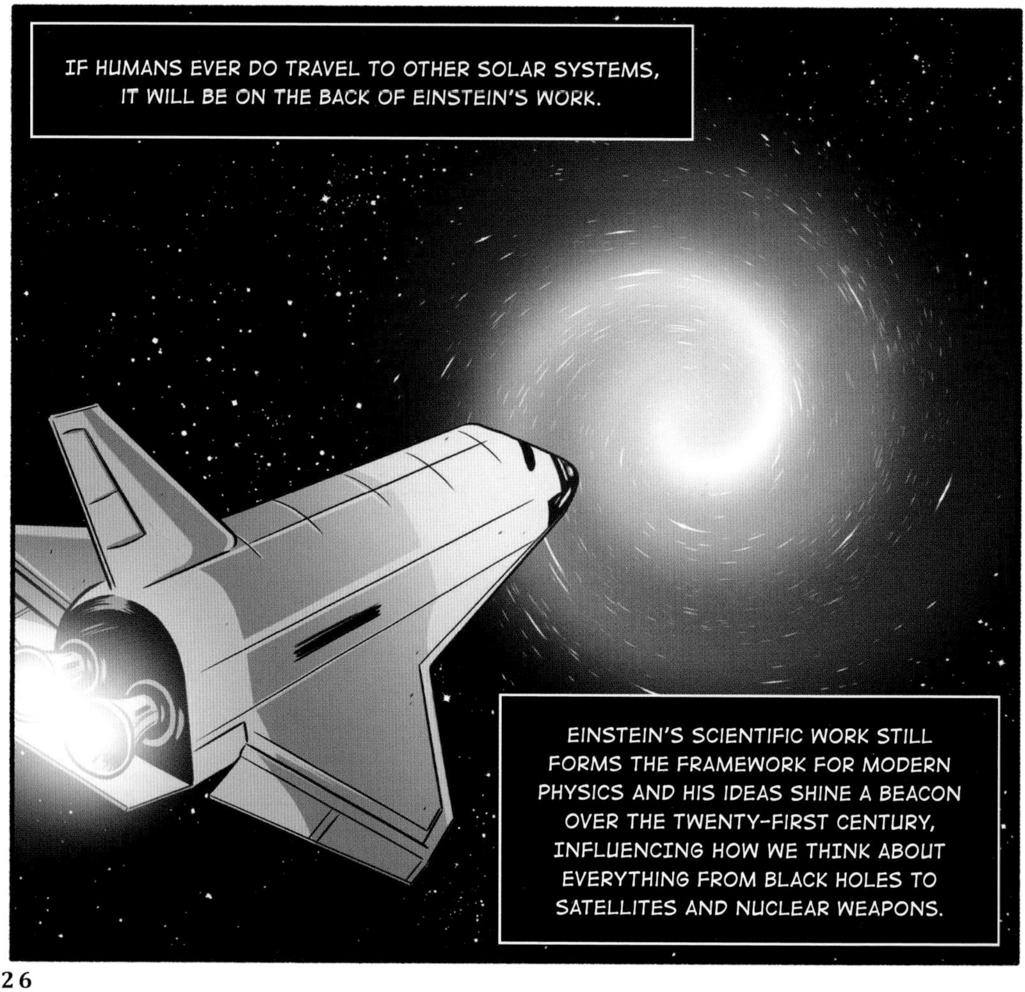
IF HUMANS EVER DO TRAVEL TO OTHER SOLAR SYSTEMS, IT WILL BE ON THE BACK OF EINSTEIN'S WORK.
EINSTEIN'S SCIENTIFIC WORK STILL FORMS THE FRAMEWORK FOR MODERN PHYSICS AND HIS IDEAS SHINE A BEACON OVER THE TWENTY-FIRST CENTURY, INFLUENCING HOW WE THINK ABOUT EVERYTHING FROM BLACK HOLES TO SATELLITES AND NUCLEAR WEAPONS.

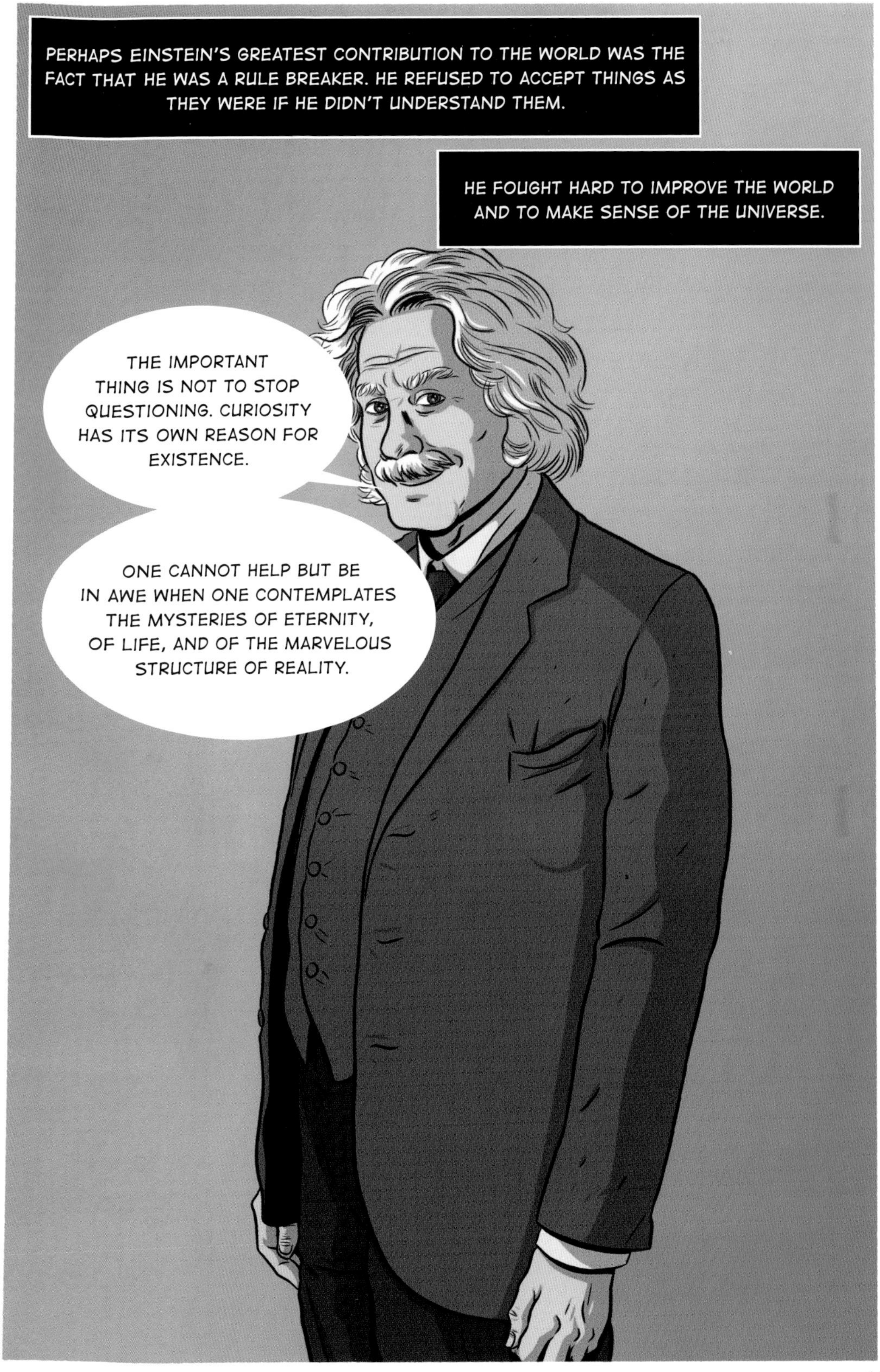
PERHAPS EINSTEIN'S GREATEST CONTRIBUTION TO THE WORLD WAS THE FACT THAT HE WAS A RULE BREAKER. HE REFUSED TO ACCEPT THINGS AS THEY WERE IF HE DIDN'T UNDERSTAND THEM.
HE FOUGHT HARD TO IMPROVE THE WORLD AND TO MAKE SENSE OF THE UNIVERSE.
THE IMPORTANT THING IS NOT TO STOP QUESTIONING. CURIOSITY HAS ITS OWN REASON FOR EXISTENCE.
ONE CANNOT HELP BUT BE IN AWE WHEN ONE CONTEMPLATES THE MYSTERIES OF ETERNITY, OF LIFE, AND OF THE MARVELOUS STRUCTURE OF REALITY.

ACKNOWLEDGMENTS

Ned Hartley: I would like to acknowledge the expressive and emotive illustrations of Tom Humberstone in giving the book such a solid foundation. I found Tom not only to be a talented illustrator, but a thoughtful and kind collaborator. I count myself very lucky to have been able to work with him. I would also like to thank editors Lucy York and Anna Southgate, script reviewer Tammy Enz, and designer Lyndsey Harwood. Thanks also go to my parents, my wonderful wife Carly, and my best inventions Violet and Hazel for their support.

Tom Humberstone: I would like to thank my parents for introducing me to comics and for encouraging my love of drawing, despite my having drawn on the back of a degree certificate when young! I would also like to thank Becky for all her support while I worked on this book.